O Captain! my Captain!

Captain! my Ca... ...fearful trip is done;
...ship has... ...the prize we
...sou... ...ll exulting,
...port... ...essel grim
...hile fo...

B

American
Literary Autographs
FROM WASHINGTON IRVING
TO HENRY JAMES

Herbert Cahoon, Thomas V. Lange,
Charles Ryskamp

with 98 Plates

$7.95

O Captain... ...the bells;
...ise up - for... ...for you the
bugle...
...or you bouquets and ribbon'd wreaths — for you
the shores a-crowding;
...or you they call, the swaying mass, their eager
faces turning:
Here Captain! dear father!
This arm beneath your head;
It is some dream that on the deck,
You've fallen cold and dead.

My Captain does not answer, his lips are pale and still,
My father does not feel my arm, he has no pulse nor will,
The ship is anchor'd safe and sound, its voyage closed
and done;
From fearful trip the victor ship comes in with
object won;
Exult O shores, and ring O bells!
But I, with mournful tread,
Walk the deck my Captain lies,
Fallen cold and dead.

Walt
Whitman
April 27 '90

American Literary Autographs

FROM WASHINGTON IRVING
TO HENRY JAMES

American Literary Autographs

FROM WASHINGTON IRVING TO HENRY JAMES

Herbert Cahoon, Thomas V. Lange,
Charles Ryskamp

DOVER PUBLICATIONS, INC., NEW YORK
in association with
THE PIERPONT MORGAN LIBRARY

Published in Canada by General Publishing Company, Ltd., 30
Lesmill Road, Don Mills, Toronto, Ontario.
Published in the United Kingdom by Constable and Company,
Ltd., 10 Orange Street, London WC2H 7EG.

*American Literary Autographs from Washington Irving to Henry
James* is a new work, first published by Dover Publications, Inc.,
in 1977 in association with The Pierpont Morgan Library.

International Standard Book Number: 0-486-23548-3
Library of Congress Catalog Card Number: 77-89415

Manufactured in the United States of America
Dover Publications, Inc.
180 Varick Street
New York, N.Y. 10014

Introduction

This book illustrates, through a series of reproductions of autograph manuscripts, letters and one or two inscriptions in books, the rise and flourishing of American literature during the nineteenth century, from Washington Irving to Henry James. It starts with the first moments that the authors of the new country reached an international audience. Appropriately, we find near the beginning a letter from Washington Irving to Walter Scott, who had encouraged him to go on with his writing. There are afterwards the final paragraphs from Irving's *Conquest of Granada* (the complete manuscript consists of 1028 leaves) and two pages from the manuscript of his *Life of George Washington*. Among the manuscripts at the end of this volume is a page from the long typescript of the scenario or outline of the first truly international American novel, Henry James's *The Ambassadors* (dated 1 September 1900). By then American literature had become a part of English—and world—literature.

Our aim is to present a popular guide to American literary autographs of this first great period. The focus of the book is on the mid-century, the years which F. O. Matthiessen has so admirably described in his book *The American Renaissance*. The major writers are illustrated with two or three selections from their most important novels or poems and letters in our collections; minor writers, many of whom were once immensely popular, are frequently represented by a page from a well-known work. One will therefore find among the poems Thomas Bailey Aldrich's "Ballad of Babie Bell," Thomas Buchanan Read's "Sheridan's Ride," Eugene Field's "Casey's Table d'hote," Fitz-Greene Halleck's "Marco Bozzaris," Samuel Woodworth's "[Old Oaken] Bucket," James Whitcomb Riley's "Dot Leedle Poy of Mine," as well as Bret Harte's "Plain Language from Truthful James (The Heathen Chinee)," John Howard Payne's "[Home,] Sweet Home," Edgar Allan Poe's "Ulalume" and a stanza from "The Raven," Julia Ward Howe's "Battle Hymn of the Republic (Army Hymn)," William Cullen Bryant's "Thanatopsis" and "To a Waterfowl," Ralph Waldo Emerson's "Concord Hymn," Henry Wadsworth Longfellow's "Children's Hour" and "Excelsior," Oliver Wendell Holmes's "Old Ironsides" and Walt Whitman's "O Captain! my Captain!" There is a page to represent Clyde Fitch's play *Barbara Frietchie* as well as John Greenleaf Whittier's poem about her, Emerson's "Behavior," Noah Webster's *Dictionary*, James Fenimore Cooper's *Deerslayer*, Mark Twain's *Life on the Mississippi* and *The Man that Corrupted Hadleyburg*, Whitman's projected Introduction to the London edition of *Leaves of Grass*, Holmes's *Autocrat of the Breakfast Table*, selections from the 39 volumes of Henry David Thoreau's *Journal* and the 18 volumes of Nathaniel Hawthorne's *Journals* and *Notebooks*, and also his *Blithedale Romance* and all that remains of the manuscript of *The Scarlet Letter*.

Most guides to historical or literary autographs are expensive books, often in several volumes. This one should be within the reach of any school or college library, young students and beginning collectors. Each entry briefly describes the manuscript from which the illustration is taken and the life and work of the author. There are comments on the particular leaf or leaves chosen and the importance of the work or the letter from which it came. We have also attempted to list the major manuscript resources for each author so that those who wish to pursue their studies further will be able to do so easily. For additional information as to the location of authors' manuscripts and letters, readers may wish to consult *American Literary Manuscripts* (University of Georgia Press, 1977).

At the end of this volume is a checklist of all of the American literary manuscript holdings, from the seventeenth century to the present, in The Pierpont Morgan Library. This will afford scholars and other libraries a ready reference to one of the most important collections of manuscripts of American literature.

Almost all of the illustrations are chosen from manuscripts in the Morgan Library. The Library's collection, however, is not as comprehensive as that formed by Mr. Clifton Waller Barrett, which is being given to the University of Virginia. In the case of six authors whose work we could illustrate only very inadequately, or not at all, we have selected letters and manuscripts from the Barrett Collection, with the gracious permission of Mr. Barrett and the University of Virginia (Nos. 2, 62, 86, 94, 97 and 98). The most outstanding of these six items is the manuscript of Stephen Crane's *Red Badge of Courage*.

It is generally recognized that of the great American collectors who were active at the end of the nineteenth century and the first part of this, J. Pierpont Morgan (1837–1913) "was the most catholic in his tastes." We think of his collecting above all in relation to many kinds of art from many thousands of years. The same is true of the written records which he gathered together, from the earliest tablets and papyri to books and manuscripts of his own contemporaries. He began by collecting autographs, specimens of the handwriting of the principal figures of his day. When still a schoolboy, before he was 15, he had acquired the autograph of President Millard Fillmore and, in response to Morgan's request, six letters from bishops of the Protestant Episcopal Church. The American collection of autographs is, therefore, the cornerstone of all of the Morgan collections—at The Pierpont Morgan Library, The Metropolitan Museum of Art and throughout the United States and the world.

By 1883, Morgan had a library with only a few fine books, but many more excellent autographs: letters of Robert Burns, Alexander Hamilton and George Washington, and one of the finest collections of autographs of the signers of the Declaration of Independence. Morgan's passion for collecting literary and historical manuscripts never abated, and it was very strong also in his son, J. P. Morgan (1867–1943). In the course of time, owing to the dazzling collections of medieval and Renaissance manuscripts, early printed books and drawings, and the wealth of English and European materials in The Pierpont Morgan Library, the importance of the American collections of manuscripts, both literary and historical, has been diminished in the public eye. Yet in both American fields, the collections of autograph manuscripts are among the half-dozen finest in the world. Especially for the years of exploration and

settlement, and then the colonial and early Federal periods, the manuscripts include a range of major documents that would be hard to equal.

The foundation of the Morgan collection of American literary manuscripts was the purchase in 1895 of the holograph of James Fenimore Cooper's *Deerslayer*. The strength of the collection lies in the manuscripts of the major authors of the mid-nineteenth century. This outstanding position was achieved in 1909 when Pierpont Morgan acquired the 263 manuscripts (including a very few letters) that had been collected by Stephen H. Wakeman (1859–1924) of New York during the previous nine years. George S. Hellman could therefore later write of the Morgan Library, "when we come to the Americans, we find very nearly all that is extant of Nathaniel Hawthorne and Henry D. Thoreau; while Poe, Whittier, Emerson, Lowell, Longfellow, Holmes and Bret Harte are represented to an extent that never again can be approached by any other collector." More recently, our most distinguished dealer in American books and manuscripts, the late John S. Van E. Kohn, wrote of the Wakeman-Morgan collection of manuscripts that for several of these authors "its overall supremacy must remain unchallenged."

Notable omissions in Wakeman's collection—not at all surprising for his time—were Melville and Emily Dickinson, but two authors were lacking whom one might have expected to find: Whitman and Mark Twain. In the years since 1909, the Morgan Library has added seven letters of Melville, whose letters and manuscripts are rare, autograph manuscripts of poems and letters of Emily Dickinson, poetical and prose manuscripts and about 50 letters of Walt Whitman and a most impressive group of Twain's manuscripts including his "Autobiography," *Life on the Mississippi* (three volumes), *Pudd'nhead Wilson* (two volumes), *The Man that Corrupted Hadleyburg* and *A Double-barrelled Detective Story*, which was purchased by the Library in 1976. In the years to come, we hope to add to our collection, to make it as representative as possible of the literary history of this country.

Since this guide and the checklist at the end of the volume may call the attention of scholars to manuscripts in the Morgan Library which they may wish to see, inquire about or have copied photographically, it should be noted that applications for cards of admission to the Reading Room are made on forms provided for the purpose; cards are readily issued to qualified and accredited scholars. Graduate students and scholars having no institutional affiliation are expected to present with their applications suitable references concerning their fitness to handle rare manuscript materials. Prior notification of visits by those from out of town is advisable in order to insure the availability of the manuscripts desired, but it is not insisted upon. The Reading Room is open from Monday through Friday, 9:30–4:45, except holidays.

This volume is above all indebted to Herbert Cahoon, Curator of Autograph Manuscripts in The Pierpont Morgan Library, who has written the entries that follow. Thomas V. Lange has made the checklist of all the American literary manuscripts in the Library. Edward Jabbour, Jr., Paul Needham, Charles V. Passela, Christine Stenstrom and J. Rigbie Turner of the Morgan Library staff, and Mr. Clifton Waller Barrett and the staff of the Alderman Library of the University of Virginia, as well as Professor Andrew Breen Myers, Dr. Gordon N. Ray and Professor Albert Robbins have been most helpful to us. It has also been a great pleasure to work with Hayward Cirker, Clarence C. Strowbridge, Stanley Appelbaum and others at Dover Publications who endeavored to make this inexpensive volume a handsome book nevertheless, and one worthy of the manuscripts that are illustrated in it. We are most grateful to The Charles Engelhard Foundation for its support of all of our publications.

CHARLES RYSKAMP
Director
The Pierpont Morgan Library

Contents

The dates are those of the particular autographs being reproduced.

American Literary Autographs

FROM WASHINGTON IRVING
TO HENRY JAMES

NOAH WEBSTER

"An American Dictionary of the English Language." Autograph
manuscript of definitions to be added to the work [n.p., n.d.]. 1 p. 27 cm.

Lexicographer and author (b. West Hartford, Conn. 1758; d. New Haven, Conn. 1843). Author of *A Grammatical Institute of the English Language* (1783–85), the first part of which became his famous "spelling book"; *Sketches of American Policy* (1785), a Federalist argument for a strong central government; *Dissertations on the English Language* (1789), which contained an essay on reformed spelling; *A Compendious Dictionary of the English Language* (1806); and *An American Dictionary of the English Language* (1828). Webster also worked for an American copyright law and helped to found Amherst College.

An American Dictionary, the product of over 20 years of incessant labor, was one of the most ambitious publications undertaken up to that time in America; Webster recorded that the printing took "15 months & 8 days." Dr. Johnson took about nine years to complete his *Dictionary* (1755) with the help of a half-dozen copyists. The definitions shown here in Webster's clear and angular hand are probably additions for the text of the second edition of *An American Dictionary*, which was published in 1841. As an author, public official, scientist, traveler and tireless worker for many causes, Webster was an apostle of what later became generally known as Americanism, a word which he was one of the first to use. The Morgan Library has a large collection of manuscript pages and corrected proof for *An American Dictionary*, as well as many letters to and from Webster. The most important collection of Webster letters and papers is in The New York Public Library.

Thor. n *In* Scandinavian Mythology, *the son of Odin & Freya & the deity that presided over all mischievous spirits of in the elements. This deity was considered the god of thunder, or was confounded with the Jupiter of the Roman's. From ϸ his name* Thor, *we have* Thursday, *& the Germans, their* Donnerstag. *See* Thursday.

Thoth. n *Among the ancient Egyptians, the deity of elo-quence, & supposed to be the inventor of writing & philosophy. He corresponded to the Mercury of the Romans.*

Thra'-nite. n *The uppermost or foremost of the three classes of rowers in an Athenian trireme.*

Thug. n [*Hindoo*, thugna *to deceive.*] *One of an association of robbers & murderers in India.*

Thor. _n_ In Scandinavian Mythology, the son of Odin & Freya & the deity that presided over all mischievous spirits & the elements. This deity was considered the god of thunder, or was confounded with the Jupiter of the Romans. From his name Thor, we have Thursday, & the Germans, their _Donnerstag_. See Thursday.

Thoth. _n_ Among the ancient Egyptians, the deity of eloquence, & supposed to be the inventor of writing & philosophy. He corresponded to the Mercury of the Romans.

Thra'nite. _n_ The uppermost or foremost of the three classes of rowers in an Athenian trireme.

Thug. _n_ [Hindoo, thug-na to deceive.] One of an association of robbers & murderers in India.
                                                             Brande.

Thu'le _n_ The name given by the ancients to the most northern part of the habitable world. This has been supposed to be some part of Norway; but the more general conjecture is, that it was Iceland.

Thurl _n_ A short communication between adits in mines.

Thus. _n_ [Gr. Θυω, to sacrifice, from its use.] The resin of the Spruce Fir.

Tic douloureux [French] A very painful affection of a nerve, occurring in sudden attacks; usually in the head.

Tide-gauge. _n_ A contrivance for registering the state of the tide continuously.

Tie. 4. A piece of timber or metal, for binding two bodies together.
    5. A character in ancient music to connect syncopated notes.

Tierce. 6. In Heraldry, a field divided into three parts.

Tiers etat, in France, the third branch or commonalty, answering to the Commons in Great Britain.

Tin'cal _n_ Rough borax, as imported from India.

CHARLES BROCKDEN BROWN

Autograph letter signed, dated Philadelphia, Jan.y 18. 1808, addressed to John B. Romeyn, a family friend. 1 p. 25 cm.

Novelist and journalist (b. Philadelphia, Pa. 1771; d. Philadelphia, Pa. 1810). In 1793 Brown gave up the practice of law for literature and became the first person in the United States to make authorship his principal profession. His novels are *Alcuin* (1798), probably the first feminist work published in America; *Wieland* (1798), an epistolary Gothic novel; *Ormond* (1799), a melodrama of rape, murder, suicide and a yellow-fever epidemic; *Arthur Mervyn* (1799–1800), a reblending of the ingredients of *Ormond; Edgar Huntly* (1799), a detective story in which Indians commit the crime; *Clara Howard* (1801); and *Jane Talbot* (1801). These novels were completed in a period of three years; Brown then turned to journalism for the rest of his life. He had been influenced by the English authors Samuel Richardson, William Godwin and Ann Radcliffe, and, in turn, his work influenced Keats, Shelley and Scott. T. L. Peacock wrote that Shelley was always searching for a summerhouse similar to the one in *Wieland* where the hero's father (like Dickens' Mr. Krook in *Bleak House*) died of "spontaneous combustion."

This letter, addressed to Dr. Romeyn, one of the most popular preachers of his day and an able theologian, is concerned with the death of Brown's father-in-law, the clergyman William Linn, which took place ten days before the letter was written. Brown is especially worried about the future education of William Linn, Jr., and fears he cannot afford to help him train for the pulpit. Young William became a lawyer instead and had a lucrative practice in Ithaca; he also wrote a biography of Thomas Jefferson that went through several editions. The best collection of Brown's papers, which are not commonly found, is in the Library of the Historical Society of Pennsylvania.

From the collection of Mr. C. Waller Barrett at the Alderman Library, The University of Virginia, Charlottesville, Virginia.

Philad. Jan.y 18. 1808. My dear Sir   Permit me to thank you for the kind letter I have lately recieved from you. The intelligence it conveyed was, indeed, equally unexpected & afflicting. The deep regret I felt at not being able to visit & console my beloved sisters, in their calamity, was alleviated by reflecting on the friendship & kindness they might justly expect to recieve from you & some other disinterested friends. Any service you may render them, will find its reward in the testimony of your own heart. Their gratitude & mine, however, will, in no small measure, be due to you.

The death of my father in law will be a heavy calamity to all his children, but it will be felt more sensibly by those that are young & unmarried. His Son William was designed for the pulpit by his father, & by the wishes of his sisters, & had his father's life been spared four or five years longer, their wishes would have probably been accomplished. As it is, I very much fear, he will be obliged to give up these desirable prospects, & pursue some way of life that may be wholly unexpensive, or, at least, [least,] less expensive to his friends. If my means were equal to my wishes, his father's death should make no change in the young man's future situation, but these, alas, are too limited to permit me to do all that is dictated by the interest of these orphans, & by my affection for them. [. . .]

I am your obliged & affectionate friend   C. B. Brown.

Philad. Jan.y 18. 1808.

My dear Sir

Permit me to thank you for the kind letter I have lately received from you. The intelligence it conveyed was, indeed, equally unexpected & afflicting. The deep regret I felt at not being able to visit & console my beloved sisters, in their calamity, was alleviated by reflecting on the friendship & kindness they might justly expect to recieve from you & some other disinterested friends. Any service you may render them, will find its reward in the testimony of your own heart. Their gratitude & mine, however, will, in no small measure, be due to you.

The death of my father in law will be a heavy calamity to all his children, but it will be felt more sensibly by those that are young & unmarried. His son William was designed for the pulpit by his father, & by the wishes of his sisters. & had his father's life been spared four or five years longer, their wishes would have probably been accomplished. As it is, I very much fear, he will be obliged to give up these desirable prospects, & pursue some way of life that may be wholly unexpensive, or, at least, least, less expensive to his friends. If my means were equal to my wishes, his father's death should make no change in the young man's future situation; but these, alas. are too limited to permit me to do all that is dictated by the interest of these orphans, & by my affection for them. I am wholly uninformed, however, as to the actual expense attending the education of a young man for the pulpit, & shall be grateful to you for any information on this head.

William formerly expressed a liking for the mercantile profession, &perhaps. this preference still continues. In such a case, perhaps his inclination ought to be complyed with even had not this disaster befallen us. I regret exceedingly my distance from Albany, which prevents a ready & speedy communication with the family: I address myself thus frankly to you from the high esteem I have of your benevolence, & the friendship I know you entertained for my father in law. This is an occasion on which. I know you will be inclined to be an active friend, & this persuasion inclines me to address you on this subject without scruple or reserve.

If William should be inclined to the mercantile life, would it be impracticable to procure him a situation with some respectable merchant in your city. I am informed it is not uncommon to take young men, of good education & connections, into compting houses, on terms very favourable to their families. If my brother's inclinations point this way, & such a situation be attainable. I do not know that any thing better could have been done for him, had his father's life been spared. May I venture to bespeak your interest for him in commending him to such a situation. if your opinion of its eligibility coincides with me.

I need not commend this unhappy family to your kindness: I am your obliged & affectionate
friend

C. B. Brown.

WASHINGTON IRVING

Autograph letter signed, dated Liverpool Oct. 15th 1817, addressed to Walter [later Sir Walter] Scott. 1 p. 24.5 cm.

Essayist, historian and biographer (b. New York City 1783; d. Irvington, N.Y. 1859). Among his works are *A History of New York . . . by Diedrich Knickerbocker* (1809), a burlesque that brought him early fame; *The Sketch Book of Geoffrey Crayon, Gent.* (1819–20), which included the celebrated stories of "Rip Van Winkle" and "The Legend of Sleepy Hollow"; *The Alhambra* (1832); and biographical studies of Columbus, Oliver Goldsmith, Mahomet and George Washington. He also wrote the fur-trade histories *Astoria* (1836) and *The Rocky Mountains (Adventures of Captain Bonneville)* (1837), both pioneering works of Western Americana. Irving was America's literary ambassador to Europe and a highly respected man of letters.

Although trained for the law, Irving gradually abandoned the profession and devoted himself to writing. In 1804 he went to Europe and traveled there for nearly two years; he returned in 1815, this time for a stay that lasted, unexpectedly, for 17 years. On August 30, 1817, while traveling in Scotland, Irving visited Scott at Abbotsford and remained there for four memorable days; they became fast friends and Scott encouraged his guest, who did not enjoy his employment in the family business, to continue to write—a happy event for American literature. When Irving returned to work in "the loathed Liverpool office" of P. & E. Irving (as he once described it), he wrote this letter to Scott and sent American editions of some of Scott's poems as a gift for his daughter Sophia.

Liverpool Oct— 15ᵗʰ 1817. My dear Sir, The parcel which accompanies this contains American editions of some of your poems. Miss Scott seemed pleased with their appearance and their lilliputian size, and perhaps a little struck with the "nigromancy" by which a quart of wine was thus conjured into a pint bottle. I told her I would send them to her when I had made my tour, and beg you will present them to her as a very poor return for the pleasure I have received from her little border songs, which still dwell in my ear. I regret that some of the volumes are rather the worse for their journey among the Scotch mountains, but I had no fairer copies at hand.

With my best remembrances to Mrs Scott and the rest of the family I am dear Sir Very faithfully Yours Washington Irving / Walter Scott Esq.

Liverpool Oct 15th 1817.

My dear sir,

The parcel which accompanies this contains american editions of some of your poems. Miss Scott seemed pleased with their appearance and their lilliputian size. and perhaps a little struck with the "necromancy" by which a quart of wine was thus conjured into a pint bottle. I told her I would send them to her when I had made my tour, and beg you will present them to her as a very poor return for the pleasure I have received from her little border songs, which still dwell on my ear. I regret that some of the volumes are rather the worse for their journey among the Scotch mountains, but I had no fairer copies at hand.

With my best remembrances to Mrs Scott and the rest of the family I am my dear sir

very faithfully
Yours.

Washington Irving.

Walter Scott Esqr.

WASHINGTON IRVING

"A Chronicle of the Conquest of Granada. By Fray Antonio Agapida."
Autograph manuscript unsigned [written in Spain 1826–28].
2 v. 20 cm.

During his second residence in Europe, Irving was invited to come to Madrid to help translate into English a work on the voyages and discoveries of Columbus. He accepted with pleasure for he had always wanted to visit Spain and had studied Spanish. Irving's planned translation became an original work and was published in 1828, but only after he had begun a history of the conquest of Granada, so richly documented in Spanish libraries and archives. These volumes, published in 1829, were an account of the winning of the last Moorish kingdom in Spain, part history, part fiction, and with humorous touches; they were based on the alleged records of a mythical Fray Antonio Agapida. Irving's sympathies were often with the highly civilized Moors and against the religious fanatics of fifteenth-century Spain, but he had an openly romantic admiration for the gallant Spanish knights, and particularly for Queen Isabella. This book was one of his favorites and he followed it with *The Legends of the Alhambra* (1832). From 1842 to 1846 Irving served as the U.S. Minister to Spain. The final paragraphs of *A Chronicle of the Conquest of Granada* are reproduced here.

The Spanish sovreigns fixed their throne in the presence-chamber of the palace, so long the seat of Moorish royalty. Hither the principal inhabitants of Granada repaired, to pay them homage and kiss their hands in token of vassallage; and their example was followed by deputies from all the towns and fortresses of the Alpuxarras, which had not hitherto submitted.

Thus terminated the war of Granada, after ten years of incessant fighting; equalling (says Fray Antonio Agapida) the far-famed siege of Troy in duration, and ending, like that, in the capture of the city. Thus ended also the dominion of the Moors in Spain, having endured seven hundred and seventy-eight years, from the memorable defeat of Roderick, the last of the Goths, on the banks of the Guadalete. ~~This glorious event took place in the~~ The authentic Agapida is uncommonly particular in fixing the epoch of this ~~great triumph of the event~~ event. This great triumph of our holy Catholic faith (says he) according to his computation took place in the beginning of January, in the year of our Lord 1492, being 3655 years from the population of Spain by the patriarch Tubal; 3797 from the general deluge; 5453 from the creation of the world, according to Hebrew calculation; and in the month ~~Rabic~~ Rabic in the eight hundred and ninety-seventh year of the Hegira, or flight of Mahomet; whom may God confound! ~~say~~ saith ~~Fray Antonio~~ the pious Agapida.

※

This great Triumph of our holy Catholic
faith (says he) took place in the beginning
of January, in the year of our Lord 1492 -
being 3655 years from the population of
Spain by the Patriarch Tubal; 3797 from
the general deluge; 5453 from
the creation of the world, according to
the Hebrew calculation; and in the seventh
year of the Hegira or flight
of Mahomet, whom may God confound!
may faith Fray Antonio Agapida.

※

The Spanish sovereigns fixed their throne
in the principal chamber of the palace, to
be the seat of learned royalty. Hither
the principal inhabitants of Granada
repaired, to lay their homage and kiss
their hands in token of vassalage; and their
example was followed by deputies from all
the towns and fortresses of the Alpuxarras,
which had not hitherto submitted.
Thus terminated the war of Granada,
after ten years of incessant fighting; equal
(says Fray Antonio Agapida) this
far-famed siege of Troy in duration, and
ending like that, in the capture of the
city. Thus ended also the dominion of
the Moors in Spain, having endured
seven hundred and seventy-eight years,
from the memorable defeat of Roderick,
the last of the Goths, on the banks of the
Guadalete. This glorious event took
place. The authentic Agapida
is uncommonly particular in fixing the
event.

WASHINGTON IRVING

"Life of George Washington." Autograph manuscript unsigned
[written at his home, "Sunnyside," early in 1859]. 20 p. 20.5 cm.

Irving began this biography in the late 1840s as a labor of love and respect for the man after whom he had been named. Although he was occasionally assisted by research workers, poor health and the immensity of the project nearly defeated him. "I must weave," he said of the book, "my web, and then die." The fifth and final volume was published in the year of his death. The autograph pages for that volume reproduced here record the final hours and death of Washington, and are written in a surprisingly clear and firm hand. The Morgan Library also has about 100 pages of manuscript materials for other portions of the *Life of George Washington.*

Irving's literary style, based often on English models, was much admired for its charm, lucidity and humor. His great contribution to American letters was to prove that an American author and his works could be honored in European literary circles as well as at home. In the process he helped establish firmly our native profession of letters. Some of his books based on indigenous themes inspired American artists and writers who came after him. Irving was the first president of the Astor Library (now a part of The New York Public Library) and served until his death. Major manuscript collections of Irving materials are in The New York Public Library, Yale University Library, Harvard University Library and the Alderman Library, University of Virginia.

[*The general continued uneasy and*] *restless but without complaining, frequently asking what hour it was."*

Further remedies were tried without avail in the evening. He took whatever was offered him, did as he was desired by the physicians and never uttered sigh or complaint.

"About ten oclock," writes M^r. Lear, "he made several attempts to speak to me before he could effect it. At length he said, "I am just going. Have me decently buried; and do not let my body be put into the vault in less than three days after I am dead." I bowed assent, for I could not speak. He then looked at me again and said, "Do you understand me?" I replied "Yes." 'Tis well said he."

"About ten minutes before he expired (which was between ten and eleven oclock) his breathing became easier. He lay quietly; he withdrew his hand from mine and felt his own pulse. I saw his countenance change. I spoke to Dr Craik who sat by the fire. He came to the bed side. The

generals hand fell from his wrist. I took it in mine and pressed it to my bosom. Dr Craik put his hands over his eyes, and he expired without a struggle or a sigh."

While we were fixed in silent grief Mrs Washington, who was seated at the foot of the bed, asked with a firm and collected voice "Is he gone?" I could not speak, but held up my hand as a signal that he was no more. "'Tis well," said she in the same voice. "All is now over; I shall soon follow him; I have no more trials to pass through."

~~*We give from M^r*~~
~~*Washington was buried in the*~~
We add ~~*a few particulars*~~ *from Mr Lears account a few particulars concerning the funeral.* ~~*Washington had*~~ *The old family vault on the estate had been opened, the rubbish cleared away and a door made to close the entrance,* ⸗ *which before had been closed with brick.* ~~*Information was received that the*~~

SAMUEL WOODWORTH

*"The Bucket." Autograph poem unsigned [New York City, c. 1840].
1 p. 25.5 cm.*

Journalist, poet and dramatist (b. Scituate, Mass. 1784; d. New York City 1842). In his youth Woodworth was a printer and later worked on the editorial staff of several newspapers and periodicals. He was the author of a novel *The Champions of Freedom* (1816) and four plays of which the third, *The Forest Rose* (1825), was a great success. In it Woodworth created the Yankee character Jonathan Ploughboy.

Woodworth's posthumous fame rests mainly on his poem generally known as "The Old Oaken Bucket," which was first published in the New York *Republican-Chronicle* (3 June 1818), of which he was the editor. It was widely reprinted and soon set to music. George S. Kaufman and Marc Connelly drew on the third line of the poem for the title of their satirical play *The Deep-Tangled Wildwood*, produced in 1923. The poem was inspired by Woodworth's nostalgic memories of a well near his boyhood home in Scituate, Mass. In a note on the back of the copy this poem which he transcribed for Mrs. James T. Fields he wrote, "I wish it were in my power to write it in a manner more deserving her [Mrs. Field's] acceptance but perhaps you are aware that for more than three years I have been laboring under the effects of a *paralysis*, that disables one and renders me unfit for writing, and almost everything else." Woodworth collections may be found in The New York Public Library and Harvard University Library.

The Bucket.

How dear to this heart are the scenes of my childhood! / When fond recollection presents them to view, / The orchard, the meadow, the deep-tangled wild-wood, / And every loved spot that my infancy knew / The wide spreading pond, the mill that stood by it / The bridge and the rock, where the cataract fell, / The cot of my father, the dairy-house nigh it, / And e'en the rude Bucket that hung in the well. / The old oaken bucket, the iron-bound, bucket / The moss-covered Bucket, that hung in the well. /

That moss-covered vessel I hail as a treasure / For often at noon, when returned from the field / I found it the source of an exquisite pleasure, / The sweetest and purest that nature can yield. / How ardent I seized it, with palms that were glowing, / And quick to the white-pebbled bottom it fell, / Then soon with the emblem of truth overflowing, / And dripping with coolness, it rose from the well. / The old oaken Bucken, the iron-bound Bucket. / The moss-covered Bucket, arose from the well. /

How sweet from the green mossy brim to receive it / As poised on the kerb, it inclined to my lips / Not a full blushing goblet could tempt me to leave it, / The sweetest that Beauty or revelry sips / And now far removed from that loved habitation, / The tear of regret will intrusively swell, / As fancy reverts to my father's plantation, / And sighs for the Bucket that hung in the well. / [The old oaken Bucket, the iron-bound bucket, / The moss-covered Bucket, that hung in the well.] /

The Bucket.

How dear to this heart are the scenes of my childhood!
  When fond recollection presents them to view
The orchard, the meadow, the deep-tangled wild-wood,
  And every loved spot that my infancy knew
The wide spreading pond, the mill that stood by it
  The bridge and the rock, where the cataract fell,
The cot of my father, the dairy-house nigh it,
  And even the rude Bucket that hung in the well.
The old oaken bucket, the iron-bound, bucket
The moss-covered Bucket, that hung in the well.

That moss-covered vessel I hail as a treasure
  For often at noon, when returned from the field
I found it the source of an exquisite pleasure,
  The sweetest and purest that nature can yield.
How ardent I seized it, with palms that were glowing,
  And quick to the white-pebbled bottom it fell,
Then soon with the emblem of truth overflowing,
  And dripping with coolness, it rose from the well.
The old oaken Bucket, the iron-bound Bucket,
  The moss-covered Bucket, arose from the well.

How sweet from the green mossy brim to receive it
As poised on the kerb, it inclined to my lips
Not a full blushing goblet could tempt me to leave it,
The sweetest that Beauty or revelry sips
And now far removed from that loved habitation,
  The tear of regret will intrusively swell,
As fancy reverts to my father's plantation,
  And sighs for the Bucket that hung in the well.

JOHN PIERPONT

"This fratricidal war." Autograph poem signed, dated Washington, D.C. 1 Nov. 1861. 1 p. 20 cm.

Unitarian clergyman, social reformer and poet (b. Litchfield, Conn. 1785; d. Medford, Mass. 1866). He published many volumes of poems and textbooks, countless single and occasional poems and sermons, and lectured ceaselessly. His books include *The Portrait* (1812), *Airs of Palestine* (1816) and *Anti-Slavery Poems* (1843). He enjoyed a busy life and his intellectual curiosity led him into many unusual byways. He invented and sometimes manufactured stoves, wooden screws and razor straps, and experimented with horticulture and spiritualism.

A brief stay in South Carolina in 1805–06 brought young Pierpont face to face with the institution of slavery, and sowed the seeds of a fiery abolitionism which remained throughout his long life. Fortunately, he lived to see the emancipation. At the age of 76 Pierpont volunteered and served for a short time as an army chaplain. To his discomfiture he was transferred to the less arduous duties of a clerkship in the Treasury Department but here he soon became interested in solving certain problems of government finance and was of great service to the Department. In Washington he retained his literary interests and never refused his autograph, and he usually added a short poem or quotation as in the example illustrated here. The Pierpont Morgan Library has a very large collection of letters, manuscripts and related materials by and about John Pierpont and his family; J. Pierpont Morgan, founder of the Morgan Library, was his grandson.

This fratricidal war/Grows on the poisonous tree,/That God and men abhor—/Accursed Slavery./And God ordains that we/Shall eat that deadly fruit,/Till we dig up the tree,/And burn its every root./

J[oh]n. Pierpont

Washington, D. C. 1 Nov. 1861

This fratricidal war,
  Grows on the poisonous tree,
That God and men abhor—
  Accursed Slavery.
And God ordains that we
  Shall eat that deadly fruit,
Till we dig up the tree,
  And burn its every root.

                              J. Pierpont

Washington D. C. 1 Nov. 1861

RICHARD HENRY DANA

"Sonnet. To a Garden-Flower sent to me by a Lady." Autograph manuscript signed [Boston, c. 1860]. 1 p. 25 cm.

Poet, essayist, and critic (b. Cambridge, Mass. 1787; d. Boston, Mass. 1879). He was the author of *The Buccaneer and Other Poems* (1827) and *Poems and Prose Writings* (1833), and a founder and an associate editor of *The North American Review*. Dana was a member of a prominent New England family and his descendants went on to achieve further distinctions in literature, government and architecture. He was the father of the author of *Two Years Before the Mast* (1840), one of the great novels of life at sea and an American classic.

Early in life Dana abandoned law and politics for literature and pursued it in a leisurely and gentlemanly fashion. His writings were well received but none of them achieved any degree of popularity. His highly regarded lectures, delivered in 1849, defending Shakespeare as the greatest poet of the English language, have never been printed. Dana's contribution to the literary development of the United States is best measured in his direct and vigorous literary criticism and his friendship with and influence on fellow poets such as Bryant. After the age of 40 he spent most of the long span of life that remained to him in dignified retirement and was a popular and respected figure in Boston society. He was a friend of James T. Fields and his family and sent Mrs. Fields this sonnet in which he talks to and tortuously anthropomorphizes a garden flower. Dana letters and manuscripts as well as those of his more famous son are to be found most abundantly in Harvard University Library and the Massachusetts Historical Society Library.

Sonnet—

To a Garden-Flower sent to me by a Lady.—

No, not in woods, nor fells, nor pastures wild, / Nor left alone to changeful Nature's care, / You open'd on the light & breath'd the air; / But one, with blush like thine & look as mild / As dewed morn, with love all undefil'd / Chose out a kindly spot, & made thy bed / Safe from the cruel blast & heedless tread, / And watch'd thy birth & took thee for her child. / And human hands solicitous have train'd / Thy slender stalk, & eyes on thee have dwelt / Radiant with thought, & human feelings rain'd / Into thy bosom, e'en till thou hast felt / That through thy life a human virtue ran,— / And now art come to greet Thy Fellow-Man. /

R H Dana

Sonnet.

To a Garden-Flower sent to me by a Lady. —

No, not in woods, nor fells, nor pastures wild,
Nor left alone to changeful Nature's care,
You open'd on the light & breath'd the air;
But one, with blush like thine & look as mild
As dewed morn, with love all undefil'd
Chose out a kindly spot, & made thy bed
Safe from the cruel blast & heedless tread,
And watch'd thy birth & took thee for her child.
And human hands solicitous have train'd
Thy slender stalk, & eyes on thee have dwelt
Radiant with thought, & human feelings rain'd
Into thy bosom, e'en till thou hast felt
That through thy life a human virtue ran, —
And now art come to greet thy Fellow-Man.

R H Dana

JARED SPARKS

Autograph letter signed, dated Cambridge, Mass. May 30, 1837, addressed to Prof. Henry Hope Reed. 1 p. 25 cm.

Clergyman, historian, educator and editor (b. Willington, Conn. 1789; d. Cambridge, Mass. 1866). Sparks was owner and editor of *The North American Review* (1824–30), and edited *The Diplomatic Correspondence of the American Revolution* (1829–30) and the writings of both Washington and Franklin. He was a professor of history at Harvard University and served as its president (1849–53). Sparks's books stimulated a great popular interest in American history, and he was one of the first native historians to recognize the value of original letters and documents for historical research.

This letter concerns the *Abridgement of the Book of Common Prayer* which Benjamin Franklin helped Lord Le Despencer (formerly Sir Francis Dashwood) to prepare, and which was published privately in 1773. The copy of the book in Philadelphia to which Sparks refers was owned by Reed's sister-in-law, Miss Bronson, and was originally given by Franklin's daughter, Mrs. Bache, to William White, first bishop of Pennsylvania, who helped prepare the first American revision of the *Book of Common Prayer*. It is now in the Morgan Library; about six other copies of the book are recorded in American libraries. The manuscript fragments by Franklin found by Sparks appear to be those now in the American Philosophical Society Library, Philadelphia; letters of Sparks are mainly in Harvard University Library and The Historical Society of Pennsylvania.

Cambridge, Mass. May 30ᵗʰ 1837 Dear Sir, Your kind favor, of the 27ᵗʰ instant, has come very apropos. *Among Franklin's papers I have lately found a fragment of the Preface to the said "Abridgment of the Book of Common Prayer", in his hand-writing, and have been puzzling myself in vain to find any clue to the book. A learned Episcopal clergyman could give me no light on the subject. It is a very curious affair, as coming from Franklin. I doubt if there is another copy in America. I shall be in Philadelphia in the autumn, and shall then hope to see & examine the book. You should take some credit to your sagacity in detecting Franklin's style in the Preface. The whole was undoubtedly written by him, and also a note to the Catechism. The fragment in my hands is nearly complete.*

Accept my thanks for your attention in this matter, and believe me to be, with great respect, Your obliged, & most ob. svt. Jared Sparks / Prof. Reed.

Cambridge, Mass. May 30th 1837

Dear Sir,

Your kind favor, of the 27th instant, has come very apropos. Among Franklin's papers I have lately found a fragment of the Preface to the said "Abridgment of the Book of Common Prayer", in his hand-writing, and have been puzzling myself in vain to find any clue to the book. A learned Episcopal clergyman could give me no light on the subject. It is a very curious affair, as coming from Franklin. I doubt if there is another copy in America. I shall be in Philadelphia in the autumn, and shall then hope to see & examine the book. You should take some credit to your sagacity in detecting Franklin's style in the Preface. The whole was undoubtedly written by him, and also a note to the Catechism. The fragment in my hands is nearly complete.

Accept my thanks for your attention in this matter, and believe me to be, with great respect,

Your obliged,
& most Ob.Sv.t
Jared Sparks

Prof. Reed.

JAMES FENIMORE COOPER

"The Deerslayer." Autograph manuscript unsigned [written in Cooperstown in 1840–41]. 261 p. 30 cm. Brown morocco.

Novelist and social critic (b. Burlington, N.J. 1789; d. Cooperstown, N.Y. 1851). Author of *The Spy* (1821), *The Pioneers* (1823), *The Last of the Mohicans* (1826), *The Prairie* (1827), *The Pathfinder* (1840), *The Deerslayer* (1841) and *Satanstoe* (1845), among many other titles. In several books, including *The American Democrat* (1838), he defended democracy as he saw it against European misconceptions, and what he felt were those of some of his fellow Americans. Cooper was master of the novel of the frontier and the first American novelist to achieve substantial recognition outside his own country.

The manuscript of Cooper's *Deerslayer* was acquired by Pierpont Morgan from an English collection in 1895, and was the first important American literary manuscript to enter his library. In plot sequence this romantic novel is the first of Cooper's five Leather-Stocking Tales. The hero, Natty Bumppo, is "Deerslayer" and he is the superb woodsman —the symbol of all that is courageous, resourceful, wise and romantic in the white men who lived in the American wilderness. The Mohican chief Chingachgook is his faithful friend, "a noble savage," and in this novel arrives with a troop of British soldiers just in time to save the day. Cooper's Indian novels represented for generations of readers throughout the western world unique aspects of the cultural history of a growing America. Yale University Library has the largest group of Cooper manuscript materials.

Deerslayer.

Chapter 1.

(For motto, turn over)

On the human imagination, events produce the effects of time. Thus, he who has travelled far and seen much, is apt to fancy that he has lived long; and the history that most abounds in important incidents, soonest assumes the aspect of antiquity. In no other way can we account for the venerable air that is already gathering around American annals. When the mind reverts to the earliest days of colonial history, the period seems remote and obscure, the thousand changes that thicken along the ~~line~~ links of recollections, throwing back the origin of the nation to a ~~time as remote~~

day so distant as ~~almost~~ seemingly to reach the mists of time; yet four lives of ordinary duration would suffice to transmit, from mouth to mouth, in the form of tradition, all that civilized man has achieved within the limits of the republic, ~~in the form of oral tradition.~~ Although New-York ~~now,~~ alone, possesses a population materially exceeding that of either of the four smallest kingdoms of Europe, or materially exceeding that of the entire Swiss Confederation, it is little more than two centuries since the Dutch commenced their settlement, rescuing the region from the savage state. Thus, what seems venerable by ~~the~~ an accumulation of changes, is reduced to familiarity when we come seriously to consider it solely in connection with time. [. . .]

On the human imagination, events produce the effects of time. Thus, he who has travelled far and
seen much, is apt to fancy that he has lived long; and the history that most abounds in important
incidents, sooner assumes the aspect of antiquity. In no other way can we account for the
venerable air that is already gathering around American annals. When the mind reverts to
the earliest days of colonial history, the period seems remote and obscure, the thousand changes
that thicken along the line links of recollection, throwing back the origin of the nation to a day so distant
as seemingly almost to reach the mists of time; and yet four lives of ordinary duration would suffice to transmit, from mouth to mouth, in the form of traditions all that civilized man has achieved within the limits of the republic, in the form of oral traditions. Although New-York now possesses a population alone, materially exceeding that of either
of the four smallest kingdoms of Europe, or materially exceeding that of the entire Swiss Confederation, it is little more than two centuries since the Dutch commenced their settle-
ment, rescuing the region from the savage state. Thus, what seems venerable by the accumulation of changes, is reduced to familiarity when we come seriously to consider it solely in connection with time.

This glance into the perspective of the past, will prepare the reader to look at the pictures
we are about to sketch, with less surprise than he might otherwise feel, and a few additional explanations may carry him back in imagination, to the precise condition of society that we
wish to delineate. It is matter of history that the settlements on the eastern shores of the Hudson, such
as Claverack, Kinderhook, and even Poughkeepsie, were not regarded as safe from Indian in-
cursion a century since, and there is still standing a residence of a younger branch of the
Van Rensselaers, on the banks of the same river, and within musket shot of the wharves of Albany, that has loop-holes constructed for defence against the same crafty enemy, although it dates
from a period scarcely so distant. Other similar memorials of the infancy of the country are
to be found, scattered through what is now deemed the very centre of American civilization, affording the plainest proofs that all we possess of security from invasion and hostile violence, is the
growth of but little more than the time that is frequently filled by a single human life.

The incidents of this tale occurred between the years 1740 and 1745, when the settled portions of the colony of New-York were confined to the four Atlantic counties, to a narrow belt of
country on each side of the Hudson, extending from its mouth to the falls near its head,
and to a few advanced "neighborhoods" on the Mohawk and the Schoharie. Broad belts
of the virgin wilderness, not only reached to the shores of the first river, but they even crossed
it, stretching away into New England, and affording secret forest covers to the noiseless
occasion of the native warrior, as he trod the secret and bloody war-path. A bird's eye view of the whole region east of the Mississippi american continent, must then have offered one vast expanse of woods, relieved by a comparatively narrow fringe of cultivation along the sea, and dotted by the glittering surfaces
of lakes, and intersected by the waving lines of rivers. In such a vast picture of solemn solitude
the district of country we wish to paint, sinks into insignificance, though we feel encouraged
to proceed by the conviction that, with slight and immaterial distinctions, he who succeeds in
giving an accurate idea of any portion of this wild region, must necessarily convey a tolerably
correct notion of the whole. Whatever may be the changes that are produced by man, the eternal round of the seasons
is unbroken. Summer and winter, seed time and harvest, return in their stated order,

JAMES FENIMORE COOPER

"Satanstoe." Autograph manuscript unsigned of chapters i–xv [written in Cooperstown in 1844]. 120 p. 32 cm. Green morocco.

This is the first page, tightly written, of approximately one half of the autograph manuscript of the first of three novels by Cooper collectively known as The Littlepage Manuscripts. They trace the history of the Littlepage family through three generations in New York State, with emphasis on the differences between the propertied and propertyless classes. The final novel in this trilogy is concerned with the Anti-Rent War in which citizens disguised themselves as Indians to intimidate the estate owners and raid their manorial tracts. The fictional Satanstoe is a neck of land in the county of Westchester which has landscape shapes and swells that resemble inverted toes. There is a tradition that Satan, making a hasty exit from a tavern in New Amsterdam, passed through the area on his way Down-East (where the Dutch and early English thought he originated), and turned everything upside down. Less fanciful than the origin of its name, *Satanstoe* is an interesting and well-written book, but it has been obscured by Cooper's novels of the frontier.

Chapter I. (Motto—turn over)

It is easy to foresee that this country is destined to undergo great and rapid changes. These that more properly belong to history, history will doubtless attempt to record, and probably with the questionable veracity ~~that is~~ and prejudice that are apt to influence the labors of that particular muse, but there is little hope that any traces of ~~the~~ American society, in its more familiar aspects, will be preserved among us, through any of the agencies usually employed for such purposes. Without a stage, in a national point of view at least, with scarcely such a thing as a book of memoirs that relates to a life passed within our own limits, and totally without light literature, to give us simulated pictures of our manners and the opinions of the day, I see scarcely ~~any~~ a mode by which the next generation will can preserve any memorials of the distinctive usages and ~~opinions~~ thoughts of this. It is true, they will have traditions of certain leading features of the colonial society, but scarcely any records; and, should the next twenty years do as much as the last, toward substituting an entirely new race, for the descendants of our own immediate fathers, it is scarcely too much to predict that even these traditions will be lost in the whirl and excitement of a throng of strangers. [. . .]

Chapter 1. (Motto — turn over)

It is easy to foresee that this country is destined to undergo great and rapid changes. Those that more properly belong to history, history will doubtless attempt to record, and probably with the usual veracity, malice and prejudice that are apt to influence the labors of that practical art; but there is little hope that any traces of the American society, in its more familiar aspects, will be preserved among us, through any of the agencies usually employed for such purposes. Without a stage, in a national point of view at least, with scarcely such a thing as a book of memoirs that relates to a life passed within our own limits, and totally without light literature, to give us similar pictures of our manners and the opinions of the day, I see scarcely any mode by which the next generation can preserve any memorials of the distinctive usages and opinions thoughts of this. It is true, they will have traditions of certain leading features of the colonial society, but none if any record; and, should the next twenty years do as much, toward revolutionizing an entirely new race, for the descendants of our own immediate fathers, it is scarcely too much to predict that even these traditions will be lost in the whirl and excitement of a thronging of strangers. Under all the circumstances, therefore, I have come to a determination to make an effort, however useless it may prove, to preserve some vestiges of household life in New York, at least, while I have endeavored to stimulate certain friends in New Jersey, and farther south, to undertake similar tasks in those sections of the country. What success will attend these last applications, is more than I can say, but, in order that the little I may do myself, shall not be lost for want of support, I have made a solemn request in my will, that those who come after me, will consent to continue this narrative, not committing to paper their own experience as I have been committing my mine, down as low at least as my grandson, if I ever have one. Perhaps, by the end of the latter's career, they will begin to publish books in America, and the fruits of our joint family labors may be thought sufficiently matured to be laid before the world.

It is possible that which I am now about to write, will be thought too homely, to relate to matters much too personal and private, to have sufficient interest for the public eye; but, it must be remembered that the loftiest interests of man are made up of a collection of those that are lowly, and, that he who makes a faithful picture of only a single important scene in the events of single life, is doing something towards painting the greatest historical piece of his day. As I have said before, the leading events of my time will find their way into the pages of far more pretending works than this of mine, in some form or other, with more or less of fidelity to the truth, and real events, and real motives, while the humbler matters it will be my office to record, will be entirely overlooked by writers who aspire to enroll their names among the Taciteses of former ages. It may be well to say here, however, I shall not attempt the historical mood at all, but content myself with giving the feelings, incidents and interests of what is purely private life, connecting them no farther with things that are of a more general nature, than is indispensable to render the narrative intelligible and accurate. With these explanations, which are made in order to prevent the person who may happen first to commence the perusal of this manuscript, from throwing it into the fire as a silly attempt to write a more silly fiction, I shall proceed at once to the commencement of my proper task.

JAMES FENIMORE COOPER

Autograph letter signed, dated New-York, Nov. 1ˢᵗ 1836, addressed to Samuel Rogers. 1 p. 24 cm.

When in London in 1828, Cooper had letters of introduction to several British literary figures of which Samuel Rogers, the poet, was one. Rogers was also a man of cultivated tastes and a fine host. He invited Cooper to his home and introduced him to his literary and artistic circle, and the two men became fast friends. Cooper writes of Rogers in his *Gleanings in Europe: England* (1837). A year before that book was published Cooper sent this letter introducing "the daughters of the late John Jay, one of the first men this country ever produced, formerly President of Congress, and they are worthy to be his daughters." Rogers survived Cooper by four years, dying at the age of 92 in 1855.

New-York, Nov. 1ˢᵗ 1836 My dear Sir, [. . .] The ladies are Mrs. Ba[n]yer (a widow) and her sister Miss Jay. They are the daughters of the late John Jay, one of the first men this country ever produced, formerly President of Congress, and they are worthy to be his daughters.

I dare not write to Lady Lansdowne in their behalf, for my own intimacy will not justify it, but if I dared I would, and yet I would rather they should know her than any other woman in London.

My wife, who always speaks of you in a manner that would make me jealous but for my own vanity, is at Cooperstown, with all her girls, the winter's campaign not having yet commenced. She does not know of my writing, or I should certainly be charged with her amitiés. I beg to be mentioned, with my regards to Miss Rogers, and Remain, Dear Sir, Your most obliged and Sincere Friend J. Fenimore Cooper / Samuel Rogers, Esquire

New-York, Nov. 1st 1836

My dear Sir,

No one can feel, more than myself, that the kindnesses he has received in his proper person, does not entitle him to claim it in behalf of others, but, ~~in your case~~ (and really I do not know whether you will consider it as an impertinence or a compliment) I have, more than once, been tempted to overlook the truth, and to fancy that your many acts of friendship to me have constituted a right to trouble you in a way, that I ~~have no right~~ ought not, to do. Two ladies, not only of my acquaintance, but of my oldest and most intimate acquaintance — two women who I confidently tell you are among the very best of their sex in this, or any other country — are going to England for their health. I am most anxious that they should see you, and they are anxious too, for the Pleasures of Memory is like an old friend to them both. As you will find good manners, good sense, and no pretension or any exactions, I hope the acquaintance, which must necessarily be short, will be productive of mutual satisfaction.

The ladies are Mrs Banyer (a widow) and her sister Miss Jay. They are the daughters of the late John Jay, one of the first men this country ever produced, formerly President of Congress, and they are worthy to be his daughters.

I dare not write to Lady Lansdowne in their behalf, for my own intimacy will not justify it, but if I dared I would, and yet I would rather they should know her than any other woman in London.

My wife, who always speaks of you in a manner that would make me feel odd but for my own vanity, is at Coopertown, with all her girls, the winter's campaign not having yet commenced. She does not know of my writing, or I should certainly be charged with her amities. I beg to be mentioned, with my regards to Miss Rogers, and

Remain,
Dear Sir,
Your most Obliged
and sincere Friend
J. Fenimore Cooper

Samuel Rogers, Esquire.

FITZ-GREENE HALLECK

"Marco Bozzaris." Autograph poem signed [n.p.] 23ᵈ April '57.
6 p. 20.3 cm.

Poet and banker (b. Guilford, Conn. 1790; d. Guilford, Conn. 1867). With Joseph Rodman Drake he wrote *The Croaker Papers*, a lively and humorous series of verses published in newspapers in 1819 and later collected. His "Elegy in Memory of Drake" (1820) and "Marco Bozzaris" (1825) were once very popular; he also wrote the long poem *Fanny* (1819)—a satire on social climbers in imitation of Lord Byron—and *Alnwick Castle* (1827). Halleck's working years were spent in banking in New York City, and included 17 as confidential clerk to John Jacob Astor. Halleck's best literary productions come from his early years; in later years his personal popularity and the comparative scarcity of good new writers kept his name alive. He always considered literature to be an avocation.

The poem was first published in *The New York Review and Athenaeum Magazine*, No. 1, June 1825, and this autograph copy, of which the first and last pages are reproduced, was written out 32 years later. It became immediately popular and was widely acclaimed, reprinted and translated into several languages (including Greek); it provided inspiration and text for elocutionists and schoolboy orators. Marco Bozzaris was a hero of the Greek War for Independence; he gained fame for the defense of Missolonghi against the Turks and was killed in action in 1823. His death in battle is the subject of Halleck's poem, and the poem itself is an expression of the friendship and admiration that the American people felt for the Greek people in their struggle for independence; the poem is, however, far from independent of the literary influence of Lord Byron, who was to die while active in the Greek cause at Missolonghi in 1824. Halleck letters and manuscripts are to be found in many American libraries.

Marco Bozzaris.

pronounced Botzare

At midnight, in his guarded tent, / The Turk was dreaming of the hour / When Greece, her knee in suppliance bent, / Should tremble at his power, / In dreams through court and camp he bore / The trophies of a conqueror, / In dreams his song of triumph heard, / Then wore his monarch's signet ring, / Then pressed that monarch's couch a king, / As wild his thoughts and gay of wing / As Eden's garden bird. /

At midnight, in the forest shades, / Bozzaris ranged his Suliote band, / True as the steel of their tried blades, / Heroes in heart and hand. / Then [. . .]

For thine her evening prayer is said / At palace couch, and cottage bed, / Her soldier, closing with the foe, / Gives, for thy sake, a deadlier blow, / His plighted maiden, when she fears / For him, the joy of her young years, / Thinks of thy fate, and checks her tears, / And she, the mother of thy boys, / Though in her eye and faded cheek / Is read the grief she will not speak, / The memory of her buried joys, / And even she who gave thee birth, / Will, by their pilgrim-circled hearth, / Talk of thy doom without a sigh, / For thou art Freedom's now and Fame's, / One of the few, the immortal names, / That were not born to die. /

Written in 1824. Copied 23ᵈ April '57, at the request of James T. Fields, Esq.

Fitz-Greene Halleck

Marco Bozzaris.

At midnight, in his guarded tent,
The Turk was dreaming of the hour
When Greece, her knee in suppliance bent,
Should tremble at his power;
In dreams, through Camp and Court, he bore
The trophies of a conqueror;
In dreams his song of triumph heard;
Then wore his monarch's signet-ring,
Then pressed that monarch's throne, a king;
As wild his thoughts, and gay of wing,
As Eden's garden bird.

At midnight, in the forest shades,
Bozzaris ranged his Suliote band,
True as the steel of their tried blades,
Heroes in heart and hand.
There

For thee her evening prayer is said
At palace-couch, and cottage-bed,
Her soldier, closing with the foe,
Gives, for thy sake, a deadlier blow;
His plighted maiden, when she fears
For him, the joy of her young years,
Thinks of thy fate, and checks her tears,
And she, the mother of thy boys,
Though in her eye and faded cheek
Is read the grief she will not speak,
The memory of her buried joys,
And even she who gave thee birth,
Will, by their pilgrim-circled hearth,
Talk of thy doom without a sigh;
For thou art Freedom's now, and Fame's,
One of the few, the immortal names,
That were not born to die.

written in 1824.   aged 23 at the signing
of
Baron J. Reily, Esq.

Fitz-Greene Halleck.

JOHN HOWARD PAYNE

"Sweet Home." Autograph manuscript of the poem signed, dated New York, Feb: 2: 1843. 1 p. 25 cm.

Actor, dramatist and diplomat (b. New York City 1791; d. Tunis 1852). Payne went to England in 1813 and remained in Europe much of his life. He wrote, translated or adapted over 60 plays. His *Brutus; or, the Fall of Tarquin* (1818) was written for the actor Edmund Kean. Other successes were *Thérèse, the Orphan of Geneva* (1821), *Charles the Second* (1824) and *Richelieu* (1826). The immortal "Home, Sweet Home" occurs in his opera *Clari; or, the Maid of Milan*, which was first produced in London on May 8, 1823. Henry Bishop wrote the music, ostensibly based on a Sicilian air, for this nostalgic ballad sung by the heroine, which recurs with variations throughout the opera as a sort of "theme song." The song became an immediate success and was soon published in sheet-music form.

In spite of his many triumphs as performer and author, Payne was constantly in debt; he had sold the copyright of *Clari* outright and received no royalties. In 1842, with the aid of his friend Daniel Webster, he obtained the post of U.S. Consul in Tunis, an office he held off and on until his death. Payne was deeply interested in the problems of the American Indian and wrote a history of the Cherokee Nation. In England he once courted the widow of Percy Bysshe Shelley, but in vain. The first two verses of "Home, Sweet Home," as shown here, were written out by Payne for James T. Fields in 1843, just before Payne left for his consular post. The principal collections of Payne materials are in the Huntington Library and Columbia University Library.

Sweet Home.

'Mid pleasures and palaces though we may roam | Be it ever so humble, there's no place like home! | A charm from the sky seems to hallow us there | Which, seek through the world, is ne'er met with elsewhere! | Home! Home! Sweet, sweet home! | There's no place like home! | There's no place like home! |

An exile from home, splendor dazzles in vain! | Oh, give me my lowly thatch'd cottage again! | The birds singing gaily, that come at my call,— | Give me them,—with the peace of mind dearer than all! | Home! Home! Sweet, sweet home! | There's no place like home! | There's no place like home! |

John Howard Payne.

At New York, Feb: 2: 1843 for James T. Fields, Esquire, Boston.

Sweet Home.

'Mid pleasures and palaces though we may roam
Be it ever so humble, there's no place like home!
A charm from the sky seems to hallow us there
Which, seek through the world, is ne'er met with elsewhere!
    'Home! Home! Sweet, Sweet home!
    There's no place like home!
    There's no place like home!

An exile from home, splendor dazzles in vain!
Oh, give me my lowly thatch'd cottage again!
The birds singing gaily, that came at my call, —
Give me them, — with the peace of mind dearer than all!
    'Home! Home! Sweet, sweet home!
    There's no place like home!
    There's no place like home!

          John Howard Payne.

At New York, Feb: 2: 1843
    for James T. Fields, Esquire, Boston.

LYDIA HUNTLEY SIGOURNEY

Autograph letter signed, dated Hartford, May 1ˢᵗ, 1840, addressed to
John Pierpont. 1 p. 23 cm.

Poet and miscellaneous writer (b. Norwich, Conn. 1791; d. Hartford, Conn. 1865). Mrs. Sigourney was one of the most popular writers of her day and published 67 volumes in just over 50 years, from *Moral Pieces in Prose and Verse* (1815) to *Letters of Life* (1866), an autobiography published after her death; she made innumerable contributions to annuals and magazines. Respected and admired by many of her contemporaries, she was known as "The Sweet Singer of Hartford"; she was also active in the cause of higher education for women. In her poetry she was preoccupied with the theme of death, and it was said that she regarded every sick child as a potential angel; even in her lifetime her elegies came to be known in certain waggish literary circles as "death's second terror."

Her letter to John Pierpont, who had published his book of poetry *The Airs of Palestine* many years before, transmitted a slip from a descendant of Pope's willow near his grotto at Twickenham and misspelled her correspondent's name. We do not know whether or not Pierpont ever sat under the shadow of the grown willow, but he was much interested in trees and gardens and would have cared for it. Mrs. Sigourney's manuscripts and letters are in many American libraries, especially Yale University Library and the Connecticut Historical Society.

Hartford, May 1ˢᵗ 1840, My dear Sir, I have recently recieved from Virginia, some slips from a descendant of Pope's celebrated willow, at Twickenham, and beg your acceptance of the one that accompanies this note. Allow it to flourish in your poetical premises, & to be refreshed by the "Airs of Palestine." May you sit under its shadow with great delight.

Please to remember me to Mʳˢ Pierpoint, and your daughter, and believe me Yours, Sir, with respect, and esteem, L. H. Sigourney

Hartford, May, 1st 1840,

My dear Sir, -

I have recently recieved from Virginia, some slips from a descendant of Pope's celebrated Willow, at Twickenham, - and beg your acceptance of the one that accompanies this note. - Allow it to flourish in your poetical premises, & to be refreshed by the "Airs of Palestine". - May you sit under its shadow with great delight. -

Please to remember me to Mr Pierpoint, and your daughter, and believe me

Yours, Sir, with respect,
and esteem,
L. H. Sigourney,

16

WILLIAM CULLEN BRYANT

"Thanatopsis." Autograph manuscript unsigned [n.p., n.d.]. 2 p. 25 cm.

Poet, essayist and editor (b. Cummington, Mass. 1794; d. New York City 1878). Among his many published works are *The Embargo* (1808), *Poems* (1821), *The Fountain* (1842), *The White-Footed Deer* (1844), *Letters of a Traveller* (1850, 1859), *Thirty Poems* (1864) and *The Flood of Years* (1878). Bryant also translated Homer and edited the influential New York *Evening Post* from 1829 until his death. He wrote mainly nature poetry, always of a high order, and his early poems are his best. He supported many liberal causes in the United States and throughout the world and, at the height of his career, was New York's leading citizen.

"Thanatopsis" was written when Bryant was 15 years of age and published in *The North American Review*, September 1817, but without the famous opening and closing lines which, when added in the *Poems* (1821), made it the first great American poem. With its cultivated melancholy reminiscent of Gray's *Elegy*, the poem became immediately celebrated and established the reputation of the poet. This is an early but undated autograph copy of "Thanatopsis" to which a signature of the author has been added. There are large collections of Bryant manuscripts in The New York Public Library and the Huntington Library.

Thanatopsis.

To him who in the love of Nature holds / Communion with her visible forms, she speaks / A various language, for his gayer hours / She has a voice of gladness and a smile / And eloquence of beauty, and she glides / Into his darker musings with a soft / And healing sympathy that steals away / Their sharpness ere he is aware. When thoughts / Of the last bitter hour come, like a blight, / Over thy spirit, and sad images / Of the stern agony and shroud and pall / And breathless darkness and the narrow house / Make thee to shudder and grow sick at heart, / Go forth, under the open sky, and list / To Nature's teachings, while, from all around, / Earth and her waters and the depths of air, / Comes a still voice;—Yet a few days and thee / The all-beholding sun shall see no more / In all his course; nor yet within the ground, / Where thy pale form was laid with many tears, / Nor in the embrace of ocean, shall exist / Thy image. [. . .]

So live that when thy summons comes to join / The innumerable caravan which moves / To that mysterious realm where each shall take / His chamber in the silent halls of Death / Thou go not, like the quarry-slave at night, / Scourged to his dungeon, but sustained and soothed / By an unfaltering trust, approach thy grave, / Like one who wraps the drapery of his couch / About him and lies down to pleasant dreams. /

William Cullen Bryant.

Thanatopsis

To him who in the love of Nature holds
Communion with her visible forms, she speaks
A various language; for his gayer hours
She has a voice of gladness, and a smile
And eloquence of beauty, and she glides
Into his darker musings, with a mild
And healing sympathy that steals away
Their sharpness, ere he is aware. When thoughts
Of the last bitter hour come like a blight
Over thy spirit, and sad images
Of the stern agony, and shroud, and pall
And breathless darkness, and the narrow house
Make thee to shudder and grow sick at heart;—
Go forth, under the open sky, and list
To Nature's teachings, while from all around—
Earth and her waters, and the depths of air,—
Comes a still voice—Yet a few days and thee
The all beholding sun shall see no more
In all his course; nor yet in the cold ground,
Where thy pale form was laid with many tears,
Nor in the embrace of ocean, shall exist
Thy image. Earth, that nourished thee, shall claim
Thy growth, to be resolved to earth again,
And, lost each human trace, surrendering up
Thine individual being, shalt thou go

To mix for ever with the elements,
To be a brother to the insensible rock
And to the sluggish clod, which the rude swain
Turns with his share, and treads upon. The oak
Shall send his roots abroad, and pierce thy mould.

Yet not to thine eternal resting place
Shalt thou retire alone, nor couldst thou wish
Couch more magnificent. Thou shalt lie down
With patriarchs of the infant world—with kings,
The powerful of the earth—the wise, the good,
Fair forms, and hoary seers of ages past,
All in one mighty sepulchre.—The hills
Rock-ribbed and ancient as the sun,—the vales
Stretching in pensive quietness between;
The venerable woods—rivers that move
In majesty, and the complaining brooks
That make the meadows green; and poured round all,
Old ocean's gray and melancholy waste,—
Are but the solemn decorations all
Of the great tomb of man. The golden sun,
The planets, all the infinite host of heaven,
Are shining on the sad abodes of death,
Through the still lapse of ages. All that tread
The globe are but a handful to the tribes
That slumber in its bosom.—Take the wings

Of morning, traverse Barca's desert sands,
Or lose thyself in the continuous woods
Where rolls the Oregon, and hears no sound,
Save his own dashings,—yet the dead are there:
And millions in those solitudes, since first
The flight of years began, have laid them down
In their last sleep—the dead reign there alone.
So shalt thou rest, and what if thou withdraw
In silence from the living, and no friend
Take note of thy departure? All that breathe
Will share thy destiny. The gay will laugh
When thou art gone, the solemn brood of care
Plod on, and each one as before will chase
His favorite phantom; yet all these shall leave
Their mirth and their employments, and shall come
And make their bed with thee. As the long train
Of ages glide away, the sons of men,
The youth in life's green spring, and he who goes
In the full strength of years, matron and maid,
And the sweet babe, and the gray headed man,—
Shall one by one be gathered to thy side,
By those who in their turn shall follow them.

So live, that when thy summons comes to join
The innumerable caravan, which moves
To that mysterious realm where each shall take
His chamber in the silent halls of death,
Thou go not, like the quarry-slave at night,
Scourged to his dungeon, but sustained and soothed
By an unfaltering trust, approach thy grave
Like one who wraps the drapery of his couch
About him, and lies down to pleasant dreams.

William Cullen Bryant.

17

WILLIAM CULLEN BRYANT

"To a Waterfowl." Autograph manuscript signed, dated Roslyn, Decr. 12th. 1877. 2 p. 25 cm.

This lyric poem was first printed in *The North American Review*, March 1818, and was collected in Bryant's *Poems* (1821). No critic writes about it without quoting Matthew Arnold, who called it "the most perfect brief poem in the language." As Bryant recollected in later years, it was written in 1815 during a journey he was making to Plainfield, Mass. He was starting out in the legal profession and was lonely and depressed by the idea of his possible failure. "To a Waterfowl" records his thoughts when he saw a lone bird making its way against the twilight sky to some unknown destination. He looks upon the bird as an inspirational lesson and feels that divine guidance will come to them both. It is a poem of intense emotion. The manuscript illustrated is one that Bryant copied out in the last year of his life.

To a Waterfowl.

Whither, midst falling dew, / While glow the heavens with the last steps of day / Far through their rosy depths dost thou pursue / Thy solitary way? /

Vainly the fowler's eye / Might mark thy distant flight, to do thee wrong, / As, darkly seen against the crimson sky, / Thy figure floats along. /

Seekst thou the plashy brink / Of weedy lake or marge of river wide, / Or where the rocking billows rise and sink / On the chafed ocean side? / [. . .]

Thou'rt gone; the abyss of heaven / Hath swallowed up thy form; yet, on my heart, / Deeply hath sunk the lesson thou hast given, / And shall not soon depart. /

He who, from zone to zone, / Guides, through the boundless sky, thy certain flight, / In the long way that I must tread alone / Will lead my steps aright. /

William Cullen Bryant.

Copied, Roslyn, Decr. 12th. 1877.

To a Waterfowl.

Whither, midst falling dew,
While glow the heavens with the last steps of day,
Far, through their rosy depths, dost thou pursue
Thy solitary way?

Vainly the fowler's eye
Might mark thy distant flight, to do thee wrong,
As, darkly seen against the crimson sky,
Thy figure floats along.

Seek'st thou the plashy brink
Of weedy lake, or marge of river wide,
Or where the rocking billows rise and sink
On the chafed ocean side?

There is a Power whose care
Teaches thy way along that pathless coast,—
The desert and illimitable air,—
Lone wandering, but not lost.

All day thy wings have fanned,
At that far height, the cold thin atmosphere,
Yet stoop not, weary, to the welcome land,
Though the dark night is near.

And soon that toil shall end;
Soon shalt thou find a summer home, and rest,
And scream among thy fellows; reeds shall bend,
Soon, o'er thy sheltered nest.

Thou'rt gone, the abyss of heaven
Hath swallowed up thy form; yet, on my heart
Deeply hath sunk the lesson thou hast given,
And shall not soon depart.

He, who, from zone to zone,
Guides, through the boundless sky, thy certain flight,
In the long way that I must tread alone,
Will lead my steps aright.

William Cullen Bryant.

Copied, Roslyn, Dec: 12th 1877.

18

WILLIAM CULLEN BRYANT

Autograph letter signed, dated New York, September 23 1862,
addressed to President Lincoln. 1 p. 22 cm.

In the fall of 1862 Cassius Marcellus Clay was ordered home from his post as Minister to Russia by President Lincoln to serve as a major-general. Clay's turbulent and psychiatrically interesting life is a story in itself, but he was a staunch abolitionist and supporter of the Union cause. Bryant took the opportunity to write Lincoln and to recommend Bayard Taylor, then Secretary of the Legation in Saint Petersburg, for the post. As a world traveler, author and diplomat, Taylor was well qualified, but Clay chose to return to Russia, where he served until 1869. In the months he spent in Russia Taylor did much to keep that country sympathetic to the Union cause. Among the infinite number of letters of recommendation for positions that have survived, this is probably one of the very few of literary importance.

September 23 1862   To Abraham Lincoln   President of the United States. Sir, If Mr. Clay is not to be reappointed as our minister to Russia, I most heartily recommend Mr. Bayard Taylor the present Secretary of Legation for that post. Mr. Taylor has many important qualifications for the place and would fill it with honor to his country. I am Sir most respectfully &c   W. C. Bryant.

Office of The Evening Post,

41 NASSAU STREET, COR. LIBERTY.

New York, September 23 1862

To Abraham Lincoln

President of the United States.

Sir.

If Mr. Clay is not to be reappointed as our minister to Russia, I most heartily recommend Mr. Bayard Taylor the present Secretary of Legation for that Post. Mr. Taylor had many important qualifications for the place and would fill it with honor to his country.

I am for sincere respectfully &c

W. C. Bryant.

19

JAMES GATES PERCIVAL

Autograph letter signed, undated, but docketed by the recipient
9 February 1843, addressed to William Greenleaf Webster. 1 p. 25.5 cm.

Poet and scientist (b. Kensington, Conn. 1795; d. Hazel Green, Wis. 1856). His literary efforts, much admired in his day, include the play *Zamor* (1815), *Poems* (1821), of which his Spenserian "Prometheus" was a part, *Prometheus Part II* (1822) and *The Dream of a Day* (1843). Percival was one of the most learned men of his day, made translations from several languages, and assisted Noah Webster in the preparation of *An American Dictionary of the English Language* (1828). He was also a medical officer and teacher of chemistry at West Point, and State Geologist of both Connecticut and Wisconsin.

An eccentric and paranoiac, Percival lived for ten years, by his own choice, in the New Haven State Hospital, where this letter was written. It is addressed to the son of Noah Webster, whom Percival was assisting in the compilation of addenda to his father's unabridged dictionary, and is a technical description of the octaves of the flute. Percival also had a considerable musical interest, wrote some songs, and is reported to have developed a theory of music, which has been lost. The largest collection of Percival materials is in Yale University Library.

Dear Sir   The question about the octave of the Flute is solved— The octave produced by blowing merely (retaining the fingering of the bass note) is that formed in a simple tube (as the Trumpet) by the Natural Harmonies or common chord, and is consequently the true natural octave— The octave formed by fingering is that formed on the principle of tuning the Flute—that is, the flute, like all instruments with fixed tuning, adapted for different Keys, has its semitones tuned equal to half a tone, but the two natural Diatonic Semitones (E to F & B to Octave) exceed half a tone by half ♮ the diesis, as the chromatic Semitones (♯ & ♭ of each tone) are less than half a tone, by the same half diesis, consequently in tuning the two Diatonic Semitones in the flute equal half a tone, there are lost in the Octave two half dieses, that is the Octave thus tuned is less ~~than~~ or flatter than the Natural Octaves by a diesis (nearly equal a quarter tone.) Q. E. D.   JG Percival / WG Webster

Dear Sir

The question about the octaves of the flute is solved — the octave produced by blowing merely (retaining the fingering of the bass note) is that formed in a simple tube (as the Trumpet) by the natural harmonies or common chord, and is consequently the true natural octave — the octave formed by fingering is that formed on the principle of tuning the Flute — that is, the flute, like all instruments with fixed tuning, adapted for different Keys, has its semitones tuned equal to half a tone, but the two natural Diatonic Semitones (E to F & B to Octave) exceed half a tone by half the diesis, as the Chromatic Semitones (# & b of each tone) are less than half a tone, by the same half diesis, consequently in tuning the two Diatonic Semitones in the Flute equal half a tone, there are lost — in the octave two half diesis, that is the octave thus tuned is less ~~than~~ or flatter than the natural octave by a diesis (nearly equal a Quarter tone.) Q.E.D.

J G Percival

W G Webster

20

JOHN PENDLETON KENNEDY

"Horse-Shoe Robinson." Autograph manuscript of a quotation from the novel, signed [Baltimore, Md. 1864]. 2 p. 20 cm.

Author and statesman (b. Baltimore, Md. 1795; d. Newport, R.I. 1870). He wrote *Swallow Barn* (1832), a picture of plantation life in Virginia; *Horse-Shoe Robinson* (1835), a tale of the American Revolution; *Rob of the Bowl* (1838), a story of colonial Maryland; and *Quodlibet* (1840), a Whig satire on politics. His biography of the Virginia politician and author William Wirt was published in 1849. Kennedy served in the U.S. House of Representatives and as Secretary of the Navy (1852–53). During his secretaryship he was influential in promoting the expedition to Japan under Commodore Perry and the second Arctic exploratory voyage of Elisha Kent Kane. He was a patron of Poe and, during Thackeray's visit to the United States in 1855–56, furnished him with information that he used in his *Virginians*, the manuscript of which is in the Morgan Library.

Horse-Shoe Robinson is a tale of Virginia and the Carolinas during the closing years of the American Revolution and is concerned with the love affair of the daughter of a Tory and an American patriot. Horse-Shoe Robinson, a blacksmith gifted with character and ability, aids the heroine (who has Republican sympathies) through many perils. Kennedy wrote out the description of Horse-Shoe Robinson (illustrated here) from his book for the benefit of a Baltimore Sanitary Fair in 1864. Kennedy's manuscripts and papers are mainly to be found in the Peabody Institute founded in Baltimore, in accordance with his advice, by the philanthropist and banker George Peabody in 1866. Peabody also gave the father of J. Pierpont Morgan his start in international banking.

The age of Horse Shoe was some seven or eight years in advance of that of Butler—a circumstance which the worthy Senior did not fail to use with some authority in their personal intercourse, holding himself, ~~to~~ on that account, to be, like Cassius, an elder if not a better soldier. On the present occasion his dress was of the plainest and most rustic description. A spherical crowned hat, with a broad brim, a coarse grey coatee of mixed cotton and wool, dark linsey-woolsey trousers adhering closely to his leg, and hob-nailed shoes constituted the principal objects that gave character to his exterior. A red handkerchief tied carelessly around his neck, with the knot hanging over his bosom communicated a certain air of jauntiness to his person. A long rifle thrown into the angle of the right arm, with the breech resting on his pommel, and a pouch of ~~deerskin~~ deerskin with a powder horn attached to it, suspended on his right side, might have warranted a spectator in taking Robinson for a woodsman or hunter from the neighboring mountains.

M.S. of Horse Shoe Robinson.

John P. Kennedy

The age of Horse Shoe was some seven or eight years in advance of that of Butler — a circumstance which he wontly in Senior did not fail to use with some authority in their several intercourse, holding himself, to — that account, to be, like Coffin, an elder if not a better soldier. On the present occasion his dress was of the plainest and most rustic description. A spherical crowned hat, with a broad brim, a coarse gray coat of mixed cotton and wool, dark linsey-woolsey trowsers ordering closely to his hip, and hob-nailed shoes constituted the principal objects that gave character to his exterior. A red handkerchief tied case-lessly around his neck, with the knot hanging over his bosom, communicated a certain air of jauntiness to his figure. A long rifle thrown into the angle of his right arm, with his head resting on his ramrod, and a hound of doubtful description,

with a powder horn attached to it, suspended on his right side, might have transmuted a skeleton in testing Robinson for a woodsman or hunter from the neighbouring mountains.

M.S. of Horse Shoe Robinson.

John P. Kennedy

21

WILLIAM HICKLING PRESCOTT

*"History of the Reign of Ferdinand and Isabella." Autograph
manuscript notes unsigned of portions of the work [n.p.,n.d.].
150 p. 24.5 cm. ¾ red morocco.*

Historian and man of letters (b. Salem, Mass. 1796; d. Boston, Mass. 1859). Prescott's histories also include *History of the Conquest of Mexico* (1843), *History of the Conquest of Peru* (1847) and *History of the Reign of Philip the Second* (1855–58). In addition to being a fine scholar, he wrote for the enjoyment of the reader and had a gift for vivid description and dramatic narrative.

As an undergraduate Prescott lost the sight of an eye as the result of a college prank and his other eye soon became sympathetically affected. He was fortunately able to afford research workers and readers, and to make notes and final copy for his books with the aid of a noctograph, a writing case for the blind. Prescott wrote on a frame traversed with brass wires indicating lines; he used an ivory or agate stylus on a carbon paper which left an impression on a sheet of paper below. The manuscript page shown here was written on the noctograph and includes materials incorporated in chapter 14 of volume II of the *History*; it can be read but only with some difficulty. The complete work, after much preliminary labor, was seven years in the writing, and was published, as Prescott's first book, at Christmas time in 1837; it was an immediate best seller and received praise from his fellow historians in America and Europe. Prescott's manuscripts are mainly in the Massachusetts Historical Society Library.

Chapter XXX

1503

We must now turn our eyes to Italy, where the sounds of war which had lately died away, were again heard in wilder dissonance than ever. Louis XII stung with mortification at his late at his late reverses, made extraordinary efforts to retrieve them in which he was readily supported by the [deletion]. In consequence, by the month of July 1503, an army consisting of over 30,000 men comprehending the

Chapter xxx

1503

[Here we must once
turn our eyes to Italy, where the scene
of war which [illegible] lately died away, was
again [illegible] in article. [illegible] Louis
[illegible] Louis XII. [illegible] with [illegible]
~~to take~~ at his late reverses, made efforts
extraordinary
to retrieve them; in which he was [illegible]
supported by the [illegible]. He [illegible]
by the month of July, 1503, an army, [illegible]
of near ~~30,000~~ men, commanding the]

22

RALPH WALDO EMERSON

"Hymn sung at the completion of the Concord Monument, 19 April, 1836." Autograph manuscript signed [written out, probably in Concord, on paper with the watermark date of 1853]. 1 p. 27 cm.

Poet, philosopher, essayist and clergyman (b. Boston, Mass. 1803; d. Concord, Mass. 1882). Author of *Nature* (1837), *The American Scholar* (1837), *Essays* (1841 and 1844), *Poems* (1847), *Representative Men* (1850) and *The Conduct of Life* (1860). He was editor of *The Dial* (1842–44) and a loyal friend to his fellow Transcendentalists. A pioneer of American thought and a leader of the American literary renaissance, Emerson was known as "the sage of Concord."

The words of the "Concord Hymn" have become part of the American tradition. The poem was written in 1836 but not sung publicly (to the tune of "Old Hundred") until July 4, 1837. This occasion was the dedication ceremony at the Old North Bridge in Concord and the words of the hymn were printed on slips of paper about six inches square and plentifully distributed among the townspeople who formed the choir. One of the singers was Henry David Thoreau and his own copy of the printed text, one of only three or four copies of this first edition known to have survived, is in the Morgan Library. The "Concord Hymn" was widely reprinted in newspapers and Emerson included it in his *Poems* (1847). The Morgan Library has autograph manuscripts of four other poems by Emerson. In his later years Emerson took an active dislike to transcribing his poems for autograph collectors, for he led a busy life as writer, lecturer and correspondent. The principal collection of Emerson manuscripts and papers is that of the Ralph Waldo Emerson Memorial Association on deposit in The Houghton Library, Harvard University, but letters and sometimes manuscripts may be found in many libraries.

Hymn sung at the completion of the Concord Monument, 19 April, 1836.

By the rude bridge that arched the flood, / Their flag to April's breeze unfurled, / Here once the embattled farmers stood, / And fired the shot heard round the world. /

The foe long since in silence slept; / Alike the conqueror silent sleeps; / And Time the ruined bridge hath swept / Down the dark stream which seaward creeps. /

On this green bank, by this soft stream, / We set today a votive stone, / That memory may their deed redeem, / When, like our sires, our sons are gone. /

Spirit, that made those heroes dare / To die, and leave their children free, / Bid Time and Nature gently spare / The shaft we raise to them and thee. /

R. W. Emerson.

Hymn sung at the completion of
the Concord Monument, 19 April, 1836.

—

By the rude bridge that arched the flood,
Their flag to April's breeze unfurled,
Here once the embattled farmers stood,
And fired the shot heard round the world.

The foe long since in silence slept;
Alike the Conqueror silent sleeps;
And Time the ruined bridge hath swept
Down the dark stream which seaward creeps.

On this green bank, by this soft stream,
We set today a votive stone,
That memory may their deed redeem,
When, like our sires, our sons are gone.

Spirit, that made those heroes dare
To die, and leave their children free,
Bid Time and Nature gently spare
The shaft we raise to them and thee.

R.W. Emerson.

23

RALPH WALDO EMERSON

"Behavior." Autograph manuscript unsigned [Concord, c. 1851].
65 p. 25 cm. Red morocco.

This is a reproduction of folio 63 recto of Number V of a series of Emerson's lectures that were first delivered in Pittsburgh in 1851 and collected in his *Conduct of Life* (1860). Emerson wrote these essays in an especially large and bold hand so that he could read the manuscript easily on the lecture platform. In *The Conduct of Life* he is concerned with the solution of the problem of the individual way of life; his language is sometimes transcendental and sometimes very practical. The Morgan Library has the manuscripts of two other lectures by Emerson that were later published as essays.

If you have not slept, or if you have slept, or if you have headach[e], or sciatica, or leprosy, or thunderstroke, I beseech you, by all angels, to hold your tongue, peace, & not pollute the morning, to which all the housemates bring serene & pleasant thoughts, by corruption & groans. Come out of the azure. Love the day. Do not leave the sky out of your landscape. The oldest the most deserving person should come very modestly into any newly awaked company, respecting the [divine communication out of which all must be presumed to have newly come.]

If ~~you have not slept~~, or if you

have slept, or if you have headach,
or thunderstroke,
or Sciatica, or leprosy, I beseech
you, by all angels, to hold your
~~peace~~
~~tongue~~, & not pollute the
morning, to which all
the housemates bring serene
& pleasant thoughts, by
corruption & groans.

Love the day. Come out of the azure. Do not leave the sky out of your landscape.
The oldest & the most deserv-
ing person should come very
modestly into any newly awaked
Company, respecting the

24

RALPH WALDO EMERSON

Autograph letter signed, dated Boston 20 Dec'. 1876, addressed to
Harrison Gray Otis Blake in Worcester. 2 p. 21.5 cm.

In this letter to Blake, Emerson turns his mind to a very practical matter. Henry David Thoreau's sister Sophia, who died in October 1876, bequeathed many of Thoreau's manuscripts, including the *Journal*, to H. G. O. Blake (1816?–1898), his friend and disciple. It fell to Emerson to arrange for the shipment of two trunks containing these manuscripts to Blake in Worcester. Emerson's powers of memory had already begun to fail and he forgot to send the keys to the trunks. The manuscripts reached Blake safely and eventually the keys. Blake edited four volumes of excerpts from Thoreau's *Journal* between 1881 and 1892. In another letter Emerson wrote Blake that Thoreau could vex tender persons by his conversation but that his books must and will find a multitude of readers. The manuscript *Journal* is now in the Morgan Library.

---

20 Dec'. 1876 My dear Sir, I have today sent by Adams's Express the two trunks containing Henry D. Thoreau's Manuscripts to your address in Worcester. On leaving the Station, I found the two keys of the trunks in my pocket, and propose to send them in this letter if Mr Adams advises it. If not, I shall send them by any the best advice I can find. . I shall be anxious about the arrival of trunks & keys until I hear from you that the entire precious property is safely in your possession With great regard, Yours, R. Waldo Emerson / H. G. Otis Blake, Esq.

BOSTON ATHENÆUM.
Beacon Street.

BOSTON, 20 Dec 187 6

My dear Sir,

I have today
sent by Adams' Express
the two trunks containing
the two Thoreau manuscripts,
Henry D. Thoreau's manuscripts in
to your address in
to your address. On leaving
Worcester, I found the
the Station, I found the
two keys of the trunks
in my pocket, and hoo-
hope to find them in this,
letter. If Mr Adams
advises it. If not, I
shall send them by any
the best advice I can
find. I shall be earnest

about the arrival
of trunks & keys until
I hear from you that
the entire (various)
the entire is safely in
your possession

With great regard,
Very faithfully
Yours,
R. Waldo Emerson

H.G.O. Blake Esq.

25

ORESTES AUGUSTUS BROWNSON

Autograph letter signed, dated Boston, Nov. 29, 1842, to Henry David Thoreau. 1 p. 25 cm.

Author, journalist and clergyman (b. Stockbridge, Vt. 1803; d. Detroit, Mich. 1876). He wrote *New Views of Christianity, Society and The Church* (1836), a condemnation of both Catholicism and Protestantism, and one of the seminal books in American Transcendentalism; *Charles Elwood; or, The Infidel Converted* (1840), a semi-autobiographical novel; *The Mediatorial Life of Jesus* (1842); *The Spirit-Rapper: an Autobiography* (1854), actually a fanciful romance about spiritual manifestations; and *The Convert* (1857), in which he gives an account of his spiritual development. Brownson was a radical and controversial writer and thinker who was greatly interested in the welfare of the working classes. He was brought up a Puritan, and became successively a Presbyterian, a Universalist minister and the organizer of his own church; in 1844 he became a Roman Catholic and, although he attempted to "Americanize" the Church, he uncompromisingly defended that faith for the rest of his life. He founded and edited the influential *Brownson's Quarterly Review* (1844–65 and 1872–75).

Brownson was very much of an individualist and had frequent disagreements with many of his friends and with himself. Brownson and Thoreau met in 1835 and remained on good terms. Late in 1842, when Thoreau was elected curator of the Concord Lyceum, he invited Brownson, among others, to lecture. In this letter Brownson declines to speak on a suggested date, but says he will lecture the last Wednesday in December, which he did. The largest group of Brownson letters and manuscripts is in the University of Notre Dame Library.

Boston, Nov. 29, 1842 My dear Sir, I regret that it is not in my power to lecture for you on the evening you name, as I am engaged for that evening to lecture in the city of New-York. If some evening, say the last Wednesday, in December, will answer your purpose, I shall be happy to lecture before your Lyceum. Yours very truly O. A. Brownson. / H. D. Thoreau.

Boston, Nov. 29. 1842

My dear Sir,

I regret that it is not in my power to lecture for you on the evening you name, as I am engaged for that evening to lecture in the city of New York. If same evening, say the last Wednesday in December, will answer your purpose, I shall be happy to lecture before your lyceum.

Yours very truly

O. A. Brownson.

H. D. Thoreau

26

NATHANIEL HAWTHORNE

"The Scarlet Letter." Title and contents leaf only [Salem, Mass. 1849].
2 p. 24.5 cm. Black morocco.

Novelist and short-story writer (b. Salem, Mass. 1804; d. Plymouth, N.H. 1864). Author of *Twice-Told Tales* (1837), *Mosses from an Old Manse* (1846), *The Scarlet Letter* (1850), *The House of the Seven Gables* (1851), *The Blithedale Romance* (1852), *Tangle-wood Tales* (1853), *The Marble Faun* (1860), *The Dolliver Romance* (1876) and *Dr. Grimshawe's Secret* (1883), the last two being published after his death. Hawthorne wrote occasional poetry and memorable short stories, and kept notebooks of major importance during his residences in England, France and Italy, as well as in the United States. His friend and Bowdoin College classmate, President Franklin Pierce, appointed him U.S. Consul in Liverpool, England in 1853 and he spent the remainder of the decade in Europe.

The Scarlet Letter, published in 1850, is one of the great literary masterpieces in the English language. The scene is seventeenth-century Salem and the story is of the effect of sin, real and symbolic, on the characters in the novel, of whom Hester Prynne, who wears the scarlet "A" for adultery, is the most prominent. This leaf with title and contents is the only surviving portion of the manuscript of *The Scarlet Letter*. Shortly before his death Hawthorne told a friend that he had thrown the manuscript in the fire, "put it up the chimney long ago. I never thought anybody would care for it." The most important collection of Hawthorne manuscripts, among which are *The Blithedale Romance, Dr. Grimshawe's Secret, The Dolliver Romance, Septimius Felton, Tanglewood Tales* and 18 volumes of his notebooks, is in The Pierpont Morgan Library.

The Scarlet Letter, a Romance. By Nathaniel Hawthorne.

Contents. / Introductory / The Custom House / I.—The Prison-Door / II—The Market Place / III—The Recognition / IV—The Interview / V—Hester at her Needle / VI—Pearl / VII—The Governor's Hall / VIII—The Elf-Child and the Minister / IX—The Leech / X—The Leech and his Patient / XI—The Interior of a Heart / XII—The Minister's Vigil / XIII—Another View of Hester / XIV—Hester and the Physician / XV—Hester and Pearl / XVI—A Forest-Walk / XVII—The Pastor and his Parishioner / XVIII—A Flood of Sunshine / XIX—The Child at the Brookside / XX—The Minister in a Maze / XXI—A New England Holiday / XXII—The Procession / XXIII—Revelation of the Scarlet Letter / XXIV.—Conclusion.

Contents.

The Scarlet Letter.

a
Romance.

By Nathaniel Hawthorne.

27

NATHANIEL HAWTHORNE

"American Notebooks." Volume containing entries for August 5, 1842–October 6, 1843. Entry for September 1 [1842]. 24 cm. Brown leather with green marbled boards.

Hawthorne's American notebooks begin with his first journalizing in 1835 and continue until his departure for England in 1853. They are followed by English notebooks (1853–58) and French and Italian notebooks (1858–62). These volumes, containing some 800,000 words, vary considerably in content and often combine diary entries, notes on reading and commonplace book transcriptions.

After Hawthorne's death, when his widow was editing selections from the notebooks for publication, she inked over certain lines and words (and even cut out pages and parts of pages) that contained language that did not fit in with her concepts of Victorian morality. Modern scholarship and the infrared lamp have been able to restore many of the obliterated words and reveal that Mrs. Hawthorne made such changes as "composed myself to sleep" for "got into bed," "praise" for "soft soap" and "luggage" for "baggage." She always expunged the words "bed" and "bosom" even when bosom was used in the description of an Egyptian mummy. When Hawthorne recorded his conversations with Melville in August 1851, she deleted the portion of a sentence that read, "and if truth must be told, we smoked cigars even within the sacred precincts of the sitting-room."

Hawthorne was a teller of tales and his notebooks do not match those of Thoreau and Emerson in philosophy or in aphorism, but he had a gift for discerning character as this sketch of Henry David Thoreau shows. Hawthorne spelled the name Thorow—the way it was pronounced.

[. . .] Sept. 1st—Thursday. *Mr. Thorow dined with us yesterday. He is a singular character—a young man with much of wild original nature still remaining in him; and so far as he is sophisticated, it is in a way and method of his own. He is as ugly as sin, long-nosed, queer-mouthed, and with uncouth and somewhat rustic, although courteous manners, corresponding very well with such an exterior. But his ugliness is of an honest and agreeable fashion, and becomes him much better than beauty. He was educated, I believe, at Cambridge, and formerly kept school in this town; but for two or three years back, he has repudiated all regular modes of getting a living, and seems inclined to lead a sort of Indian life among civilized men—an Indian life, I mean, as respects the absence of any systematic effort for a livelihood. He has been for some time an inmate of Mr. Emerson's family; and, in requital, he labors in the garden, and performs such other offices as may suit him— being entertained by Mr. Emerson for the sake of what true manhood there is in him. Mr. Thorow is a keen and delicate observer of nature—a genuine observer, which, I suspect, is almost as rare a character as even an original poet; and Nature, in return for his love, seems to adopt him as her especial child, and shows him secrets which few others are allowed to witness. He is familiar with beast, fish, fowl, and reptile, and has strange stories to tell of adventures, and friendly passages with these lower brethren of mortality. Herb and flower, likewise, wherever they grow, whether in garden or wild wood, are his familiar friends. [. . .]*

in the world, that we may safely take the word of any mortal, when they say that they need our assistance; and even should we be deceived, still the good to ourselves, resulting from a kind act, is worth more than the trifle by which we purchase it. It is desirable, I think, that such persons should be permitted to roam through our land of plenty, scattering the seeds of tenderness and charity—as birds of passage bear the seeds of precious plants from land to land, without ever dreaming of the office which they perform.

Sept. 1st. Thursday. Mr. Thoreau dined with us yesterday. He is a singular character—a young man with much of wild original nature still remaining in him; and so far as he is sophisticated, it is in a way and method of his own. He is as ugly as sin, long-nosed, queer-mouthed, and with uncouth and somewhat rustic, although courteous manners, corresponding very well with such an exterior. But his ugliness is of an honest and agreeable fashion, and becomes him much better than beauty. He was educated, I believe, at Cambridge, and formerly kept school in this town; but for two or three years back, he has repudiated all regular modes of getting a living, and seems inclined to lead a sort of Indian life among civilized men—an Indian life, I mean, as respects the absence of any systematic effort for a livelihood. He has been for some time an inmate of Mr. Emerson's family; and, in requital, he labors in the garden, and performs such other offices as may suit him—being entertained by Mr. Emerson for the sake of what true manhood there is in him. Mr. Thoreau is a keen and delicate observer of nature—a genuine observer, which, I suspect, is almost as rare a character as even an original poet; and Nature, in return for his love, seems to adopt him as her especial child, and shows him secrets which few others are allowed to witness. He is familiar with beast, fish, fowl, and reptile, and has strange stories to tell of adventures and friendly passages with these lower brethren of mortality. Herb and flower, likewise, wherever they grow, whether in garden or wild wood, are his familiar friends. He is also

28

NATHANIEL HAWTHORNE

*"The Blithedale Romance." Autograph manuscript signed, dated
Concord, Mass. May 1852. 206 leaves. 24.5 cm. Black leather
with gray cloth boards.*

Brook Farm was the name of a celebrated experiment in communistic or cooperative living—sometimes called the "Transcendental Picnic"—that was established on a farm in West Roxbury, Mass., about nine miles from Boston, on April 1, 1841. George Ripley was the leader of the community, and most of the Concord intellectuals, with the exception of Emerson and Thoreau, were actively interested in the progress of Brook Farm. Hawthorne invested some money in the experiment and went there to live; he soon found that the lack of privacy was incompatible with his work as a writer and left to marry Sophia Peabody and to live happily at the Old Manse in Concord. In 1852 he published *The Blithedale Romance* in which, as he wrote in the preface, he "ventured to make free with his old, and affectionately remembered home, at Brook Farm, as being, certainly, the most romantic episode of his own life.—essentially a day-dream and yet a fact—and thus offering an available foothold between fiction and reality."

The character Zenobia, beautiful and passionate, is imaginatively based on Margaret Fuller, and Miles Coverdale, the narrator, is a fictional self-portrait. The tale itself is joyous, and pleasant for the most part, in spite of Zenobia's suicide by drowning, and discusses many issues of the day, such as prison reform, women's rights and spiritualism.

While at Brook Farm Hawthorne wrote a delightful series of letters to his future wife in which he euphemistically called the inexhaustible manure pile the "gold mine" and referred to the "transcendental heifer, belonging to Miss Margaret Fuller." Shown here is the opening page of *The Blithedale Romance*, which introduces both Coverdale and Old Moodie, who is later revealed as the father of Zenobia and her half-sister Priscilla. The name "Henderson" at the top left refers to one of the compositors who set the book in type from this manuscript.

I
Old Moodie.

The evening before my departure for Blithedale, I was returning to my bachelor-apartments, after attending the wonderful exhibition of the Veiled Lady, when an elderly man of rather shabby appearance met me in an obscure part of the street.

"Mr. Coverdale," said he, softly, "can I speak with you a moment?"

As I have casually alluded to the Veiled Lady, it may not be amiss to mention, for the benefit of such of my readers as are unacquainted with her now forgotten celebrity, that she was a phenomenon in the mesmeric line; one of the earliest that had indicated the birth of a new science, or the revival of an old humbug. Since those times, her sisterhood have grown too numerous to attract much individual notice; nor, in fact, has any one of them ever come before the public under such skilfully contrived circumstances of stage-effect, as those which at once mystified and illuminated the remarkable performances of the lady in question. [...]

I
Old Moodie.

The evening before my departure for Blithedale, I was returning to my bachelor-apartments, after attending the wonderful exhibition of the Veiled Lady, when an elderly man of rather
shabby appearance met me in an obscure part of the street.

"Mr Coverdale," said he, softly, "can I speak with you a
moment?"

As I have casually alluded to the Veiled Lady, it may not be
amiss to mention, for the benefit of such of my readers as are
unacquainted with her now forgotten celebrity, that she was a
phenomenon in the mesmeric line; one of the earliest that had
indicated the birth of a new science, or the revival of an old
humbug. Since those times, her sisterhood have grown too numerous to attract much individual notice; nor, in fact, has
any one of them ever come before the public under such skilfully
contrived circumstances of stage-effect, as those which at once
mystified and illuminated the remarkable performances of the
lady in question. Now-a-days, in the management of his subject, 'clairvoyant,' or 'medium', the exhibitor affects the simplicity and openness of scientific experiment; and even if he pro-
fess to tread a step or two across the boundaries of the spiritual world, yet carries with him the laws of our actual life, and
extends them over his preternatural conquests. Twelve or fifteen
years ago, on the contrary, all the arts of mysterious arrangement,
of picturesque disposition, and artistically contrasted light and
shade, were made available in order to set the apparent
miracle in the strongest attitude of opposition to ordinary
facts. In the case of the Veiled Lady, moreover, the interest of
the spectator was further wrought up by the enigma of her identity, and an absurd rumor (probably set afloat by the exhibitor,

29

WILLIAM LLOYD GARRISON

"The Free Mind—A Prison Sonnet." Autograph manuscript signed
[n.p.] 1878. 1 p. 23.5 cm.

Author, founder and editor of *The Liberator* (1831–65), and radical abolitionist (b. Newburyport, Mass. 1805, d. New York City 1879). His books include *Thoughts on African Colonization* (1832), *Sonnets* (1843) and a *Selection* (1852) from his writings and speeches. Garrison was the son of an immigrant family who grew up in poverty and who became (in Vernon Parrington's phrase) "the flintiest character amongst the New England militants." A founder of the American Anti-Slavery Society (1833), he was also its president for many years. After the Civil War Garrison campaigned for world peace, temperance, women's suffrage and the rights of the American Indian. He fought injustice and prejudice.

In 1830 Garrison was convicted of criminal libel and spent seven not unprofitable weeks in jail in Baltimore, Maryland. He had the leisure to write if not always the materials, and this sonnet and many others were first written on the walls of his prison cell—as indicated on this fair copy that he made for Mrs. James T. Fields, the author whose Boston home was a social center for literary personages. "The Free Mind" is Garrison's finest poem and, although it is indebted to the prison poetry of Richard Lovelace, it is impressive in its own right. Through the years he made numerous copies of it for autograph collectors and others, and the Morgan Library also has one that he wrote out for Jacob Heaton, the Quaker abolitionist, in 1853. Garrison's firm, clear hand presents no obstacles for the reader. Manuscripts and letters of Garrison are in many institutions, but the largest collection is in the Boston Public Library.

The Free Mind—A Prison Sonnet.*

High walls and huge the body *may confine, / And iron grates obstruct the prisoner's gaze, / And massive bolts may baffle his design, / And watchful keepers mark his devious ways; / Yet scorns th' immortal* mind *this base control; / No chains can bind it, and no cell enclose: / Swifter than light it flies from pole to pole, / And in a flash from earth to heaven it goes! / It leaps from mount to mount, from vale to vale / It wanders, plucking honeyed fruits and flowers; / It visits home, to hear the fire-side tale, / Or in sweet converse pass the joyous hours: / 'Tis up before the sun, roaming afar, / And in its watches wearies every star! /*

[1878.]   *W^m. Lloyd Garrison.*

*Pencilled impromptu on the wall of my prison-cell in Baltimore, Md., April, 1830.

The Free Mind — A Prison Sonnet.*

High walls and huge the body may confine,
  And iron grates obstruct the prisoner's gaze,
And massive bolts may baffle his design,
  And watchful keepers mark his devious ways;
Yet scorns th' immortal mind this base control;
  No chains can bind it, and no cell enclose:
Swifter than light it flies from pole to pole,
  And in a flash from earth to heaven it goes!
It leaps from mount to mount, from vale to vale
  It wanders, plucking honeyed fruits and flowers;
It visits home, to hear the fire-side tale,
  Or in sweet converse pass the joyous hours:
'Tis up before the sun, roaming afar,
And in its watches wearies every star!

[1878.]   Wm. Lloyd Garrison.

---

* Pencilled impromptu on the wall of my prison-cell in Baltimore, Md., April, 1830.

ROBERT MONTGOMERY BIRD

"Have Much Delight." Autograph letter signed, in rhyme, dated Philadelphia, Feby. 26th 1839. 1 p. 12.5 cm.

Dramatist, novelist, editor and physician (b. Newcastle County, Del. 1806; d. Philadelphia, Pa. 1854). His most famous play was *The Gladiator* (1831), based on the story of Spartacus, which was acted by Edwin Forrest over a thousand times; he also wrote for Forrest *Oralloossa* (1832)—about the assassination of Pizarro—*The Broker of Bogota* (1834) and the revision of *Metamora* (1836). Forrest's failure to keep financial agreements turned Bird to the writing of fiction and he produced *The Hawks of Hawk-Hollow* (1835), *Sheppard Lee* (1836) and his finest novel, *Nick of the Woods* (1837), designed to correct the romantic literary idea that the American Indian was a noble savage. Although troubled by poor health, Bird was part owner of and helped to edit the Philadephia *North American* from 1847 until his death.

The occasional poem shown here is one in which Bird accepts a dinner invitation from the prominent Wistar family of Philadelphia. Its charm obviously saved it from destruction and it is pasted in a copy of the first edition of *Nick of the Woods* formerly owned by the Philadelphia lawyer and author Edward D. Ingraham. Although trained as a physician, Bird gave up the profession because he did not like to collect fees from his patients. Edwin Forrest not only cheated him out of royalties on his plays but refused to let the plays be published; they were not edited and printed until 1917 and 1919. Only in his novels did Bird find some degree of profit and recognition. His manuscripts and papers are in the University of Pennsylvania Library.

Have much delight / To accept invite / For Wistar Party on Saturday night / And am, in a word, / Your humble-come-tumble, / R. M. Bird / Phil. Feby. 26th 1839.

Have much delight
To accept invite
For Wistar Party on Saturday night,
And am, in a word,
Your humble servant,
R.M. Bird.

Phil. Feby. 26th
1839.

31

WILLIAM GILMORE SIMMS

Autograph letter signed, dated Woodlands, April 4, 1852 to Frederick Saunders. 1 p. 25 cm.

Novelist, poet, editor and critic (b. Charleston, S.C. 1806; d. Charleston, S.C. 1870). He was the leading Southern man of letters of his time and a prolific author among whose novels are *The Yemassee* (1835), *The Partisan* (1835), *Mellichampe* (1836) and *Eutaw* (1856), all about the Revolutionary War in South Carolina; *Views and Reviews* (1845) is a volume of criticism. His books of poems include *Poems: Descriptive, Dramatic, Legendary, and Contemplative* (1853). He also published histories of South Carolina and biographies of Francis Marion, Captain John Smith and Nathanael Greene. He was a devoted South Carolinian and especially fond of aristocratic Charleston, whose social leaders, until his final years, often snubbed him because of his humble origins.

Frederick Saunders (1807–1902), to whom the Simms letter reproduced was written, was an English publisher sent to New York City in 1837 to try to arrange an international copyright agreement. He remained as journalist and author and was librarian of The Astor Library for over 20 years. At the end of his life he helped in the formation of The New York Public Library. Simms writes from his plantation home to congratulate Saunders on his book *Memories of the Great Metropolis* and mentions his own poor health. Simms defended slavery and tried to explain the Southern position to the North in a lecture tour of 1856; his audiences were at first hostile and later just stayed away. After the Civil War, during which "Woodlands" was burned, Simms had to write constantly to make a living and was unable to maintain his literary standards. The most important collection of his works is in the University of South Carolina Library.

Woodlands April 4, 1852   F. Saunders, Esq.   Dear Sir: I am here at the plantation, measurably invalided; at all events lying pretty much upon mine oars, counselled to a months holiday if possible. If, in that time, I can accomplish the things I designed to send you, you shall surely have them. I have all the will to serve you, and sincerely hope for the ability. If in a week, I can forward you any thing, by any effort, such is my real anxiety to serve you, I shall certainly dedicate myself to the task. I said a civil thing or two anent "The Great Metropolis" and so did Richards in the Gazette. It is certainly a most admirable manual in this modern Babylon. Your cheap library is certainly remarkably cheap & remarkably good. It is wonderfully if you should make money by such prices. Is it in the way of M\u0072 Putnam to procure one back numbers of the Shakespeare & Percy Society publications? I have a large number of both collections, but incomplete. Excuse the brevity of my letter; I find, as well with business as with brain policy I must economize my epistolary labours. Yours truly   W. Gilmore Simms

Woodlands April 4. 1852.

J. Saunders, Esq.

Dear Sir:

I am here at the plantation, measurably invalided; at all events lying pretty much upon mine oars,
constrained to a months holiday if possible. If, in that
time, I can accomplish the things I designed to send
you, you shall surely have them. I have all the will to
serve you, and sincerely hope for the ability. If in a
week, I can forward you any thing, by any Effort, such
is my real anxiety to serve you, I shall certainly dedicate myself to the task. I said a civil thing or two anent
"The Great Metropolis" and so did Richards in the Gazette. It
is certainly a most admirable Manual in the modern Babylon. Your cheap library is certainly remarkably cheap &
remarkably good. It is wonderfully if you should make
money by such prices. Is it in the way of Mr. Putnam to
procure me back numbers of the Shakespeare & Percy Society
publications? I have a large number of both collections,
but incomplete. Excuse the brevity of my letter; I feel, as
well with business as with brain policy I must economize,
my epistolary labours.

Yours truly

W. Gilmore Simms

32

HENRY WADSWORTH LONGFELLOW

"The Children's Hour." Autograph manuscript signed [n.p., n.d.].
4 p. 22.5 cm.

Poet (b. Portland, Me. 1807; d. Cambridge, Mass. 1882). Among his many popular books are *Outre-Mer* (1835), *Hyperion* (1839), *Voices of the Night* (1839), *Ballads and Other Poems* (1841), *Evangeline* (1847), *The Song of Hiawatha* (1855), *The Courtship of Miles Standish* (1858), *Tales of a Wayside Inn* (1863), *The Hanging of the Crane* (1874) and *Ultima Thule* (1880–82). His translation of Dante's *The Divine Comedy* (1865–67) has stood the test of time.

Longfellow was a precocious student who published his first poem at the age of 13 and graduated from Bowdoin College, where Hawthorne was a classmate, when he was 18. He traveled widely and mastered most of the European languages with rapidity and fluency; it was said that only Dutch resisted him. He taught modern languages at Harvard for 18 years before retiring to a placid life of writing, travel and coping with an ever-increasing correspondence.

"The Children's Hour" was first published in *The Atlantic Monthly* (September 1860). In 1843 Longfellow married for the second time and he and his bride were given by her father as a wedding gift Craigie House, Washington's former headquarters in Cambridge. The three "blue-eyed banditti" who are the subjects of the charming poem are the Longfellow daughters. And the charms of this poem were such that, according to George S. Hellman, who sold the celebrated Wakeman collection of American literary manuscripts to Pierpont Morgan, Mr. Morgan purchased the entire collection after reading it. This autograph copy of the memorable poem was written out by Longfellow soon after publication. The most important collection of Longfellow manuscripts and papers is in Harvard University Library.

The Children's Hour.

Between the dark and the daylight, / When the night is beginning to lower, / Comes a pause in the day's occupations, / That is known as the Children's Hour. /

I hear in the chamber above me / The patter of little feet, / The sound of a door that is opened, / And voices soft and sweet. /

From my study I see in the lamplight, / Descending the broad hall stair, / [Grave Alice and laughing Allegra / And

Edith with golden hair. /   ...]

[I have you fast in my fortress / And will not let you depart, /] But put you down into the dungeons / In the round tower of my heart. /

And there will I keep you forever, / Yes, forever and a day, / Till the walls shall crumble to ruin, / And moulder in dust away! /

Henry W. Longfellow.

But, put you down into the dungeons
In the round tower of my heart.

And, there will I keep you forever,
Yes, forever and a day,
Till the walls shall crumble to ruins,
And moulder in dust away!

Henry W. Longfellow

The Children's Hour

Between the dark and the daylight,
When the night is beginning to lower,
Comes a pause in the day's occupation,
That is known as the Children's Hour.

I hear in the chamber above me
The patter of little feet,
The sound of a door that is opened,
And voices soft and sweet.

From my study I see in the lamplight,
Descending the broad hall stair,

33

HENRY WADSWORTH LONGFELLOW

"The Arrow and the Song." Autograph manuscript signed, dated [n.p.]
1870. 1 p. 21.5 cm.

This popular poem was first published in Longfellow's *Belfry of Bruges and Other Poems* (1845). In it the poet likens his craft to the shooting of arrows into the air—with happy results for the poet. Longfellow wrote of the composition of the poem: "October 16, 1845. Before church, wrote 'The Arrow and the Song,' which came into my mind as I stood with my back to the fire, and glanced on to the paper with arrow's speed. Literally an improvisation." The poem has appeared in many anthologies and the Morgan Library has an autograph musical setting of it, by Charles François Gounod, that is apparently unpublished.

The Arrow and the Song.

I shot an arrow into the air, / It fell to earth I knew not where, / For so swiftly it flew, the sight / Could not follow it in its flight. /

I breathed a Song into the air, / It fell to earth I knew not where; / For who hath sight so keen and strong, / That it

can follow the flight of song.

Long, long afterward in an oak / I found the arrow still unbroke, / And the song, from beginning to end, / I found again in the heart of a friend. /

1870.   *Henry W. Longfellow*

The Arrow and the Song.

—

I shot an arrow into the air,
It fell to earth I knew not where,
For so swiftly it flew, the sight
Could not follow it in its flight.

I breathed a Song into the air,
It fell to earth I knew not where;
For who hath sight so keen and strong,
That it can follow the flight of song.

Long, long afterward in an oak
I found the arrow still unbroke,
And the Song, from beginning to end,
I found again in the heart of a friend.

Henry W. Longfellow

1870.

34

HENRY WADSWORTH LONGFELLOW

"Excelsior." Autograph manuscript signed, dated Cambridge,
December 8 1858. 4 p. 23 cm.

"Excelsior" was first published in *Ballads and Other Poems* (1841), a famous volume that also contained "The Skeleton in Armor," "The Wreck of the Hesperus" and "The Village Blacksmith." The inspiration for the poem is said to have come from a reproduction of the seal of the State of New York, which has the motto "Excelsior." According to a note on Longfellow's original draft in Harvard University Library, the poem was finished at three o'clock on the morning of September 28, 1841. It depicts the unswerving purpose of a man of genius, climbing the mountain of his career and ignoring temptations and warnings. He dies at the top and "Excelsior" becomes a promise of immortality. The poem was so successful that it was often parodied, most memorably by Bret Harte in his "Sapolio."

Excelsior

The shades of night were falling fast, / As through an Alpine village passed, / A youth who bore, 'mid snow and ice, / A banner with the strange device / Excelsior! /

His brow was sad; his eye beneath / Flashed like a faulchion from its sheath, / And like a silver clarion rung / The accents of that unknown tongue / Excelsior! / [. . .]

There in the twilight cold and gray, / Lifeless but beautiful he lay, / And from the sky serene and far, / A voice fell, like a falling star, / Excelsior! /

Henry W. Longfellow.

Cambridge. December 8 1858.

Excelsior.

The shades of night were falling fast,
As through an Alpine village passed
A youth, who bore, 'mid snow and ice,
A banner with the strange device,
Excelsior!

His brow was sad; his eye beneath,
Flashed like a falchion from its sheath,
And like a silver clarion rung
The accents of that unknown tongue,
Excelsior!

In happy homes he saw the light
Of household fires gleam warm and bright;

Above, the spectral glaciers shone,
And from his lips escaped a groan,
A voice fell, like a falling star,
Excelsior!

Henry W. Longfellow.

Cambridge. December 2.
1852

35

JOHN GREENLEAF WHITTIER

"Barbara Frietchie." Autograph manuscript signed [n.p., n.d.].
3 p. 23.5 cm.

Poet and editor (b. Haverhill, Mass. 1807; d. Hampton Falls, N.H. 1892). Author of *Legends of New England in Prose and Verse* (1831); *Moll Pitcher* (1832); *Leaves from Margaret Smith's Journal* (1848), an excellent picture of colonial times and perhaps Whittier's best writing in prose; *Songs of Labor* (1850); *The Panorama* (1856), which includes the first book printings of "The Barefoot Boy" and "Maud Muller"; *In War Time* (1864); *Snow-Bound* (1866), his finest poem and an American classic; *The Tent on the Beach* (1867); and *Among the Hills* (1869). For short periods of time he was the editor of several periodicals. Whittier was born and lived an earnest Quaker; he was a staunch abolitionist and wrote many poems against slavery.

"Barbara Frietchie," one of Whittier's most celebrated poems, was first published in *The Atlantic Monthly* (October 1863). "Yon grey head," Mrs. Frietchie, aged 96, is said to have flown the American flag during the occupation of Frederick, Maryland by General "Stonewall" Jackson and his Confederate troops in 1862. Whittier later learned that it was a much younger Mrs. Mary Quantrell who had raised the flag on her house and that Barbara Frietchie, who achieved the immortality, had followed her in another act of courage. Mrs. Quantrell's defiance was acknowledged by the General and his men who raised their hats, "To you, madam, and not to your flag!" But Whittier wrote in good faith and when the new information reached him it was too late to change the poem. In Clyde Fitch's drama, described later in these pages, Barbara Frietchie is a young girl. This is an early draft of the poem and Whittier's signature has been added to the manuscript. His many surviving letters and manuscripts are in numerous collections, especially The Essex Institute and the Swarthmore College Friends Historical Library.

Barbara Frietchie.

~~Lapped in~~ *Up from the meadows rich with corn, / Clear in the cool September morn, /*

The clustered spires of Frederick stand / Green-walled by the hills of Maryland. /

Round about ~~it~~ them orchards sweep / Apple & peach-tree fruited deep, /

Fair as ~~the~~ a garden of the Lord / To the eyes of the famished rebel horde, /

On that pleasant morn of the early fall / When Lee marched over the mountain wall,— /

Over the mountains winding down, / Horse & foot, into Frederick town. /

Forty flags with their silver stars / Forty flags with the crimson bars, /

Flapped in the morning wind: the sun / Of noon looked down, & saw not one. /

Up rose old Barbara Frietchie then / Bowed with her fourscore years & ten. /

Bravest ~~& truest~~ of all in Frederick town, / She took up the flag the men hauled down! / [. . .]

John G. Whittier

Barbara Frietchie.

Up from the meadows rich with corn,
Clear in the cool September morn,

The clustered spires of Frederick stand
Green-walled by the hills of Maryland.

Round about them orchards sweep
Apple & peach tree fruited deep,

Fair as the garden of the Lord
To the eyes of the famished rebel horde,

On that pleasant morn of the early fall
When Lee marched over the mountain wall,—

Over the mountains winding down,
Horse & foot, into Frederick town.

Forty flags with their silver stars,
Forty flags with their crimson bars,

Flapped in the morning wind; the sun
Of noon looked down, & saw not one.

Up rose old Barbara Frietchie then,
Bowed with her fourscore years & ten;

Bravest of all in Frederick town,
She took up the flag the men hauled down;

"Who touches a hair of yon grey head
Dies like a dog! March on!" he said.

All day long through Frederick street
Sounded the tread of marching feet:

All day long that free flag tost
Over the heads of the rebel host.

Ever its torn folds rose & fell
On the loyal winds that loved it well;

And through the hill-gaps sunset light
Shone over it with a warm good-night.

Barbara Frietchie's work is o'er,
And the Rebel rides on his raids no more.

Honor to her! and let a tear
Fall, for her sake, on Stonewall's bier.

Over Barbara Frietchie's grave,
Flag of Freedom and Union, wave!

And ever the stars above look down
On thy stars below in Frederick town!

Peace and order and beauty draw
Round thy symbol of light & law;

John G. Whittier

36

JOHN GREENLEAF WHITTIER

*Autograph letter signed, dated Amesbury, Mass. 10th Mo 30 1886, to
the Editor of the "[Boston Evening] Transcript." 1 p. 18 cm.*

Whittier's poem "The Bartholdi Statue" was first published in the New York weekly *The Independent* for October 28, 1886. The *Boston Evening Transcript* quickly reprinted it and the author just as quickly wished to see it in a slightly revised version. He either added or corrected the additional stanza which appears here in manuscript and attached it with a clipping of the poem to his letter. In the final version in Whittier's *Poetical Works* the third manuscript line appears as "In peace, beneath thy Colors Three," instead of "In peace, across the severing sea,"—a definite improvement. It was on October 28, 1886 that President Grover Cleveland dedicated Bartholdi's statue of *Liberty Enlightening the World* on Bedloe's Island in New York harbor. The name of the island has been changed to Liberty Island and the Statue of Liberty is now a National Monument; it is a symbol of freedom, and commemorates French-American friendship.

Amesbury, Mass 10th Mo 30 1886   Will the Editor of the Transcript publish this corrected version of "The Bartholdi Statue"? The little poem was hastily written, and I failed to see a the proof before it was in print. J. G. W. 10th Mo 30. 1886

O France, the beautiful!—to thee / Once more a debt of love we owe; / In peace, across the severing sea, / We hail a later Rochambeau. /

Amesbury, Mar 10th Nov 30 1886

Will the Editor of the Transcript
publish this corrected version
of "The Bartholdi Statue"? —
The little poem was hastily
written, and I failed to see
a ~~the~~ proof. before it was in
print.   J. G. W.

~~10th Mo 30, 1886~~

THE BARTHOLDI STATUE.

BY JOHN GREENLEAF WHITTIER.

The land, that, from the rule of Kings,
  In freeing us, ~~itself~~ made free,
Our Old World Sister, to us brings
  Her sculptured Dream of Liberty:

Unlike the shapes on Egypt's sands
  Uplifted by the toil-worn slave,
On Freedom's soil with freemen's hands
  We rear the symbol free hands gave.

O France, the beautiful! — to thee
  Once more a debt of love we owe;
In peace, across the severing sea,
  We hail a later Rochambeau!

Rise, stately symbol! holding forth
  Thy light and hope to all who sit
In chains and darkness! Belt the earth
  With watch-fires from thy torch uplift!

Reveal the primal mandate still
  Which Chaos heard and ceased to be,
Trace on mid-air th' Eternal Will
  In signs of fire: "Let man be free!"

Shine far, shine free, a guiding light
  To Reason's ways and Virtue's aim,
A lightning flash the wretch to smite
  Who shields his license with thy name!

OAK KNOLL, 10th Mo., 22d, 1886.
        —From the Independent of Oct. 28.

37

EDGAR ALLAN POE

Autograph letter signed "Poe" [New York, N. Y., February 3, 1845]
addressed to John Augustus Shea. 1 p. 27 cm. Decorated brown
morocco gilt.

Poet, short-story writer and critic (b. Boston, Mass. 1809; d. Baltimore, Md. 1849). Author of *Tamerlane* (1827), *Al Aaraaf* (1829), *Poems* (1831), *The Narrative of Arthur Gordon Pym* (1838), *Tales of the Grotesque and Arabesque* (1840), *The Murders in the Rue Morgue* (1843), *Tales* (1845) and *The Raven* (1845). He was on the staff of and contributed to several important magazines.

The poems and stories of Poe are, in some degree, familiar to every American, and his position in American letters is secure; to the French he is one of the great seminal figures of modern literature. "The Raven" is his most famous poem and Poe himself regarded it as a masterpiece. It was first printed in the New York *Evening Mirror* for January 29, 1845, which had been granted permission to print it in advance of publication in *The American Review* for February, which appeared a few days later. Poe is said to have received 15 dollars in payment from *The American Review*, which would have been fair compensation at space rates of the time. Among the numerous reprintings of the poem was one in the New York *Daily Tribune* for February 4, 1845 and for this Poe made the changes in lines 60–66 that are written out in this letter to J. A. Shea, who was on the staff of the newspaper. This is the only part of "The Raven" existing in a manuscript meant for the printer. The changes were duly incorporated and Poe continued to make other changes in the poem for the rest of his life. The only complete autograph manuscript of "The Raven," which Poe copied out at the request of a Dr. S. A. Whittaker, is now in The Free Library of Philadelphia. There are six autograph lines in the Library of the University of Texas at Austin, which also has Poe's corrected copy of the first edition. The leading repositories of Poe manuscripts are The Free Library of Philadelphia, the University of Texas Library, The New York Public Library and the Morgan Library.

Dear Shea, Lest I should have made some mistake in the hurry I transcribe the whole alteration.

Instead of the whole stanza commencing "Wondering at the stillness broken &c—substitute this

Startled at the stillness broken by reply so aptly spoken, / "Doubtless", said I, "what it utters is its only stock and store / Caught from some unhappy master whom unmerciful Disaster / Followed fast and followed faster till his songs one burden bore— / Till the dirges of his Hope the melancholy burden bore, / 'Nevermore—ah, nevermore!' " /

At the close of the stanza preceding this, instead of "Quoth the raven Nevermore", substitute "Then the bird said "Nevermore". Truly yours Poe

Dear Shea,

Lest I should have made some mistake in the hurry I transcribe the whole alteration.

Instead of the whole stanza commencing "Wondering at the stillness broken &c – substitute this

Startled at the stillness broken by reply so aptly spoken,
"Doubtless", said I, "what it utters is its only stock and store
Caught from some unhappy master whom unmerciful Disaster
Followed fast and followed faster till his songs one burden bore –
Till the dirges of his Hope the melancholy burden bore,
            "Nevermore – ah, nevermore!'"

At the close of the stanza _preceding_ this, instead of "Quoth the raven Nevermore", substitute "Then the bird said "Nevermore".

            Truly yours
                Poe

38

EDGAR ALLAN POE

"Ulalume—A Ballad." By Edgar A. Poe. Autograph manuscript signed
[written at Old Point Comfort, Virginia, September 10, 1849].
5 p. 24.5 cm. Blue morocco.

Although not the most famous of Poe's poems, "Ulalume" is considered by many critics to be his greatest and most original. It was first published in *The American Review* for December 1847 and is most easily described as a lyrical ballad lamenting the death of the poet's beloved "Ulalume." The autograph manuscript of this poem in the Morgan Library, of which the first page is reproduced, was written out for Miss Susan V. Ingram, who was the most appreciative listener in a party where Poe read it on the moonlit evening of September 9, 1849 at Old Point Comfort, Virginia. Miss Ingram told Poe, "I understand it and it is lovely," and Poe sent her this copy the following day. With it was a note from him saying in part, "I would endeavor to explain to you what I really meant—or what I fancied I meant by the poem, if it were not that I remembered Dr. Johnson's bitter and rather just remarks about the folly of explaining what, if worth explanation, should explain itself." "Ulalume" remains a poem of much mystery of meaning and has had a considerable influence on symbolist poetry in France and England.

Early in this century Miss Ingram sold this Poe autograph for $100 because she needed money; it was later acquired at auction by J. P. Morgan. In 1913 Miss Ingram visited Mr. Morgan's Library to see once again the poem that Poe had written out for her over 60 years before, and a month before his tragic death. The Morgan manuscript of "Ulalume" is accepted by modern scholars as the definitive text of the poem.

Ulalume—A Ballad.

By Edgar A. Poe.

The skies they were ashen and sober;/ The leaves they were crispéd and sere—/ The leaves they were withering and sere:/ It was night, in the lonesome October/ Of my most immemorial year:/ It was hard by the dim lake of Auber/ In the misty mid region of Weir:—/ It was down by the dank tarn of Auber,/ In the ghoul-haunted woodland of Weir./ [...]

Ulalume — A Ballad.
By Edgar A. Poe.

The skies they were ashen and sober;
  The leaves they were crispèd and sere—
  The leaves they were withering and sere:
It was night, in the lonesome October
  Of my most immemorial year:
It was hard by the dim lake of Auber,
  In the misty mid region of Weir:—
It was down by the dank tarn of Auber,
  In the ghoul-haunted woodland of Weir.

Here once, through an alley Titanic,
  Of cypress, I roamed with my Soul—
  Of cypress, with Psyche, my Soul.
These were days when my heart was volcanic
  As the scoriac rivers that roll—.
  As the lavas that restlessly roll
Their sulphurous currents down Yaanek,
  In the ultimate climes of the Pole—
That groan as they roll down Mount Yaanek,
  In the realms of the Boreal Pole.

Our talk had been serious and sober,
  But our thoughts they were palsied and sere—
  Our memories were treacherous and sere;

39

EDGAR ALLAN POE

"Hans Phaall   A Tale by Edgar A. Poe" [*n.p., n.d.*]. *20 p. 19.5 cm.*
Blue morocco.

This tale was first published in *The Southern Literary Messenger* for June 1835, six months before Poe became its editor, and is one of the earliest examples of science fiction in American literature. The complete title is "The Unparalleled Adventures of One Hans Pfaal" and the story describes an imaginary voyage to the moon.

It is in the form of a long letter, carried from the moon by a mystic messenger to the States' College of Astronomers in Rotterdam, in which Hans Pfaal tells of his voyage in a balloon while breathing with the help of a "condenser." On the moon he found great extremes of heat and cold, a volcanic surface and strange cities with crowds of ugly people. If the College will permit him to return home, pardon him for certain offenses and reward him, he will tell them many more tales of his voyage, the most momentous ever conceived by any denizen of earth. The College is ready to pardon and pay him but no messenger can be sent back to the moon because the messenger has disappeared. And so Poe's tongue-in-cheek story, basically preposterous but told with gifted imagination, is unmasked. There is a coda-like comment that Hans Pfaal has been seen drunk in a suburban tippling house.

Poe wrote this tale in his "roman script," a hand quite different from the clear script he used for his poems; the manuscript is slightly incomplete, lacking several paragraphs. The Morgan Library has two other manuscripts of tales by Poe, and autograph copies of his poems "Annabel Lee" and "The Bells." The Library also has a large portion of the autograph manuscript of his revised version of "Tamerlane," which in its printed first edition has become a touchstone of literary rarity.

HANS PHAALL

A Tale by Edgar A. Poe

[*Quotation from Tom O'Bedlam's Song crossed out*]

BY *late accounts from Rotterdam that city seems to be in a singularly high state of philosophical excitement. Indeed phenomena have there occurred of a nature so completely unexpected, so entirely novel, so utterly at variance with pre-conceived opinions, as to leave no doubt on my mind that long ere this all Europe is in an uproar, all Physics in a ferment, all Dynamics and Astronomy together by the ears.*

It appears that on the — day of — (I am not positive about the date) a vast crowd of people, for purposes not specifically mentioned, were assembled in the great square of the Exchange in the goodly and well-conditioned city of Rotterdam. The day was warm—unusually so for the season—there was hardly a breath of air stirring—and the multitude were in no bad humour at being now and then besprinkled with friendly showers of momentary duration. These occasionally fell from large white masses of cloud which chequered in a fitful manner the blue vault of the firmament. Nevertheless about noon a slight but remarkable agitation became apparent in the assembly; the clattering of ten thousand tongues succeeded; and in an instant afterwards ten thousand faces were upturned towards the heavens, ten thousand pipes descended simultaneously from the corners of ten thousand mouths, and a shout which could be compared to nothing but the roaring of Niagara resounded long, loud, and furiously, through all the environs of Rotterdam. [...]

HANS PHAALL
A Tale by Edgar A. Poe

~~[struck-through lines]~~

BY late accounts from Rotterdam that city seems to be in a singularly high state of philosophical excitement. Indeed phenomena have there occurred of a nature so completely unexpected, so entirely novel, so utterly at variance with pre-conceived opinions, as to leave no doubt on my mind that long ere this all Europe is in an uproar, all Physics in a ferment, all Dynamics and Astronomy together by the ears.

It appears that on the —— day of —— (I am not positive about the date) a vast crowd of people, for purposes not specifically mentioned, were assembled in the great square of the Exchange in the goodly and well-conditioned city of Rotterdam. The day was warm — unusually so for the season — there was hardly a breath of air stirring — and the multitude were in no bad humour at being now and then besprinkled with friendly showers of momentary duration. These occasionally fell from large white masses of cloud which chequered in a fitful manner the blue vault of the firmament. Nevertheless about noon a slight but remarkable agitation became apparent in the assembly; the clattering of ten thousand tongues succeeded; and in an instant afterwards ten thousand faces were upturned towards the heavens, ten thousand pipes descended simultaneously from the corners of ten thousand mouths, and a shout which could be compared to nothing but the roaring of Niagara resounded long, loud, and furiously, through all the environs of Rotterdam.

The origin of this hubbub soon became sufficiently evident. From behind the huge bulk of one of those sharply-defined masses of cloud already mentioned, was seen slowly to emerge into an open area of blue space, a queer, heterogeneous, but apparently solid body of substance, so oddly shaped, so outré in appearance, so whimsically put together, as not to be in any manner comprehended, and never to be sufficiently admired by the host of sturdy burghers who stood open-mouthed and thunderstruck below. What could it be? In the name of all the vrows and

40

OLIVER WENDELL HOLMES

"The Autocrat of the Breakfast-Table. Every Man his own Boswell."
Autograph manuscript signed of parts iv–xii [n.p., 1857–58].
306 p. 25 cm. Green morocco gilt.

Physician and man of letters (b. Cambridge, Mass. 1809; d. Boston, Mass. 1894). His best-known literary works are *Poems* (1836); *The Autocrat of the Breakfast-Table* (1858); *The Professor at the Breakfast-Table* (1860); *Elsie Venner* (1861), the first and best of his "medicated novels"; *The Poet at the Breakfast-Table* (1872); *Before the Curfew* (1888); and *Over the Teacups* (1891). His most important medical works are *Homeopathy and its Kindred Delusions* (1842) and *The Contagiousness of Puerperal Fever* (1843), which is said to have saved more lives than any American publication of the nineteenth century. Holmes's career was in medicine and it brought him much professional fame. From 1847 to 1882 he was Parkman Professor of Anatomy and Physiology at Harvard but found time for extensive writing and lecturing, and a full social life; his conversational brilliance and wit endeared him to a host of friends.

The Autocrat had its beginning in papers which Holmes published in 1831–32, but he took up the work more seriously in 1857. The book is a series of essays and dialogues that take place at mealtimes in a Boston boardinghouse, and introduces various New England types, who are treated with geniality and gentle humor. Some of Holmes's memorable single poems are introduced in *The Autocrat*, including "The Deacon's Masterpiece" and "The Old Man Dreams." Holmes's own favorite, "The Chambered Nautilus," reproduced here, appeared in the fourth episode of *The Autocrat* when it was first published in the February 1858 issue of *The Atlantic Monthly*, a magazine which he had named. The nautilus is a mollusk that enlarges its shell as it grows and, in this poem, symbolizes human endeavor; the soul is exhorted to build "more stately mansions" "as the swift seasons roll." When Whittier read the poem he said it was "booked for immortality," an observation assisted by Eugene O'Neill's play *More Stately Mansions*. Large collections of Holmes manuscripts and letters are in Harvard University Library, the Huntington Library, the Morgan Library, and many other institutions.

The chambered Nautilus.

This is the ship of pearl, which, poets feign, / Sails the unshadowed main; / The venturous bark that flings / On the sweet summer wind its purpled wings / In gulfs enchanted where the siren sings, / And coral reefs lie bare / Where the cold sea-maids rise to sun their streaming hair. / [. . .]

Build thee more stately mansions, O my Soul, / As the swift seasons roll! / Leave thy low-vaulted past! / Let each new temple, nobler than the last / Shut thee from Heaven with a dome more vast, / Till thou at length art free, / Leaving thine outgrown shell by life's unresting sea! /

The Chambered Nautilus.

This is the ship of pearl, which, poets feign,
Sails the unshadowed main;
The venturous bark that flings
On the sweet summer wind its purpled wings
In gulfs enchanted, where the Siren sings,
And coral reefs lie bare,
Where the cold sea-maids rise to sun their streaming hair.

Its webs of living gauze no more unfurl;
Wrecked is the ship of pearl!
And every chambered cell,
Where its dim dreaming life was wont to dwell,
As the frail tenant shaped his growing shell,
Before thee lies revealed,—
Its irised ceiling rent, its sunless crypt unsealed!

Year after year beheld the silent toil
That spread his lustrous coil;
Still, as the spiral grew,
He left the last year's dwelling for the new,
Stole with soft step its shining archway through,
Built up its idle door,
Stretched in his last-found home, and knew the old no more.

Thanks for the heavenly message brought by thee,
Child of the wandering sea,
Cast from her lap, forlorn!
From thy dead lips a clearer note is born
Than ever Triton blew from wreathèd horn!
While on mine ear it rings,
Through the deep caves of thought I hear a voice that sings:—

Build thee more stately mansions, O my soul,
As the swift seasons roll!
Leave thy low-vaulted past!
Let each new temple, nobler than the last,
Shut thee from heaven with a dome more vast,
Till thou at length art free,
Leaving thine outgrown shell by life's unresting sea!

41

OLIVER WENDELL HOLMES

"Old Ironsides." Autograph poem signed, dated Boston, Jan. 21ˢᵗ 1865.
1 p. 22 cm.

"Old Ironsides" is the popular name of the U.S. frigate *Constitution*, launched in 1797, which played an important part in the War of 1812 and, under the command of Isaac Hull, won a famous sea battle with the British ship *Guerrière*. In 1830 the Navy determined that the *Constitution* was no longer seaworthy and ordered her to be broken up and sold. Holmes, one year out of Harvard and studying law, read the notice in a newspaper and indignantly wrote out the impetuous stanzas of "Old Ironsides." He sent them to *The Boston Daily Advertiser*, which printed the poem on September 16, 1830. Soon reprinted throughout the country, it stirred a national crusade, and the name of Oliver Wendell Holmes, who had just come of age, was known to a large part of the people of the United States. The Secretary of the Navy rescinded his order and the tattered ensign was not torn down. The *Constitution* was rebuilt and continued in active service for many years; it is now on exhibition at the navy yard in Charleston, Mass. Holmes wrote out this copy of the poem in the final weeks of the American Civil War.

Old Ironsides.

Ay, tear her tattered ensign down! / Long has it waved on high, / And many an eye has danced to see / That banner in the sky; / Beneath it rung the battle shout, / And burst the cannons' roar;— / The meteor of the ocean air / Shall sweep the clouds no more! /

Her deck, once red with heroes' blood, / Where knelt the vanquished foe, / When winds were hurrying o'er the flood / And waves were white below, / No more shall feel the victors' tread, / Or know the conquered knee;— / The harpies of the shore shall pluck / The eagle of the sea! /

O better that her shattered hulk / Should sink beneath the wave; / Her thunders shook the mighty deep, / And there should be her grave; / Nail to the mast her holy flag, / Set every threadbare sail, / And give her to the god of storms, / The lightning and the gale! /

Oliver Wendell Holmes
Boston Jan. 21ˢᵗ 1865.

Old Ironsides.

Ay, tear her tattered ensign down!
  Long has it waved on high,
And many an eye has danced to see
  That banner in the sky;
Beneath it rung the battle shout,
  And burst the cannon's roar; —
The meteor of the ocean air
  Shall sweep the clouds no more!

Her deck, once red with heroes' blood,
  Where knelt the vanquished foe,
When winds were hurrying o'er the flood
  And waves were white below,
No more shall feel the victor's tread,
  Or know the conquered knee; —
The harpies of the shore shall pluck
  The eagle of the sea!

O better that her shattered hulk
  Should sink beneath the wave;
Her thunders shook the mighty deep,
  And there should be her grave;
Nail to the mast her holy flag,
  Set every threadbare sail,
And give her to the god of storms,
  The lightning and the gale!

                    Oliver Wendell Holmes
                      Boston Jan. 21st 1865.

42

MARGARET FULLER (MARCHESA [MARCHIONESS] OSSOLI)

Autograph letter signed "Margaret," dated Florence, 10th May 1850, addressed to William Wetmore Story. 4 p. 18.5 cm.

Author, editor, transcendentalist and social reformer (b. Cambridgeport, Mass. 1810; d. off Fire Island, N.Y. 1850). The most important woman of letters of her day, she wrote *Summer on the Lakes* (1844), *Woman in the Nineteenth Century* (1845) and *Papers on Literature and Art* (1846); she was editor of *The Dial* (1841–42). Margaret Fuller was accepted into the Concord transcendentalist circle as an equal of Emerson and Thoreau and it was there that her great talent for conversing became apparent. The ladies' classes she taught for five years in Boston came to be known as "conversations." She also spent two years in New York City on the staff of Horace Greeley's *Tribune*.

In 1846 Margaret Fuller went to Europe and met some of the leading literary personalities of the time. In Italy she fell in love with the Marchese (Marquis) Ossoli; they announced their marriage when their son was one year old. The Ossolis were followers of Mazzini in his quest for Italian independence and unity, and when the French troops entered Rome in April 1849, they fled to Florence; she spent the winter in writing a history of the Revolution in which they had taken part. On May 17, 1850 the Ossolis sailed for New York with the manuscript. They were all lost when their ship, which carried a vast amount of marble, went down off Fire Island. In this farewell letter, written a week before sailing, to the sculptor and author William Wetmore Story, there is the ominous and prophetic phrase "look out for news of shipwreck." There are important collections of Margaret Fuller manuscripts and letters in Harvard University Library and the Boston Public Library.

Florence 10th May 1850. My dear William I wrote you a letter & then burnt it because many disturbances prevented my saying what I should, yet fear that this will be no better. We are upon the move & my head is full of boxes, bundles, pots of jelly & phials of medicine [.] I never thought much about a journey for myself, except to try & return all the things, books, especially I had been borrowing, but about my child I feel anxious lest I should not take what is necessary for his health & comfort on this long voyage where omissions are irreparable. The unpropitious weather, rain from the 4 April up to the present time delays us now from day to day as our ship the "Elisabeth" (look out for news of shipwreck) cannot finish taking in her cargo till come one or two good days. Mean while I have been hoping to get a few lines from Emelyn to tell me where you are & what are your arrangements & answering a letter I sent to the care of Greene & Co more than a fortnight ago &c—

I leave Italy with most sad & unsatisfied heart, hoping indeed to return, but fearing that may not in my "cross biassed lot" be permitted till strength of feeling & keenness of perception be less [than during those bygone rich if troubled years.]

Florence 10th May 1850.

My dear William

43

HORACE GREELEY

"Recollections of a Busy Life. By Horace Greeley. No. XXXIII. Europe—The World's Exposition." Autograph manuscript signed [n.p., n.d.]. 7 p. 23 cm.

Journalist, social reformer, author and political leader (b. Amherst, N.H. 1811; d. Pleasantville, N.Y. 1872). Greeley founded the influential *New-York Tribune* in 1841 and edited it until his death. He was a Member of Congress from New York (1848–49) and Democratic candidate for the presidency in 1872, but was badly defeated by Grant in the election. As an antislavery advocate he supported the administration during the Civil War and afterwards promoted general amnesty and universal suffrage. His books include *Glances at Europe* (1851), *The American Conflict* (1866), *Recollections of a Busy Life* (1868) *and Essays on Political Economy* (1870).

Even in his lifetime Greeley's odd appearance, high-pitched voice and almost illegible handwriting were subjects of popular humor. It was said that a letter in which he dismissed an employee was so indecipherable that the employee used it as a letter of recommendation. The first page of his chapter on the Great Exhibition held in Hyde Park in 1851 has its difficulties in word and letter formation but is not beyond retrieval. Greeley was a friend of most of the leading writers of his time. He acted for many years as Thoreau's unofficial literary agent; Margaret Fuller worked for him on the *Tribune* and for a while lived in his household. Greeley manuscripts and letters are available in many American libraries.

Recollections of a Busy Life.

By Horace Greeley.

No. XXXIII.

Europe—The World's Exposition

The year 1851 was signalized by the first grand Exposition of the productions of All Nations' Art and Industry. It was held in Hyde Park, London, once at the extreme west end of that metropolis, but long since enveloped by a steady, imperial growth in we commerce, wealth and population. Prince Albert, the Queen's husband, having been placed at the head of the enterprise, the Queen did her best to ensure its success; and her influence, exerted to the utmost, was extended far beyond her Court and those who aspire to shine bask in its beams. A portion of the Tory Aristocracy stood aloof, or only visited the Exposition as careless sightseers; but the Royal Family, the Liberal Aristocracy, the manufacturing, commercial and more intelligent Laboring classes, were united and enthusiastic in their efforts to secure the success of the grand undertaking. I think judge that the habitual frigid[ity of British toward foreigners was never before so thoroughly set aside or overcome.]

Recollections of a Busy Life.
By Horace Greeley.
No. XXXIII.
Europe — The World's Exposition.

The year 1851 was signalized by the first grand Exposition of the Productions of All Nations' Art and Industry. It was held in Hyde Park, London, once at the extreme west end of that metropolis, but long since enveloped by the steady, immortal growth in its commerce, wealth and population. Prince Albert, the Queen's husband, having been placed at the head of the enterprise, the Queen did her best to ensure its success; and her influence, exerted to the utmost, extended far beyond her Court and those who arbitrate to shine back in its beams. A portion of the Tory Aristocracy stood aloof, or only visited the Exposition as a careless sight-seer; but the Royal Family, the Liberal Aristocracy, the Manufacturing, Commercial and more intelligent Laboring Classes, were united and enthusiastic in their efforts to secure the success of the grand undertaking. I judge that he but not rigid.

44

HARRIET BEECHER STOWE

Autograph letter signed, dated Hartford, Feb'. 16. 1889, addressed to
James Russell Lowell. 1 p. 20.5 cm.

Novelist (b. Litchfield, Conn. 1811; d. Hartford, Conn. 1896). Author of *Uncle Tom's Cabin* (1852), the great book of American antislavery literature which was printed in many languages all over the world, and a second attack on slavery, *Dred: A Tale of the Great Dismal Swamp* (1856), an account of the demoralizing influence of slavery on the whites. She also wrote *Sunny Memories of Foreign Lands* (1854), and novels of New England including *The Minister's Wooing* (1859), *The Pearl of Orr's Island* (1862), *Oldtown Folks* (1869), and *Poganuc People* (1878), based on her own childhood. Her book *Lady Byron Vindicated* (1870), accusing Lord Byron of incest, was not well received, especially in England.

When President Lincoln met Mrs. Stowe during the course of the Civil War, he greeted her with the words, "So you're the little woman who wrote the book that made this great war!" There is much truth in this statement, for probably no other work of literature has so influenced the course of history as *Uncle Tom's Cabin*. It solidified antislavery sentiment in the North and made the burning issue of slavery a moral one. Mrs. Stowe once averred that "God wrote the book, I took His dictation."

The letter reproduced here was sent to James Russell Lowell offering him congratulations on his seventieth birthday. Mrs. Stowe mentions being old but she was to outlive Lowell by five years. Her manuscripts and letters may be found in The Nook Farm Research Library, the Huntington Library and many other collections.

Hartford Feb'. 16. 1889   Dear Mr Lowell   I am one of the thousands who have laughed & wept over your magic verses & the impression still remains tho now I am old, & biblically speaking "well stricken" in years.

I rejoice in the notice that is about to be taken of your birthday. Please count me among the number of congratulating friends   Ever Yours   H B Stowe

Hartford Feb 16. 1889

Dear Mr Lowell

I am one of the
thousands who have laughed
& wept over your magic verses
& the impression still remains
tho now I am old, & biblically
speaking "well stricken" in
years.

I rejoice in the notice
that is about to be taken
of your birth-day. please count
me among the number of
congratulating friends

Ever Yours

H. R. Thorn

45

HENRY DAVID THOREAU

"Journal. October 22 1837 — November 3 1861." Autograph manuscript in 39 volumes written in notebooks of various sizes.

Essayist, naturalist and poet (b. Concord, Mass. 1817; d. Concord, Mass. 1862). Author of "Civil Disobedience" (published in E. P. Peabody's *Aesthetic Papers*, 1849), *Walden; or, Life in the Woods* (1854) and the monumental *Journal*. Thoreau did not seek nor find fame during his lifetime, but to citizens of the twentieth century he is a profoundly influential figure. His intellectual and spiritual life, his great love of nature and his fight against slavery and what he believed to be unjust taxation have made him a mentor for our times.

One of the most dramatic lines in Thoreau's *Journal* is the simple statement illustrated here: "Walden Sat. July 5th—45 Yesterday I came here to live." The *Journal* that Thoreau kept for nearly 25 years contains over two million words and is one of the great treasures of American literature; in the vault of the Morgan Library it is still carefully kept in the stout box of pine that Thoreau made for it with his own hands. The *Journal* furnished material for *A Week on the Concord and Merrimack Rivers* (1849) and *Walden*, the two books which Thoreau published during his lifetime, and for other volumes issued after his death; the *Journal* itself was edited and published in 1906 and a new edition is in preparation. The collection of Thoreau manuscripts in the Morgan Library is the largest and most important in existence.

Walden Sat. July 5th—45 Yesterday I came here to live. My house makes me think of some mountain houses I have seen, which seemed to have a fresher auroral atmosphere about them as I fancy of the halls of Olympus. I lodged at the house of a saw-miller last summer, on the Caatskill mountains, high up as Pine Orchard in the blueberry & raspberry region, where the quiet and cleanliness & coolness seemed to be all one, which had their ambrosial character. He was the miller of the Kanterskill [Kaaterskill] Falls, They were a clean & wholesome family inside and out—like their house. The latter was not plastered—only lathed and the inner doors were not hung. The house seemed [. . .]

Walden Sat. July 5ᵗ '45

Yesterday I came here to live.
My house makes me think
of some mountain house I have
seen, which seemed to have a
purer auroral atmosphere
about them as I fancy of the
halls of Olympus. I lodged at
the house of a saw-miller
last summer, on the Catskill
mountains, high up as Pine
Orchard in the blueberry &
raspberry region, where the
quiet and cleanliness & coolness seemed to be all one,
which had this ambrosial
character. He was the miller
of the Kauterskill Falls,
They were a clean & wholesome
family inside and out —
like their house. The latter
was not plastered — only lathed
and the inner doors were
not hung. The house seemed

46

HENRY DAVID THOREAU

*"Walden." Autograph manuscript unsigned of pages 109–110, a
portion of the chapter on "Reading," in the first edition (1854).
2 p. 23 cm.*

Few literary masterpieces are so eagerly and closely read as *Walden*; the book attracts
readers and sometimes becomes a part of their lives. In his small house at Walden Pond
Thoreau's reading was part of his search for truth, and it was serious reading. In this
chapter he confessed, "I read one or two shallow books of travel in the intervals of my
work, till that employment made me ashamed of myself, and I asked myself where it
was then that *I* lived." "Reading" is only one chapter of *Walden*, which is a magnificent
record of nature, a philosophy of life and a basic and memorable introduction to Thoreau's
originality and genius.

Thoreau did most of his writing for *Walden* in the years 1846–48 and again 1851–
54; he drew heavily upon his *Journal* at every stage of writing and rewriting. He was not
a hermit at Walden Pond but made occasional visits to see Emerson, who owned the
property on which his house was built, to lecture in Concord and to eat an apple or two
with friends; he also received visitors. *Walden* was first printed in 1854 in an edition of
2000 copies and had a modest sale; it was not until 1889 that reader interest made possible
the publication of a new, carefully designed edition. Since that date Thoreau's reputation
has grown and hardened; he and his major works, especially *Walden*, become more
central to our way of life as years pass by. The manuscript of *Walden* (seven drafts written from 1846 to 1854) and the author's corrected proof for the work are in the Huntington Library. The undated draft page illustrated here has lines crossed out which were
not included in the book.

---

*[. . . the heroic writers of antiquity. They seem as solitary,
and the letter in which] they are printed as rare and curious
as ever. It is even worth the expense of youthful days and
costly hours if you learn only some words of an ancient
language which are raised out of the trivialness of the
street, to be perpetual suggestions and provocations. It is
not in vain that the Every farmer loves remembers &
repeats the few Latin words which he has learned heard.*

*Men We sometimes speak as if the study of the classics
would at length make way for more modern and practical
studies, but the brave and adventurous student will always*

*study classics in whatever language they may be written,
and however ancient they may be. [for they have to be
studied in the same spirit in which we study nature. They
are to a great extent only valuable commentaries on her
works, or in one sense, her own finest fruits—never ancient,
and never modern.] For what are the classics but the noblest
recorded thought of man? They are the only oracles which
have are not decayed & there are such answers to the most
modern inquiry in [them as Delphi and Dodona never
gave.]*

they are printed as rare and curious
as ever. It is even worth the expense of youthful days and costly
hours if you learn only some words
of an ancient language which are
raised out of the triviateness of the
street, to be perpetual suggestions
and provocations. Every farmer loves
to repeat the few Latin words which he
has learned.

Men sometimes speak as if the
study of the classics would at length
make way for more modern and
practical studies, but the brave
and adventurous student will always study classics in whatever language
they may be written, and however
ancient they may be — for they
have to be studied in the same
spirit in which we study nature.
They are to a great extent only valuable commentaries on her works, or
in one sense, her own finest fruits —
never ancient, and never modern.
What are the classics but the
noblest recorded thoughts of man?
they are the only oracles which have
not decayed & there are such answers
to the most modern inquiries in

47

HENRY DAVID THOREAU

Autograph letter signed, dated Boston, May 6. '57 addressed to
Richard F. Fuller. 2 p. 22.5 cm.

Richard Frederick Fuller (1821–69) was the younger brother of Margaret Fuller. In 1841, he decided to give up the world of business and enter Harvard. He needed tutoring and took up residence in Concord so that he might study with Thoreau. The latter enjoyed Fuller's companionship for there were too few young men with intellectual leanings in Concord; Fuller profited from it too and after several months of study was admitted to Harvard. Thoreau thanks Fuller for the gift of a music box with a view of Lucerne on the cover. Although the script does not differ greatly from Thoreau's regular hand he mentions that it is written with "one of the 'primaries' of my osprey's wings." Fuller became a clergyman, an army chaplain during the Civil War and a minor poet.

[*Whatever we may think of it, it is a part of the harmony of the spheres you have sent me*] *which has condescended to serve us Admetuses, and I hope I may so behave that this may always be the tenor of your thought for me.*

If you have any strains, the conquest of your own spear or quill to accompany these, let the winds waft them also to me.

I write this with one of the "primaries" of my osprey's wings, which I have preserved over my glass for some state occasion and now it offers.

Mrs. Emerson sends her love—Yr friend, Henry D. Thoreau

which has condescended to serve as
Adventures, and I hope I may
so behave that this may always
be the tenor of your thoughts for me.
     If you have any steam, the
conquest of your own spear or quill
& accompany these, let the winds
waft them also to me.
     I write this with one of the
"primaries" of my osprey's wing,
which I have preserved one my
glass for some state occasion
and now it offers.
     Mrs. Emerson sends her love—
               Yr friend,
                    Henry D. Thoreau

48

JAMES T. FIELDS

Autograph letter signed, dated Boston, May 6. '57, addressed to
George William Curtis. 1 p. 20 cm.

Publisher, author and editor (b. Portsmouth, N.H. 1817; d. Boston, Mass. 1881). Fields wrote *Poems* (1849) and much occasional verse, *Yesterdays with Authors* (1872) and *In and Out of Doors with Charles Dickens* (1876). He was editor of *The Atlantic Monthly* from 1861 to 1870, and a partner in the publishing firm of Ticknor & Fields, which was absorbed by what is now Houghton Mifflin Company in 1878.

Fields traveled extensively in Europe and was a friend and adviser of many of the leading English and American authors of his day. His wife, Annie Adams Fields, had a famous literary salon in their home on Charles Street in Boston, and kept an album containing poems copied out for her by their authors; she bequeathed this to J. P. Morgan for his library.

In this letter to George William Curtis at *Putnam's Monthly Magazine*, Fields offers a poem that John Greenleaf Whittier had sent to Dix and Edwards, publishers of the magazine, just at the time of their business failure. Curtis was also associated editorially with the recently founded *Harper's Weekly* (he later became editor) and accepted the poem, "My Namesake," for that periodical; it was published in the issue of May 23, 1857. The most important collection of Fields letters and manuscripts is in Harvard University Library.

Boston, May 6. '57. My dear Curtis, Some weeks ago Whittier sent to "Putnam's Magazine" a poem called the "Namesake" Dix & Edwards write it has never been received. Please to let me know if you would like it now? It is, I think, Whittier's best poem. There are between thirty & forty verses of four lines each. It is almost entirely autobiographical, and is one of the finest pictures of a serene Quaker life I have ever read. He must have fifty dollars for it, as entre nous, *he is in special need, just now. It should appear in the June number, if possible Let me hear from you by return mail if you want it, as I have undertaken to dispose of it for him, if you do not want it for Putnam. Very Truly Yours, James T. Fields.*

Boston, May 6. '57.

My dear Curtis,
                    Some weeks ago
Whittier sent to "Putnam's Magazine"
a poem called the "Namesake" Dix
& Edwards write it has never been received? Please to let me know
if you would like it now? It is, I think,
Whittier's best poem. There are between thirty & forty verses of four lines
each. It is almost entirely autobiographical, and is one of the finest
pictures of a serene Quaker life I have
ever read. He must have fifty dollars
for it, as entre nous, he is in especial
need, just now. It should appear
in the June number, if possible Let
me hear from you by return of mail
if you want it, as I have undertaken
to dispose of it for him, if you do not want
it for Putnam. Very Truly Yours,
                    James T. Fields

49

JAMES RUSSELL LOWELL

"The Washers of the Shroud." Autograph poem unsigned [n.p., n.d.].
6 p. 21 cm.

Poet, essayist and diplomat (b. Cambridge, Mass. 1819; d. Cambridge, Mass. 1891). His poetical works include *Poems* (1844), followed (all in 1848) by *A Fable for Critics*, clever and entertaining criticism of his fellow American authors; *The Vision of Sir Launfal*; and *The Biglow Papers (First Series)*, condemning the war with Mexico. *The Biglow Papers (Second Series)*, published in 1862, was concerned with the issue of slavery; both series are partly in prose. His other writings include *Among My Books* (1870 and 1876), *My Study Windows* (1871), *Democracy and Other Addresses* (1887) and *Political Essays* (1888). Lowell helped to edit *The Atlantic Monthly* and *The North American Review*, and served as U.S. Minister to both Spain and Great Britain, where he made many friends for his country and himself. He taught the French and Spanish languages at Harvard College for over 30 years.

When James T. Fields became editor of *The Atlantic Monthly* in 1861 he asked Lowell, who had just given up the editorship, for a contribution. With the Civil War very much on his mind he completed within a few days "The Washers of the Shroud." In it Lowell abandoned his generally pacifist attitude and took the position that sometimes justice must resort to force—"For the sheathed blade may rust with darker sin." The opening and final pages of his manuscript are reproduced here, the latter showing a significant alteration. The poem was printed in *The Atlantic Monthly* for November; at about the same time that the poem was published Lowell learned of the death of a favorite nephew at the Battle of Ball's Bluff. The principal repository for Lowell manuscripts and letters is Harvard University Library, but there are important collections in a number of other libraries.

The Washers of the Shroud.

Along a riverside, I know not where, / I walked last night in mystery of dream; / A chill creeps curdling yet beneath my hair / To think what chanced me by the pallid gleam / Of a moon-wraith that waned through haunted air. / [...]

So said I, with clenched hands & passionate pain, / Thinking of dear ones by Potomac's side; / Again the loon laughed, mocking, & again / The echoes bayed far down the night & died / While waking I recalled my wandering brain. /

"Tears may be ours, but proud, for those who win
Death's royal purple in the Enemy's lines;
Peace, too, brings tears, o'mid the battle-din;
The wisest ear some tott'ring hope divines
For the dreaded ... ... sin.

"God, give us peace, not such as lulls to sleep,
But soul on High, astir with purpose stout,
And let our chief ... ...
Her posts all set up, his battle-lanterns lit,
And her ... thunders gathering for their leap!"

So said I, with clenched hands of passionate pain,
Thinking I heard once by Potomac's side;
Again the love laughed, mocking, o'er again
The echoes ... far down the night ...
While wailing I recalled my wandering brain.

The Watchers of the Strand.

1

Along a sorrowful ..., I knew not where,
I walked last night in mystery of dream;
A child crept nestling yet beneath my hair
To think what chanced me by the pallid gleam
Of a moon-... that waved through haunted air.

2

Pale fireflies poised within the ...
Their ..., drawing ... of light;
The love, that seemed to rock some golden flight,
laughed, of the echoes bubbling in affright,
Like Ocean's hounds fled baying down the night?

3

There all was silent till there rose my ...
A moment in the stream that choked my breath;
Was it the ... plash of a wading deer?
But something said, "This is the Stream of Death,
The sisters weave a shroud — ill thing to hear!"

50

JAMES RUSSELL LOWELL

*"The Trustee's Lament." Autograph poem signed [n.p., n.d.]. 1 p.
24.5 cm.*

"The Trustee's Lament" was first published in *The Atlantic Monthly* (August 1858), of which Lowell was editor, and for which Hennessy, whose name appears in another hand at the top left of this reproduction, was a compositor. Lowell appears to have been a trustee of the Dudley Astronomical Observatory in Albany, New York, somewhat to his discomfiture as he describes it in this amusing piece of verse. He did not see fit to include this in any of his books.

The Trustee's Lament.

Per aspera ad astra.

*(Scene: outside the gate of the Astronomical Observatory
at Albany)*

There was a time when I was blest; / The stars might rise in East or West / With all their sines & wonders, / I cared for neither great nor small, / As pointedly unmoved by all / As, on the top of steeple tall, / A lightning-rod at thunders. /

What did I care for Science then? / I was a man with fel-lowmen / And called the Bear the Dipper, / Segment meant piece of pie,—no more, / Cosine—the parallelogram that bore / John Smith & Co above a door, / Arc—what called Noah skipper. /

No axes weighed upon my mind, / (Unless I had a few to grind,) / And, as for my astronomy, / Had Hedgecock's quadrant then been known, / I might a lamp-post's height have shown / By gas-tronomic skill,—if none / Find fault with the metonymy. /

J. R. Lowell

Hennessy   The Trustee's Lament.

Per aspera ad astra.

[Scene: outside the gate of the Astronomical Observatory at Albany.]

There was a time when I was blest;
The stars might rise in East or West
     With all their sines & wonders,
I cared for neither great nor small,
As pointedly unmoved by all
As, on the top of steeple tall,
     A lightning-rod at thunders.

What did I care for Science then?
I was a man with fellowmen
     And called the Bear the Dipper,
Segment meant piece of pie, – no more,
Cosine – the parallelogram that bore
John Smith & Co above a door,
     Arc – what called Noah skipper.

No axes weighed upon my mind,
(Unless I had a few to grind,)
     And, as for my astronomy,
Had Hedgcock's quadrant then been known,
I might a lamp-post's height have shown
By gas-tronomic skill, – if none
     Find fault with the metonymy.

51

JULIA WARD HOWE

"Army Hymn." Autograph manuscript unsigned [n.p., n.d.]. 2 p. 24.5 cm.
Autograph letter signed, dated Boston, November 14, 1873, addressed to Mrs. Gordon Lester Ford. 2 p. 20 cm.

Author and reformer (b. New York City 1819; d. Middletown, R.I. 1910). She wrote a *Memoir of Dr. Samuel Gridley Howe* (1876), her husband, a *Life of Margaret Fuller* (1883) and books of verse, travel sketches and essays. She is famous for her "Battle Hymn of the Republic" (1862). Mrs. Howe devoted much of her life to charity and public service in many causes, especially women's suffrage and world peace.

This is an undated transcript of "The Battle Hymn of the Republic," of which the first page is reproduced, made by Mrs. Howe for Mrs. James T. Fields. "Army Hymn" was another title of the poem. The poem was originally written in the early hours of November 19, 1861, while Mrs. Howe was visiting an army camp near Washington, D.C. with a party headed by Governor Andrew of Massachusetts; she set it down either in the camp or in Willard's Hotel. She composed to the tune of the popular song "John Brown's Body" or "Glory Hallelujah," but the "Glory Hallelujah" chorus does not appear in this manuscript nor in the earliest printed versions of the poem. *The Atlantic Monthly* bought the poem for four dollars and it was published in the February 1862 issue of that magazine. An earlier publication in the *New-York Daily Tribune*, January 14, 1862, has been noted; it may have been set up from advance proofs of the magazine. These lines, in great measure because of their musical setting, became immensely popular, and Mrs. Howe became the most honored woman of her day. Her autograph signature is also shown here, on the second page of a letter written to Mrs. Gordon Lester Ford in 1873. Manuscripts and letters of Mrs. Howe are in many libraries, and Harvard University Library has a special collection.

Army Hymn.

Mine eyes have seen the glory of the coming of the Lord; / He is trampling out the vintage where the grapes of wrath are stored, / He hath loosed the fateful lightning of His terrible swift sword; / His truth is marching on. /

I have seen Him in the watchfires of an hundred circling camps; / They have builded Him an altar in the evening dews and damps, / I can read His righteous sentence by the dim and flaring lamps; / His day is marching on. / [. . .]

[My only excuse for these delays is that I am almost at my wit's ends with things needing to be done, and] ought to have, but cannot have, a private secretary. I will answer your letter presently in my official capacity, and as fully as I can.

Meantime believe me, with grateful remembrance of your kind hospitality, Yours sincerely   Julia Ward Howe.

Army Hymn.

Mine eyes have seen the glory of the coming of the Lord;
He is trampling out the vintage where the grapes of wrath are stored;
He hath loosed the fateful lightning of His terrible swift sword;
His truth is marching on.

I have seen Him in the watchfires of an hundred circling camps;
They have builded Him an altar in the evening dews and damps;
I can read His righteous sentence by the dim and flaring lamps;
His day is marching on.

I have read a fiery gospel writ in burnished

52

WALT WHITMAN

["Leaves of Grass.] Introduction to the London Edition." Autograph manuscript unsigned [Washington, D.C. 1867]. 14 p. 19.5 cm. Green morocco.

Poet (b. West Hills, near Huntington, Long Island, N.Y. 1819; d. Camden, N.J. 1892). Author of *Leaves of Grass* (1855), which was revised and augmented with additional poems in eight later editions published during his lifetime; *Drum-Taps* (1865); *Democratic Vistas* (1871); *Two Rivulets* (1876); *Specimen Days & Collect* (1882–83); *November Boughs* (1888); *Good-Bye My Fancy* (1891); and other works. Whitman wrote personal and universal poetry of power, beauty and optimism at a time when America was not entirely prepared to receive it, but he has come to be regarded as America's national poet and his *Leaves of Grass* is one of the great books of American literature.

In his early years Whitman worked at many different occupations, but was mainly interested in journalism. He served as a nurse during the Civil War and was employed as a clerk in the U.S. Department of the Interior until dismissed by the secretary because of the nature of certain poems in *Leaves of Grass*. Whitman also worked in the office of the U.S. attorney general but, after a paralytic stroke in 1873, he spent the rest of his days living frugally in his small house in Camden, N.J., but receiving many visitors.

William Michael Rossetti was a champion of Whitman's poetry in England and in 1868 edited and published a selection of his poems in London, which enjoyed a considerable popularity. With slight modifications Rossetti included the notable Preface to the 1855 edition of *Leaves of Grass*. When he learned of Rossetti's publishing intentions Whitman tried, in a roundabout manner, to get him to use the "Introduction" of which two pages are reproduced here, but it was too late. Whitman had written the highly favorable "Introduction" himself and attempted to pass it off as the work of his friend William D. O'Connor. He also tried to have it used on two later occasions when there were English editions of his poems or rumors of them, appropriately changing his stated age each time, but without success. Important Whitman collections are in the Library of Congress, Duke University Library, the Alderman Library, University of Virginia, Yale University Library and The New York Public Library.

Introduction to the London Edition.

America—that new world in so many respects besides its geography—has perhaps afforded nothing even in the astonishing products of the fields of its politics, its mechanical invention, material growth, & the like, more original, more autochthonic, than its late contribution in the field of literature, the Poem, or poetic writings, of named Leaves of Grass, *which in the following pages, we*

present to the British public. [...]

He The Poet is now in his 49th 53d 62d year, & is pourtrayed by one who knows him intimately, as tall in stature, with shapely limbs, slow of movement, florid & clear face, bearded & gray, blue eyes, an expression of great equanimity, of decided presence [& singular personal magnetism.]

11

to Southerners as well as north-
erner, not to the Richmond
fell, & Lee capitulated...

he lingers even yet as too
few, regards even the costumes of manner & looks—
even new, the said legacy
bequeathed by these vast armies,
the long Companies & sanguinary
battles.

The Poet

62 He is now in his
prime of year, & is pourtrayed ?
one who knows him int—
mately as tall in stature,
with shapely limbs, slow of
movement, florid & clear face,
bearded & gray, blue eyes,
an expression of great e gra—
nimity, of decided presence

"Leaves of Grass" 1881

<u>Introduction to the</u>
<u>London Edition.</u>

America — that new world
in so many respects besides
its geography — has perhaps
afforded nothing even in the
astonishing product of the
field of Poet. to Politics, its
fresh aural invention, material growth & the like,
more original, more autoch-
thonous, than its late contri—
bution in the field of Literature,
& return to poetic writings.
the Poem, or Poetic writings.
named Leaves of Grass, which
in the following pages, we pre-
x sent to the British Public.

53

WALT WHITMAN

["November Boughs.] Diary of the War." Autograph manuscript signed with initials [Washington, D.C.] September 1863 – April 29 1866. 23 p. Written on paper of various sizes. Green morocco gilt.

"Diary of the War" is actually a title of convenience for this manuscript which consists of extracts from letters that Whitman wrote to his mother during the Civil War. These extracts, which were printed in the "Last of the War Cases" chapter of *November Boughs* (1888), were Whitman's selection from this correspondence written out for his publisher in Philadelphia. After Whitman's death the letters were published in full as *The Wound Dresser* (1898), edited by Richard Maurice Bucke, one of Whitman's literary executors, and show some differences from the texts in *November Boughs*. Whitman's humanity and compassion is evident in all of these entries, and especially in this account of the last days of Charles Cutter, aged 17. This manuscript was given by Whitman to Thomas Donaldson on the poet's last birthday, May 31, 1891; Donaldson, a Philadelphia lawyer, was a close friend and was instrumental in presenting Whitman with a horse and phaeton which cheered his final years.

[Yesterday I spent a good part of the afternoon with a] young soldier of 17. Charles Cutter, of Lawrence City, Mass., 1ˢᵗ Mass. Heavy Artillery, Battery M.; he was brought to one of the hospitals mortally wounded in abdomen. Well, I thought to myself, as I sat looking at him, it ought to be a relief to his folks if they could see how little he really suffered. He lay, very placid, in a half lethargy, with his eyes closed. As it was ~~very~~ extremely hot, and I sat a good while silently fanning him, and wiping the sweat, at length he opened his eyes quite wide and clear, and looked inquiringly around. I said, "What is it, my boy? Do you want any thing?" He answered quietly, with a good-natured smile, "O, nothing; I was only looking around to see who was with me." His mind was somewhat wandering, yet he lay in an evident peacefulness that sanity and health might have envied.

I had to leave for other engagements. He died, I heard afterward, without any special agitation, in the course of the night.

young soldier of 17. Charles
Cutter. of Lawrence City. Mass..
1st Mass. Heavy Artillery. Battery
M.; he was brought to one of the
hospitals mortally wounded in
abdomen. Well. I thought to myself. as I sat looking at him.
it aught to be a relief to his folks
if they could see how little he
really suffered. He lay. very placid,
in a half lethargy. with his eyes
closed. As it was extremely very hot and
I sat a good while silently fanning
him, and wiping the sweat, at
length he opened his eyes quite
wide and clear, and looked inquiringly around. I said, "What
is it, my boy? Do you want any
thing?" He answered quietly. with
a good-natured smile. "O. nothing:
I was only looking around to see
who was with me." His mind was
somewhat wandering, yet he lay
in an evident peacefulness that.
sanity and health might have envied.

I had to leave, for other engagements. He died, I heard afterward.
& special agitation, in the course.
of the night.

54

WALT WHITMAN

"O Captain! my Captain!" Autograph manuscript signed, dated
[Camden, N.J.] April 27 '90. 1 p. 26.5 cm.

This memorial of President Lincoln is the best known but least characteristic poem from Whitman's pen; it is one of the few poems he wrote using conventional rhyme and meter. It became so much more popular than his other poems that Whitman once remarked, "I'm almost sorry I ever wrote the poem." This did not prevent him from writing out this fair copy for Dr. S. Weir Mitchell of Philadelphia. The latter proposed to help Whitman in his poverty and illness by offering him $100 for an autograph transcript of "O Captain!" and made his offer through a mutual friend, Horace Howard Furness, the Shakespearean scholar. Furness wrote Mitchell that when he mentioned the proposal to Whitman, "he was silent for some minutes. Then he looked up with really a genuine irradiation in his face. 'Why,' said he, 'that's quite a bonanza! Yes I'll do it.' " Whitman later wrote Dr. Mitchell that the money "is opportune & will do me much good." "O Captain!" was first published in the New York *Saturday Press*, November 4, 1865, and collected in the *Drum-Taps* "Sequel" (1865) and in *Passage to India* (1871). Whitman wrote three other poems in memory of Abraham Lincoln, including the great threnody "When Lilacs Last in the Dooryard Bloom'd." The manuscript draft of "O Captain!," which shows much reworking, is in the Library of Congress.

O Captain! my Captain!

O Captain! my Captain! our fearful trip is done; / The ship has weather'd every rack, the prize we sought is won; / The port is near, the bells I hear, the people all exulting, / While follow eyes the steady keel, the vessel grim and daring, / But O heart! heart! heart! / O the bleeding drops of red, / Where on the deck my Captain lies, / Fallen cold and dead. /

O Captain! my Captain! rise up and hear the bells; / Rise up—for you the flag is flung—for you the bugle trills; / For you bouquets and ribbon'd wreaths—for you the shores a-crowding; / For you they call, the swaying mass, their eager faces turning; / Here Captain! dear father! / This arm beneath your head; / It is some dream that on the deck / You've fallen cold and dead. /

My Captain does not answer, his lips are pale and still, / My father does not feel my arm, he has no pulse nor will, / The ship is anchor'd safe and sound, its voyage closed and done; / From fearful trip the victor ship comes in with object won; / Exult O shores, and ring O bells! / But I, with mournful tread, / Walk the dead [sic] my Captain lies / Fallen cold and dead. /

Walt Whitman
April 27 '90

O Captain! My Captain!

O Captain! my Captain! our fearful trip is done,
The ship has weather'd every rack, the prize we
        sought is won;
The port is near, the bells I hear, the people all exulting,
While follow eyes the steady keel, the vessel grim
        and daring;
    But O heart! heart! heart!
      O the bleeding drops of red,
        Where on the deck my Captain lies,
          Fallen cold and dead.

O Captain! my Captain! rise up and hear the bells;
Rise up — for you the flag is flung — for you the
        bugle trills;
For you bouquets and ribbon'd wreaths — for you
        the shores a-crowding;
For you they call, the swaying mass, their eager
        faces turning;
    Here Captain! dear father!
      This arm beneath your head;
        It is some dream that on the deck,
          You've fallen cold and dead.

My Captain does not answer, his lips are pale and still,
My father does not feel my arm, he has no pulse nor will,
The ship is anchor'd safe and sound, its voyage closed
        and done,
From fearful trip the victor ship comes in with
        object won;
    Exult O shores, and ring O bells!
      But I, with mournful tread,
        Walk the deck my Captain lies,
          Fallen cold and dead.

Walt Whitman
April 27 '90

55

HERMAN MELVILLE

Autograph letter signed, dated Pittsfield [Mass.] Nov 24ᵗʰ 1853,
addressed to Harper & Bros., his publishers. 1 p. 22 cm.

Novelist, poet and short-story writer (b. New York City 1819; d. New York City 1891). He published five novels, including *Typee* (1846), before his *Moby-Dick* (1851), the symbolic story of the search for the white whale and one of the great novels of world literature. Melville continued to write and publish until his death, at which time he left his *Billy Budd* in manuscript, but received little recognition from critics or the general public during his lifetime.

Surviving letters of some American nineteenth-century authors may be counted in the thousands, but only about 275 letters of Melville are known. This letter is concerned with a book on "Tortoises and Tortoise Hunting," for which Melville obtained an advance from the Harpers (in spite of the "Declined" marked on the letter), but which was never completed. Portions of the book, however, were actually written and found their way into his sketches, "The Encantadas, or Enchanted Isles," which were first published, not in *Harper's New Monthly Magazine* but in *Putnam's Monthly Magazine,* in 1854. The principal repositories of Melville materials are The Houghton Library of Harvard University, The New York Public Library and the Berkshire Athenaeum; Melville's surviving contracts with the firm of Harper & Bros. are in Columbia University Library.

Pittsfield Nov 24ᵗʰ 1853 Gentlemen:— In addition to the work which I took to New York last Spring, but which I was prevented from printing at that time; I have now in hand, and pretty well on towards completion, another book—300 pages, say—partly of nautical adventure, and partly—or, rather chiefly, of Tortoise Hunting Adventure. It will be ready for press some time in the coming January. Meanwhile, it would be convenient, to have advanced to me upon it $300.—My acct: with you, at present, can not be very far from square. For the abovenamed advance—if remitted me now—you will have security in my former works, as well as security prospective, in the one to come, (The Tortoise-Hunters) because if you accede to the aforesaid request, this letter shall be your voucher, that I am willing your house should publish it, on the old basis— half-profits. Reply immediately, if you please, And Beleve Me, Yours   Herman Melville

Pittsfield Nov 24ᵗʰ 1853

Gentlemen : — In addition to the work which
I took to New York last Spring, but which I was
prevented from printing at that time; I have now
in hand, and pretty well on towards completion,
another book — 300 pages, say — partly of nautical
adventure, and partly — or rather chiefly, of Tortoise
Hunting Adventure. It will be ready for press
some time in the coming January. Meanwhile,
it would be convenient, to have advances to me
upon it ⅌ 300. — My acct: with you, at
present, can not be very far from square. For
the aborenamed advance — if remitted me now —
you will have security in my former works, as
well as security prospective, in the one to come,
(The Tortoise - Hunters) because if you accede
to the aforesaid request, this letter shall be
your voucher, that I am willing your house should
publish it, on the old basis — half - profits.
　　　Reply immediately, if you please,
　　　And Believe Me, Yours
　　　　　Herman Melville

56

THOMAS BUCHANAN READ

*"Sheridan's Ride." Autograph manuscript signed [n.p., n.d.]. 4 p.
23 cm.*

Poet and painter (b. near Guthriesville, Pa. 1822; d. New York City 1872). His works include *Paul Redding* (1845), a novelette and his one book of prose; *Poems* (1847); *The House by the Sea* (1855); *The Wagoner of the Alleghanies* (1862); and *A Summer Story, Sheridan's Ride, and Other Poems* (1865). Read's only poems that are remembered today are "Sheridan's Ride" and "Drifting," but he was regarded by contemporary critics as one of the chief poets of America. His reputation as a painter has also declined, but he painted a picture of "Sheridan's Ride" and numerous portraits; Longfellow, Mrs. Browning and George Peabody were among his subjects.

In October 1864, while Sheridan was away and in conference with Grant, his troops at Cedar Creek, Virginia, were threatened by the forces of Jubal Early; but Sheridan rode 20 miles in record time from Winchester to turn back Early and defeat him. During the Civil War, Read was on the staff of General Lew Wallace and made many patriotic speaking and recital tours through the North. The American actor James Edward Murdoch, who was traveling with him, recited "Sheridan's Ride" on the same day that Read wrote it. The Alderman Library, University of Virginia, and The Historical Society of Pennsylvania have collections of Read manuscripts and letters.

Sheridan's Ride

Up from the South at break of day, / Bringing to Winchester fresh dismay, / The affrighted air with a shudder bore / Like a herald in haste to the chieftain's door, / The terrible grumble and rumble and roar / Telling the battle was on once more— / And Sheridan twenty miles away! /

And wider still those billows of war / Thundered along the horizons bar,— / And louder yet into Winchester rolled / The roar of that red sea uncontrolled / Making the blood of the listener cold, / As he thought of the stake in that fiery fray / And Sheridan twenty miles away! /

But there is a road from Winchester town— / A good broad highway leading down; / And there, thro' the flush of the morning light, / [A steed as black as the steeds of night / Was seen to pass, as with eagle flight. / . . .]

[Be it said, in letters both bold and bright:] / "Here is the steed that saved the day / By carrying Sheridan into the fight / From Winchester, twenty miles away!" /

T. Buchanan Read

Sheridan's Ride

Up from the South at break of day,
Bringing to Winchester fresh dismay,
The affrighted air with a shudder bore
Like a herald in haste to the chieftain's door,
The terrible grumble and rumble and roar
Telling the battle was on once more —
And Sheridan twenty miles away!

And wider still those billows of war
Thundered along the horizon's bar,
And louder yet into Winchester rolled
The roar of that red sea uncontrolled
Making the blood of the listener cold,
As he thought of the stake in that fiery fray
And Sheridan twenty miles away!

But there is a road from Winchester town —
A good broad highway leading down;
And there, thro' the flush of the morning light,

"Here is the steed that saved the day
By carrying Sheridan into the fight
From Winchester, twenty miles away!"

T. Buchanan Read

57

EDWARD EVERETT HALE

"Of the Chief:—and To Him." Autograph poem signed, dated
[*Boston*] *Aug 29. 1884. 2 p. 21 cm.*

Author and clergyman (b. Boston, Mass. 1822; d. Boston, Mass. 1909). His most famous book is *The Man Without a Country* (1865), the fictional story of Philip Nolan, a U.S. Navy officer who expressed a desire never to hear the name of his country again. Hale also wrote scholarly histories and biographies, historical and Utopian novels, and a variety of miscellaneous works. Some of these are *If, Yes, and Perhaps* (1868); *Sybaris and Other Homes* (1869), a tract on social hygiene; *Ten Times One Is Ten* (1871); *In His Name* (1873), a story of the twelfth-century Waldenses; *Franklin in France* (1887–88); *A New England Boyhood* (1893), based on his own memories; and *James Russell Lowell and His Friends* (1899). Hale was pastor of the South Congregational Church in Boston for nearly 50 years, active in civic and philanthropic causes, and an American pioneer in urging the formation of a kind of United Nations.

This poem, which is both capricious and serious, is a tribute to Oliver Wendell Holmes on his seventy-fifth birthday and has references to his writings. Hale and Holmes were friends in Boston and the physician-poet contributed to the magazine *Old and New* when it was edited by Hale. On one occasion Hale importuned Holmes for more contributions and received the reply, "You are such a *polycephalous* and *polycheirous* producer that you hardly realize the limitations of a common mortal with only one pair of hemispheres and two hands." Hale's manuscripts and letters are scattered in many libraries, but there are special collections in Harvard University Library, the New York State Library and the American Antiquarian Society.

Of the Chief:—and To Him.

He taught me my geology; / From him I knew / How, in their Rabble Rout, / The crazy Crew / Of Giants threw / Their pudding and their plumbs about. / [...]

Blessings and thanks and praise, / In stumbling prose, in sweetest lays;— / And if grief come / Even to a prophet poet's home:— / To him some measure of the peace and faith / The hope and strength which conquer Death, / Which in our darker days, / With all a poet's prophecy / And all a prophet's poetry, / And all a wise man's wisdom, he / Has sent to comfort you and me. /

E. E. Hale

Aug 29. 1884—

Of the Chief:— and To Him.

He taught me my geology;
From him I knew
How in their Rattle Root,
The Crazy Crew
Of Scouts threw
Their history and their plumets about.

He taught no modesty;
In sitting at his feet
I said that I
Would never try
To be
So funny as is he:

And this—dear Critic,—will account for me

And, how to headstrong, he
Knew taught the world,— to be
Wise in such wise as wisdom's self is wise;—
Yet playful, kind and true;
To mingle old and new,
And with the mixture brew,
With fittest reason
The brew to season,
Then taste out nothing for me and you.

But when the war cloud growls & lowers
Above the lands,
The poet stands
And tells the Coward how to try,—
And tells the bravest how to die:
Inspires songs, and cheers his troops & ours!

Blessings and thanks and praise,
In stirring hours, in sweetest lays;—
And if grief came
Even to a habit poet's home;—
To him some measure of the peace and faith
To him hope and strength which conquer death.
Which in our darker days,

With all a poet's prophecy
And all a prophet's poetry,
And all a wise man's wisdom, he
Has sent to comfort you and me.

E. E. Hale

Aug 29. 1884 —

58

FRANCIS PARKMAN

•

Tribute to James Russell Lowell signed, dated Boston, 16 Feb. 1889.
1 p. 17 cm.

Historian (b. Boston, Mass. 1823; d. Boston, Mass. 1893). His most important works are *The California and Oregon Trail* (1849), *Pioneers of France in the New World* (1865), *The Jesuits in North America* (1867), *The Discovery of the Great West* (1869), *Montcalm and Wolfe* (1884) and *A Half-Century of Conflict* (1892).

Parkman was born to a prominent New England family and, after his graduation from Harvard College, traveled extensively in Europe. He followed this with a strenuous six months' journey westward which was recorded in his greatest book, *The California and Oregon Trail*. In spite of the title, Parkman never saw California or Oregon, but he recorded superb descriptions of Indian customs. Throughout his life Parkman suffered from a series of nervous and physical ailments; as with the historian Prescott, these particularly affected his eyesight, and for many years he was unable to read. His reputation as a historian rests on the series of volumes, published over four decades, known collectively as *France and England in North America*, the history of the long contest for dominance that culminated in the French and Indian Wars. This classic of nineteenth-century historiography combined massive research, a vigorous but controlled narrative style and a poetical, almost mystical insight into the conditions of life in the North American wilderness before its conquest by European civilizations. The largest collection of Parkman's papers is in Harvard University Library.

We all know Mr. Lowell's brilliant quality as poet, critic, scholar, and man of the world; but that in him which touches me most strongly belongs to his relations to his country,—his keen and subtle yet kindly recognitltion of her virtues and her faults and the sympathetic power with which in the day of her melancholy triumph, after the Civil War, he gave such noble expression to her self-devotion, sorrows, and hopes.

Boston, 16 Feb. 1889.

Francis Parkman

We all know Mr. Lowell's brilliant quality as poet, critic, scholar, and man of the world; but that in him which touches me most strongly belongs to his relations to his country, — his keen and subtle, yet kindly recognition of her virtues and her faults and the sympathetic power with which in the day of her melancholy triumph, after the Civil War, he gave such noble expression to her self-devotion, sorrows, and hopes.

Francis Parkman

Boston, 16 Feb. 1889.

59

GEORGE WILLIAM CURTIS

"Our new Livery, & other things. a Letter from Mrs Potiphar to Miss Caroline Pettitoes." Autograph manuscript unsigned of chapter 2 of his "Potiphar Papers" (1853) [n.p., n.d.]. 44 p. 25 cm. Brown morocco.

Essayist, editor and political reformer (b. Providence, R.I. 1824; d. New Brighton, Staten Island, N.Y. 1892). Other books by Curtis are *Nile Notes of a Howadji* (1851), *Prue and I* (1857) and a posthumous collection, *Literary and Social Essays* (1894). Curtis, an independent spirit and moving force in nineteenth-century America, is almost forgotten in this century. He was the ablest leader of the Civil Service reform movement, fought against slavery and for women's rights, and insisted on the public duty of educated men.

As a young man Curtis imbibed the influences of Brook Farm and traveled in the Near East as a newspaper correspondent. He published several books based on his travels and in 1863 became editor of *Harper's Weekly*, an office he retained until his death. He wrote for the magazine himself and worked closely with the leading writers and artists (especially Thomas Nast) of his day. *The Potiphar Papers* is a gentle satire on high society and features the newly rich social climber, Mrs. Potiphar, and her adviser, the Reverend Cream Cheese. These names and the autograph page illustrated here about the Easter bonnet give the flavor of the sketches, which were very popular in their day. The Morgan Library has 12 manuscripts by Curtis, and other manuscripts and letters may be found in many American libraries.

Our new Livery, & other things.
a Letter from Mrs Potiphar to Miss Caroline Pettitoes.

My dear Caroline.—Lent came so frightfully early this year that I was very much afraid my new bonnet ~~a l'Ip~~ à l'Imperatrice would not be out from Paris soon enough. But fortunately it arrived just in time, & I had the satisfaction of taking down the pride of M^{rs} Crœsus who fancied ~~she~~ hers would be the only stylish hat in church the first Sunday.—She could not keep her eyes away from me, ~~but~~

and I sat so unconcerned and so ~~constantly~~ calmly looking at the D^r. that she was quite ~~frantic~~ vexed. But whenever she turned away I ~~took~~ ran my eyes over the whole congregation, and would you believe that almost without an exception ~~the~~ people had their old things? However I suppose they forgot how soon Lent was coming. As I was ~~coming~~ passing out of church M^{rs} Crœsus brushed by me:—¶ "Ah!" said she "good morning. Why! bless me! You've got that pretty hat I saw at [Lawson's."]

Our new Livery, & other things.
a Letter from Mrs Potiphar to Miss Caroline
Pettitoes.

New York.

My dear Caroline. -

Lent came so frightfully early
this year that I was very much afraid my new
bonnet ~~à~~ à l'Imperatrice would not
be out from Paris soon enough. But fortunately it arrived just in time, & I had the
satisfaction of taking down the pride of
Mrs Croesus who fancied ~~this~~ hers would be
the only stylish hat in church the first
Sunday. - She could not keep her eyes away
from me, ~~and~~ I sat so unconcerned and so
calmly
~~constantly~~ looking at the Dr. that she was
veiled
quite ~~frantic~~. But whenever she turned
away I ~~did~~ ran my eyes over the whole
congregation, and would you believe that almost without an exception the people had
their old things? However I suppose they
forgot how soon Lent was coming. As I was
passing
~~coming~~ out of church Mrs Croesus brushed by
me: - ¶ "Ah!" said she "good morning, why!
bless me! You've got that pretty hat I saw at

60

BAYARD TAYLOR

Autograph letter signed, dated Gotha, Germany, April 22, 1873,
addressed to [Whitelaw] Reid. 1 p. 22 cm.

Poet, novelist and traveler (b. Kennett Square, Pa. 1825; d. Berlin, Germany 1878). His many books include *Views A-Foot* (1846); *Rhymes of Travel* (1849); *Eldorado* (1850), about the gold rush in California; *A Visit to India, China, and Japan* (1855); *At Home and Abroad* (1860); *Hannah Thurston* (1863), a love story set in Ptolemy, N.Y.; *John Godfrey's Fortunes* (1864), an autobiographical record; *The Story of Kennett* (1866), about his home town; and *Lars: A Pastoral of Norway* (1873), a long poem dedicated to Whittier in which Lars comes to America and adopts the Quaker faith.

Bayard Taylor was raised in a strict, quiet Quaker household which bred in him, in reaction, an intense desire to see the world. At 19 he sailed to Europe and spent two years wandering there; the story of his travels, *Views A-Foot*, went through many editions. He continued to mix journalism, poetry and travel for many years, earning a reputation in the United States as a modern-day Marco Polo. Following the death of his first wife after only two months of marriage, Taylor spent several years in Africa and the Orient, attached for part of the time to Commodore Perry's squadron. His poetry was of great popularity in its time: he was commissioned to write the Gettysburg Ode and the Centennial Ode. It is now all forgotten. His most important achievement was his translation of Goethe's *Faust* (1870–71), which was published to remarkable acclaim and long remained as the standard translation into English; the autograph manuscript of most of part two of this translation is in the Morgan Library. This letter to the editor of the New York *Tribune* sends a travel piece and discusses his plans to visit the Vienna Exposition with the painter and journalist William J. Stillman and the journalist Eugene V. Smalley. The largest collection of Bayard Taylor materials is in Cornell University Library.

Gotha, Germany. April 22, 1873. My dear Reid: Here you have another letter about the studios in Rome. I shall add a brief one about the artists in Florence, and that will be as much, I think, as the Tribune now needs from Italy.

I leave here to-night for Vienna. Smalley will have already told you that everything is arranged, and if we do not get ahead it will simply be because other papers have adopted precisely the same plans—a thing not to be prevented. I shall give to the Exposition all the time I can possibly spare from my History (which must be finished in August), but do not see how I can remain in Vienna beyond May 20th. However, Stillman and E. V. Smalley are both excellent men, and if we launch the reports properly, there need be no shortcomings afterwards.

I still delight in the vitality and vigor of the Trib. Pray let me know more about the new building, when you have any time to spare. This will be my address all summer. Love to all friends. Ever faithfully yours, Bayard Taylor.

Gotha, Germany.
April 22, 1873.

My dear Reid:

Here you have another letter about
the studios in Rome. I shall add a brief
one about the artists in Florence, and that
will be as much, I think, as the Tribune
now needs from Italy.

I leave here to-night for Vienna.
Smalley will have already told you that
everything is arranged, and if we do not
get ahead it will simply be because other
papers have adopted precisely the same
plans — a thing not to be prevented. I shall
give to the Exposition all the time I can
possibly spare from my History (which
must be finished in August), but do
not see how I can remain in Vienna beyond May
20th. However, Stillman and E.V. Smalley
are both excellent men, and if we launch
the reports properly, there need be no
shortcomings afterwards.

I still delight in the vitality and
vigor of the Trib. Pray let me know more
about the new building, when you have
any time to spare. This will be my
address all summer. Love to all friends.
                Ever faithfully yours,
                Bayard Taylor.

61

LEW WALLACE

Autograph letter signed, dated Crawfordsville, Nov. 26. 1888, to
James McCormick Dalzell. 1 p. 26 cm.

Author, soldier and statesman (b. Brookville, Ind. 1827; d. Crawfordsville, Ind. 1905). His books include *The Fair God* (1873), written under the influence of *The Conquest of Mexico* of Prescott; *Ben-Hur: A Tale of the Christ* (1880), which achieved amazing popularity as a novel and in stage and motion-picture adaptations (the famous chariot race became a feature attraction in circus performances); and *The Prince of India* (1893), among others. Wallace was a major-general during the Civil War and later served as governor of New Mexico and U.S. minister to Turkey. He was deeply interested in art, music and literature.

While practicing law in his home state in 1888, Wallace had occasion to send this reply to James McCormick Dalzell, generally known as "Private Dalzell" for he had published his Civil War autobiography under that name. Dalzell was apparently seeking a post in the pension bureau and had written Wallace before—vaguely. Now Wallace replies in no uncertain terms. The most important group of Wallace letters and manuscripts, including the manuscript of *Ben-Hur*, is in the Lilly Library, Indiana University. Twenty-seven pages necessary to complete the manuscript of *Ben-Hur* were presented to the Lilly Library at its dedication ceremonies in 1960 by the Morgan Library and Harper & Bros.

Crawfordsville, Nov. 26. 1888. My Dear Dalzell. Again!
And still you don't say what you want.
If a place in the pension bureau, say so, and forward
your application, with all the backing you can command.

Dont rely upon my being appointed Secretary of War.
I am not an applicant, and will not be. Yours truly   Lew.
Wallace / Private Dalzell.

Crawfordsville, Nov. 26, 1888.

My Dear Dalzell.

Again!

And still you don't say what you want.

If a place in the pension bureau, say so, and forward your application, with all the backing you can command.

Dont rely upon my being appointed Secretary of War. I am not an applicant, and will not be.

Yours truly

Lew. Wallace

Private Dalzell.

62

HENRY TIMROD

Autograph letter signed, dated Columbia, March 26ᵗʰ [1867],
addressed to Paul Hamilton Hayne. 4 p. 20.5 cm.

Poet (b. Charleston, S.C. 1828; d. Columbia, S.C. 1867). His most famous single poems are "Ethnogenesis," "The Cotton Boll," "A Cry to Arms," "Carolina" and the Magnolia Cemetery "Ode." *Poems* (1860) was his only book published during his lifetime. Timrod's poems, based on classical models but written with great emotional intensity, celebrated the cause of the South during the Civil War, and he was known as the "Poet Laureate of the Confederacy." He earned a living as a private tutor on plantations and as an editor, but was financially ruined by the war and succumbed to tuberculosis in his thirty-ninth year.

Paul Hamilton Hayne was Timrod's lifelong friend and posthumous editor. The letter of which the first and last pages are reproduced here was written about six months before Timrod's death and is partly concerned with the trip to New York City which he was never destined to take. He also writes warmly of their friend William Gilmore Simms. The largest collection of Timrod materials is in the University of South Carolina Library.

From the Collection of Mr. C. Waller Barrett at the Alderman Library, The University of Virginia, Charlottesville, Virginia.

Columbia March 26ᵗʰ My dear Paul, I would have answered your letter before, but for the sickness of my wife. She has had a bad hemorrhage of the lungs. I need not say that until this was arrested and until she began to mend, I was in no condition to write.

If I go North, I shall be glad to avail myself of your introductions. Whipple, I should especially like to meet, and they say that Fields is a genial fellow. But alas! Where shall I get the golden or paper wings to waft me thither. Yet I shall need but little, and shall [endeavour to raise it by hook or crook....]

[How the fellow hugs] himself in the idea that he has

tripped you in your argument ~~against~~ on sonnets—by dwelling upon the necessity of a defence. As if it has not been occasionally necessary to defend even poetry itself against fools.

Strange how Simms sticks to an idea once formed. I bet you that yet go on quoting that passage as Middleton's to the day of his death. Dear old fellow, he is though— and very kind to me.

I have other letters to write to-day, or I would make this longer. Remember me to Mrs Hayne and believe me as always affectionately yrs Henry Timrod

Columbia March 28th
[1867]

My dear Paul,

I received your answer...

Henry Irwin

63

HELEN HUNT JACKSON

Autograph letter signed with initials, dated New York The Berkeley, April 2ᵈ—1884, addressed to Mrs. Quinton. 4 p. 20.5 cm.

Poet and novelist (b. Amherst, Mass. 1830; d. Colorado Springs, Colo. 1885). She wrote *Verses. By H. H.* (1870; enlarged and revised, 1874); *Mercy Philbrick's Choice* (1876), based in part on the life of Emily Dickinson; *A Century of Dishonor* (1881), an account of the government's mistreatment of the American Indians; and *Ramona* (1884), a romance on the same theme, among other works. Much of her early writing of poems, reviews, articles and stories was anonymous or pseudonymous.

Helen Hunt Jackson, born Fiske, was the daughter of an Amherst professor and was a neighbor and school friend of Emily Dickinson. Her first husband (an Army officer) and two children all died before she was 35, at which time she took up a literary career. After marrying her second husband, W. S. Jackson, she moved to Colorado Springs, where she developed an interest in the Indians and their cause. *A Century of Dishonor* was sent to each member of Congress, and the next year Mrs. Jackson was appointed by the government to report on the condition and treatment of the Mission Indians of California. Mrs. Jackson's last and most popular novel, *Ramona*, dealt with injustices to Indians, but its continuing appeal has been as an historical romance of Spanish California. In this letter she writes of the completion of *Ramona*, its serialization and book publication, and discusses plans for its distribution among members of a church association. A large group of Mrs. Jackson's letters and manuscripts is in the Huntington Library.

New York The Berkeley April 2ᵈ—1884 Dear Mrs. Quinton—My story is done—170,000 (or more) words.— It is called "Ramona."—It is to run as a serial in the Christian Union beginning the 1ˢᵗ of May. It will take six months.—I am going to strike for the churches this time. I do not dare to think I have written a second Uncle Tom's Cabin—but I do think I have written a story which will do be a good strike for the Indian cause.—[...]

[But I think the Branch Associations ought all to have the] story to read as it comes out.—to read it at their monthly meetings.—Is not this a good idea?—Yrs ever—H.J.

story to read as it comes out, — to
read it at their monthly meetings. —
Is not this a good idea? —
  Yrs ever — H.J.

New York
The Berkeley
March 24
1884

Dear Mrs. Quinton —
  My story
is done — 170. ovo (or more)
words — or so called
"Ramona." —
Or to run as aserial
in the Christian Union
beginning the 15t May,
or will take six months —
— I am going to strike
for this elucled this time.
I do not dare to think
I have within a few
weeks Louis Larus — but —
I do think I have
writin a story article
will be a good Brothe
for the Indian Cause. —

64

EMILY DICKINSON

*"The sun kept stooping—stooping—low—." Autograph poem signed
"Emily" [Amherst, Mass. c. 1860]. 1 p. 18.5 cm.*

Poet (b. Amherst, Mass. 1830; d. Amherst, Mass. 1886). Only seven of her poems were published during her lifetime. Volumes edited by others and published since her death include *Poems* (1890), *Poems: Second Series* (1891), *The Single Hound* (1914), *Further Poems* (1929), *Bolts of Melody* (1945) and *Poems* (1955), the definitive collection. Her delicate and revealing verses, many of them mystical in tone, have been called the finest written by a woman.

Emily Dickinson wrote 1775 poems during her lifetime that have survived to be edited and collected; the manuscripts of nearly all of them are extant, often in drafts and fair copies which she sent to friends. One of these friends was the soldier and author Thomas Wentworth Higginson, to whom she wrote in 1862, beginning a correspondence that lasted for the rest of her life; Higginson was a friendly mentor but lacked critical insight and did not help Miss Dickinson on her way to a literary career which might have begun in her lifetime. This copy of "The sun kept stooping" was written out in pencil and sent to Susan Gilbert Dickinson, "Sue," who was her close friend and who had married her brother in 1856. There is another manuscript of this work with some variant readings in The Houghton Library, Harvard University, which has a large group of Emily Dickinson's manuscripts and papers. There are other collections of her work in the Boston Public Library and in The Jones Library.

The sun kept stooping—stooping—low— / The Hills to meet him—rose— / On his part—what Transaction! / On their part—what Repose! /

Deeper and deeper grew the stain / Upon the window pane— / Thicker and thicker stood the feet / Until the Tyrian /

Was crowded dense with Armies— / So gay—so Brigadier— / That I felt martial stirrings / Who once the Cockade wore— /

Charged, from my chimny corner— / But nobody was there! /

                                                        Emily.

The sun kept stooping - stooping - low.
the Hills to meet him - rose -
On his part - what Transaction!
On their part - what Repose!

Deeper and deeper grew the stain
Upon the window pane -
thicker and thicker stood the feet
Until the Tyrian.

Was crowded dense with Armies -
So gay; so Brigadier -
that I felt martial stirrings
Who once the Cockade wore -

Charged from my Chimney Corner -
But Nobody was there!

Emily.

65

EMILY DICKINSON

Autograph letter signed "Emily," undated [Amherst, Mass. c. 1883]
addressed to "Dear Girls." 2 p. 20.5 cm.

This letter written in pencil was sent to her niece, Martha Dickinson, and one of her friends. It is in Miss Dickinson's later handwriting in which the letters are widely separated and there is considerable space between the lines. It may have been sent next door or to the home of Martha's friend in Pittsfield, Mass. when she was visiting there. For Emily Dickinson the sound of "your voices—mad and sweet—as a Mob of Bobolinks" could have come from either place. The printed text of the poem that concludes the letter has two more lines as published in *Poems* (1896), and these have been added in the transcription.

Dear Girls, I hope you are having superb times, and am sure you are, for I hear your voices—mad and sweet—as a Mob of Bobolinks. I send you my love—which is always new for Rascals like you, and ask instead a little apartment in your Pink Hearts—call it Endor's Closet.

If ever the World should frown on you—he is old you know—give him a Kiss, and that will disarm him—if it dont—tell him from me,

Who has not found the Heaven—below— / Will fail of it above, / For Angels rent the House next our's / Wherever we remove— / [God's residence is next to mine, / His furniture is love.] / Lovingly, Emily.

Dear Girls.
I hope you
are having superb
times, and am
sure you are.
for I heard your
voices, mad and
sweet - as a Mob
of Bobolinks.
I send you my
love, which is
always new for
Rascals like you.
and ask instead
a little apartment
in your Pink Hearts-

Call it Enoch's
Closet. If ever the World
should frown on
you - he is glad-
you know - give
him a kiss, and
that will disarm
him - "if it don't-"
tell him - from me.
who has not found
-the Heaven - below-
will fail of it, Above-
for Angels rent next ours',
-the House next ours'
wherever we remove -
Lovingly, Emily.

66

MARY MAPES DODGE

"Hans Brinker, or, The Silver Skates." Autograph manuscript page from chapter xxviii signed [n.p., n.d.]. 1 p. 22 cm.

Author of children's books and editor (b. New York City 1831; d. Onteora Park, N.Y. 1905). In addition to *Hans Brinker* (1866) she wrote *The Irvington Stories* (1865), *A Few Friends and How They Amused Themselves* (1869), *Rhymes and Jingles* (1875), *Donald and Dorothy* (1883) and *The Land of Pluck* (1894). Mrs. Dodge was editor of the children's magazine *St. Nicholas* (1873–1905) and made her name and that of the magazine household words.

This familiar story of a Dutch boy and girl gives a picture of Holland, with its canals, dikes, windmills and wooden shoes, that has become stamped indelibly on the American mind. Hans and his sister Gretel are children in a Dutch village whose father has been injured in a fall from scaffolding on a dike. Gretel wins the prize in a skating competition and persuades a famous physician to treat and cure her father, which he does. In the final chapter the children are described as they became in later life: Hans a successful doctor and Gretel a noted singer and beauty. The page of text reproduced here has some of the conversation of young Dutch people and an English friend during a visit to the great museum, the Mauritshuis, in The Hague. Mrs. Dodge never visited Holland but read many books and articles on the country, especially J. L. Motley's *The Rise of the Dutch Republic*. She states in her preface that many of the incidents in the book were drawn from life—presumably from information provided her by Dutch friends. Dutch words and phrases, translated in footnotes, add flavor to the text. There are manuscripts and letters of Mrs. Dodge in the Alderman Library, University of Virginia (including several more pages of *Hans Brinker* in her autograph), and the Huntington Library, among other repositories.

[Ben,] ~~could readily believe as he looked upon it, that the Silent Prince~~ true to his greatness of character, had been exceedingly simple in his attire. ~~but~~ His aristocratic ~~ins~~ prejudices were however decidedly shocked when Lambert told him of the way in which William's ~~bride fourth wife~~ bride had first entered the Hague. ~~She said~~ 'The beautiful Louisa de Coligny, whose father and former husband ~~bo~~ both had ~~both~~ fallen at the Massacre of St. Bartholomew, was coming to ~~marry~~ be fourth wife to the Prince, and of course,' said Lambert, [']we Hollanders were too gallant to allow the lady to enter the town on foot. No sir, we sent (or rather my ancestors ~~did~~ sent) a clean, open post-wagon to meet her, with a plank across it for her to sit upon![']

"Very gallant indeed!" exclaimed ~~Carl~~ Ben ~~almost~~ with almost a sneer in his polite laugh—["]and she the daughter of an ~~Cardinal, too,~~ Admiral of France!"

"Was she? Upon my word I had nearly forgotten that. But, you see Holland had very plain ways in the good old time, in fact we are a very simple, frugal people to this day. The van Gend establishment, ~~well~~ is ~~quite an~~ a decidedly exception you ~~must now~~ know."

"A very agreeable exception, I think," said Ben.

"Certainly, certainly. But, between you and ~~I~~ me, Mynheer van Gend, though he has wrought his own fortunes can afford to be magnificent, and yet be frugal."

"Exactly so," said Ben ~~solemnly~~ profoundly; at the same time stroking his upper lip and chin, which latterly had been showing delightful and un[mistakable signs of coming dignities.]

~~and nearly believe he looked upon it, that in then him~~ still
true to his greatness of character, had been exceedingly
simple in his attire, ~~but~~ His aristocratic ~~was~~ prejudices
were, however, decidedly ~~shocked~~ shocked when Lambert told him of
the way in which William ~~bride, quiet~~ had just entered the Hague.

¶ ~~She was~~ The beautiful Louisa de Coligny, whose father
and former husband ~~to~~ both had ~~both~~ fallen at the Massacre
of St. Barthol~~omew~~omew, was coming to ~~marry~~ be fourth wife to the Prince, and
of course, said Lambert, we Hollanders were too gallant
to allow the lady to enter the town on foot. No sir, we
sent (or rather my ancestors ~~did~~ sent) a clean, open post-
wagon to meet her, with a plank across it for her
to sit upon!

"Very gallant indeed!" exclaimed Carl ~~almost~~ Ben with almost a
sneer in his polite laugh — and she the daughter of an
~~Cardinal, two~~ Admiral of France!"

"Was she? Upon my word I had nearly forgotten that — But, you
see Holland had very plain ways in the good old time,
in fact we are a very simple, frugal people to this day
The van Gend establishment, ~~and~~ is ~~quite~~ a decided, an exception
you ~~and we~~ know —"

"A very agreeable exception, I think," said Ben.

"Certainly, certainly. But, between you and I, Mynheer van
Gend, though he has wrought his own fortunes can
afford to be magnificent, and yet be frugal."

"Exactly so," said Ben ~~solemnly~~ profoundly; at the same time smoking his upper
lip and chin, which latterly had been showing delightful and un-

67

LOUISA MAY ALCOTT

*"Jack and Jill: A Village Story." Autograph manuscript unsigned of
one leaf of the novel [Concord, Mass. 1879]. 1 p. 24.5 cm.*

Author, especially of books for young people, poet and daughter of Bronson Alcott (b. Germantown, Pa. 1832; d. Boston, Mass. 1888). She wrote *Flower Fables* (1855); *Hospital Sketches* (1863), based on her experiences as an untrained army nurse during the Civil War; *Little Women* (1868–69), an immediate and enduring success that gave her family financial independence; *An Old Fashioned Girl* (1870); *Little Men* (1871); *Jack and Jill* (1880); and *Jo's Boys* (1886). Members of her family and Concord friends often served as models for her characters. Miss Alcott twice visited Europe and was active in both women's suffrage and the temperance movement; she had a great sympathy for people, especially boys and girls.

As she began to write *Jack and Jill*, Miss Alcott wrote in her journal, "Have no plan yet but a boy, a girl, and a sled, with an upset to start with. Vague idea of working in Concord young folks and their doings." The page shown here, which corresponds to page 6 in the first edition of 1880, describes a sledding scene and gives a glimpse of daredevil Jill and honest, blue-eyed Jack. The Morgan Library also has a letter which Miss Alcott wrote on the death and funeral of Thoreau. This letter, which was published in facsimile by the Library in 1962, is a sensitive expression of grief and of high confidence in Thoreau's permanence. Large collections of the manuscripts and letters of Louisa May Alcott are to be found in Harvard University Library and the Alderman Library, University of Virginia.

[*"They are lovely warm, and they do fit. Must be too small for your paws, so I'll knit you a new pair for Christmas, and make you wear them, too," said Jill, putting on the mittens with a nod of thanks, and ending her] speech with a stamp of the her rubber boots to enforce her threat.*

Jack laughed & up they trudged to the hill top spot whence the three coasts diverged.

"Now which will you have?" he asked with a steady warning look in the honest blue eyes which often unconsciously controlled naughty Jill against her will.

"That one," & the red mitten pointed firmly to the perilous path just tried.

"You will do it?"

"I will!"

"Come on then, & hold tight."

Jack's smile was gone now & he waited without a word while Jill tucked herself up, then took his place in front & off they went on the brief, breathless trip straight into the drift by the fence below.

"I don't see anything very awful in that. Come up & have another. Joe is watching us & I'd like to show him that we are n't afraid of anything," said Jill, with a defiant glance at a distant boy who had paused to watch the descent.

speech with a stamp of the (her) rubber boot to enforce her threat.

Jack laughed & up they trudged to the (shed) where the three coasts diverged. "Now which will you have?" he asked with a (warning) look in the honest blue eyes which often unconsciously controlled naughty Jill against her will.

"That one." & the red mitten pointed firmly to the perilous path just tried.

"You will do it?"

"I will!"

"Come on then, & hold tight."

Jack's smile was gone now & he waited without a word while Jill tucked herself up, then took his place in front & off they went on the long, breathless trip straight into the drift by the fence below.

"I don't see anything very awful in that. Come up & have another. Joe is watching us & I'd like to show him that we are not afraid of anything." said Jill, with a defiant glance at a distant boy who had paused to watch the descent.

HORATIO ALGER

*"How Johnny bought a Sewing-Machine." Autograph manuscript
signed [New York, 1866]. 14 p. 25 cm. Citron morocco.*

Unitarian clergyman and author (b. Revere, Mass. 1834; d. Natick, Mass. 1899). Alger
wrote over one hundred books for boys including the *Ragged Dick* (1867), *Luck and
Pluck* (1869) and *Tattered Tom* (1871) series, and was by far the most successful American author in this field. Most of his adult years were spent as chaplain to the Newsboys'
Lodging House in New York City, to which he devoted his affection, time and money,
and where, in turn, he found material for his books. His stories of rags to riches through
honesty, hard work, character and courage had a profound influence on the younger generation of his time.

This early story may be the only surviving fully autograph manuscript by Alger. It
was first published in the Boston magazine *Our Young Folks* in August 1866. Johnny
hopes to pick enough cranberries to buy his mother a sewing machine and save her from
toiling early and late with her needle. One morning he saves a little girl from drowning
and is duly rewarded by her grateful father with a sewing machine for his mother, a
hundred-dollar bill and a promised future job in his store, as shown in the denouement on
this final page. The reader shares in the general rejoicing, but never learns whether
Johnny marries the girl he rescued. Warmhearted, but none too virtuous himself, Alger
died poor in spite of his voluminous output of best sellers. The largest collection of Alger
letters is in the Huntington Library.

---

*[Mrs.] Cooper found that it worked admirably, and would
lighten her labors more even than she had hoped.*

*"But you hav'n't opened your letter," she said with a
sudden recollection.*

"So I hav'n't," said Johnny.

*What was his surprise when opening it to discover the
same hundred dollar bill which Mr. Barclay had originally
given him, accompanied by the following note.*

*"My dear young friend, I have bought your mother a
sewing-machine, which I send by express today. I hope it
will please you both, and prove very useful. I also send you
a hundred dollars which I wish you to use for yourself.
The sewing-machine will be none the less your present*
*to your mother, since both that and the money are a very
insufficient recompense for the service you have rendered
me. Continue to love and help your mother, and when you
are old enough to go into a store I will receive you into
mine. Your friend, Henry Barclay."*

*There was great joy in the little cottage that evening.
Johnny felt as rich as a millionaire, and could not take
his eyes from the corner where the handsome new sewing-machine had been placed. And his mother, happy as she
was in her present, was happier in the thought that it had
come to her through the good conduct of her son.*

Horatio Alger, Jr.

Cooper found that it worked admirably, and would lighten her labors more even than she had hoped.

"But you haven't opened your letter," she said with a sudden recollection.

"So I haven't," said Johnny.

What was his surprise on opening it to discover the same hundred dollar bill which Mr. Barclay had originally given him, accompanied by the following note.

"My dear young friend,

I have bought your mother a sewing-machine, which I send by express today. I hope it will please you both, and prove very useful. I also send you a hundred dollars which I wish you to use for yourself. The sewing-machine will be none the less your present to your mother, since both that and the money are a very insufficient recompense for the service you have rendered me. Continue to love and help your mother, and when you are old enough to go into a store I will receive you into mine.

Your friend,

Henry Barclay."

There was great joy in the little cottage that evening. Johnny felt as rich as a millionaire, and could not take his eyes from the corner where the handsome new sewing-machine had been placed. And his mother, happy as she was in her present, was happier in the thought that it had come to her through the good conduct of her son.

Horatio Alger, Jr.

69

FRANK STOCKTON

Autograph letter signed, dated Charlottesville, Va., Aug. 29: 1884,
addressed to Oliver Wendell Holmes. 2 p. 21 cm.

Novelist and story writer (b. Philadelphia, Pa. 1834; d. Washington, D.C. 1902). His novels, often humorous, include *Rudder Grange* (1879), *The Casting Away of Mrs. Lecks and Mrs. Aleshine* (1886) and *The Squirrel Inn* (1891), in which one character is engaged in translating Dickens into ancient Greek.

Although Stockton spent the first part of his life as a wood engraver, he appears to have been more a craftsman than artist. In 1867 he began contributing children's stories to the *Riverside Magazine for Young People*, which were gathered together as *Ting-a-Ling* in 1870. He became a frequent contributor to other children's periodicals, and assistant editor of *St. Nicholas* when Mary Mapes Dodge founded it in 1873.

The sudden success of *Rudder Grange* (a typical and fanciful tale of a young couple living on a derelict river barge) ended Stockton's editorial work, and he devoted the remainder of his life to writing. His short story "The Lady or the Tiger?" is a classic which Stockton was never able to equal. In it he poses the unanswered dilemma of whether a barbaric princess, forced to decide, would give up her lover to another woman or to a tiger who would eat him. Stockton's whimsy was in marked contrast to the crises facing America in the 1880s, and he was held in high esteem for that reason. In this letter of congratulation to Dr. Holmes he invokes, with his happy Virginia family, the hope of an eternal breakfast table. There is a special collection of Stockton letters and manuscripts in the Alderman Library, University of Virginia.

My dear Dr. Holmes, As around the head of a family,—say of Virginia,—gather his cousins, his second cousins, and his cousins so far removed that he never heard of them, wishing him joy and good fortune, so come we all upon this your birth-day, and would be glad to come any other day if we could find a decent excuse for it, to wish you, not all unselfishly, many years of life, and strength, and work.

And when, on some morning farther removed than the remotest of your literary kin, you shall push back your chair, fold up your napkin, and, rising from the table, say: "After this I breakfast without you": we will look at each other and smile, and each think to himself with a little comfortable vanity: "Not if St. Peter be the man of discernment I take him to be." Very sincerely Frank R. Stockton

Charlottesville. Va.
Aug. 29: 1884.

My dear Dr. Holmes,

As around the head of a family — Say of Virginia — or rather his cousins, his second cousins, and his cousins so far removed that he never heard of them — wishing him joy and good fortunes, so come we all upon this your birth-day and would be glad to come any other day if we could find a decent excuse for it. I wish you, not all jung delightful many years of life, and strength, and work.

And when, on some morning farther removed than the rest longest of your library him! your whole push back your chair (fold up your napkin, and, rising from the table, say:

"After this I breakfast without you", we will look at each other and smile, and each think is himself with a little comfort-able vanity. "Not if Mr Peter be the man of discernment I take him to be."

Very sincerely
(Frank H. Stockton)

Charlottesville, Va.
Aug. 29: 1857.

70

SAMUEL LANGHORNE CLEMENS (MARK TWAIN)

"Pudd'nhead Wilson   A Tale by Mark Twain." Autograph manuscript signed, dated Florence, March 1893. 2 v. 28 cm. Red morocco.

Author, journalist and humorist (b. Florida, Mo. 1835; d. Redding, Conn. 1910). One of America's greatest and best-known writers. Some of his works are *The Innocents Abroad* (1869), *The Gilded Age* (1873, written with Charles Dudley Warner), *The Adventures of Tom Sawyer* (1876), *A Tramp Abroad* (1880), *The Prince and the Pauper* (1882), *Life on the Mississippi* (1883), *The Adventures of Huckleberry Finn* (1884), *A Connecticut Yankee in King Arthur's Court* (1889), *The Tragedy of Pudd'nhead Wilson* (1894), *Personal Recollections of Joan of Arc* (1896), *The Man that Corrupted Hadleyburg* (1900) and *The Mysterious Stranger* (1916).

The scene of this tale is a small Missouri town in the 1830s in which the lawyer David Wilson acquires the nickname of "Pudd'nhead" from the townspeople because they cannot understand either his wisdom or his eccentricity. Pudd'nhead later solves a murder mystery and a case of transposed identities by a comparison of fingerprints, one of the earliest examples in fiction of the use of this technique; he thus redeems himself in the eyes of his fellow citizens. The manuscript of *The Tragedy of Pudd'nhead Wilson* was acquired from the author by Pierpont Morgan in 1909; Mark Twain was an occasional visitor to the Library and a friend of the Morgan family. In a letter of September 15, 1909 to Mr. Morgan he wrote, "one of my high ambitions is gratified—which was to have something of mine placed elbow to elbow with that august company which you have gathered together to remain indestructible in a perishable world."

Illustrated here is the page of Pudd'nhead Wilson's calendar that introduces the book and a highly entertaining page with a key to signs that will enable Mark Twain to avoid writing out weather conditions each time they occur in the tale. The key to signs and many other pages of this manuscript were not used in *Pudd'nhead Wilson* when it was published in 1894.

The major collections of Mark Twain manuscripts and letters are in the University of California Library, Stanford, the Alderman Library, University of Virginia, and Yale University Library.

Pudd'nhead Wilson

A TALE

By Mark Twain

There is no character, howsoever good & fine, but it can be destroyed by ridicule, howsoever poor & witless. Observe

the ass, for instance: his character is about perfect, he is the choicest spirit among all the humbler animals, yet see what ridicule has brought him to. Instead of feeling complimented when we are called an ass, we are left in doubt.— Pudd'nhead Wilson's Calendar. [...]

1

Pudd'nhead Wilson

A TALE

By Mark Twain.

There is no character, however good & fine, but it can be destroyed by ridicule, however poor & witless. Observe the ass, for instance: his character is about perfect, he is the choicest spirit among all the humbler animals, yet see what ridicule has brought him to. Instead of feeling complimented when we are called an ass, we are left in doubt. — Pudd'nhead Wilson's Calendar.

To Printer. Please make free similes of these signs & use them at chapter-tops — one & sometimes two. It is not necessary that they fit the weather in chapter always.

Key to Signs used in this book. (3)

To save the space usually devoted to explanations of the state of the weather in books of this kind, the author has substituted a simple system of weather-signs — the reader glancing at the head of a chapter will instantly convey to the reader's mind a perfect comprehension of the kind of weather which is going to prevail below.

The signs & their meanings here follow:

Sunny.

Rainy.

Snow.

Pitch Dark.

Starlight.

Moonlight.

Fog.

When two or more signs occur together, the weather is going to be more, or more yet, or still more variable, according to number of signs employed.

71

SAMUEL LANGHORNE CLEMENS
(MARK TWAIN)

"Life on the Mississippi." Autograph manuscript unsigned [n.p., n.d.].
3 v. 22 cm. Brown cloth.

Mark Twain published the early chapters of this autobiographical narrative in *The Atlantic Monthly* for 1875; the complete work did not appear in book form until 1883. The mighty Mississippi and its people were for Mark Twain a liberal education and a highway of American humor; he wrote that on the river he had become personally familiar with about all the different types of human nature. This manuscript lacks the chapter that was later incorporated into *The Adventures of Huckleberry Finn* and some other chapters, but the two pages illustrated here give a capsule-like description of Huck; some pages of this manuscript were not included in the first edition of the book. In addition to numerous clippings and a drawing of a crossing lamp on the river, Mark Twain has added to these volumes a letter from Captain Isaiah Sellers of May 4, 1859 concerning the flooding of the Mississippi. Clements may have acquired his pseudonym from this river pilot, the "patriarch of the craft," although he did not use it until several years later when he began life as a writer in Virginia City, Nevada. The Mississippi River was the keystone of his great literary career.

[The book is a story which details some] passages in the life of an ignorant village boy—Huck Finn, son of the town-drunkard of my time out West, there. He has run away from his persecuting father, & from a persecuting good widow who wishes to make a nice, truth-telling, respectable boy of him; & with him a slave of the widow's has also escaped. They have found a fragment of a lumber raft, (it is high water & dead summer time,) & are floating down the river by night & hiding in the willows by day—

bound for Cairo, whence the negro will seek freedom in the heart of the free States. But in a fog, they pass Cairo without knowing it. By & by they begin to suspect the truth, & Huck Finn is persuaded ~~resolves~~ to end the dismal suspense by ~~making a risky dash for information:~~ swimming down to a huge raft which they have seen [in the distance ahead of them, creeping aboard ~~in~~ under cover of the darkness, & gathering the needed information by eavesdropping.]

68

by night & hiding in the
willows by day — bound
for Cairo, whence the
negro will seek freedom
in the heart of the free
States. But in a fog, they
pass Cairo without
knowing it. By & by
they begin to suspect the
truth, & that Finn is pursuing
them, & that their Finn
resolves to end the dismal
suspense by making
a plucky dash for my or—

notation:

67

passages in the life of
an innocent boy — village
sneak Finn, son of the
town-drunkard of my
time out West, there.
He has run away from
his persecuting father,
to form a perfect cutting
good widow who wishes
truth-telling, respect-
to make a nice, truthful
boy of him; & with
him a slave of the widow's
has also escaped. They
have formed a (it is high water & the summer time)
a lumber raft, & are
floating down the river

72

SAMUEL LANGHORNE CLEMENS (MARK TWAIN)

"The Man that Corrupted Hadleyburg." Autograph manuscript signed, dated Vienna, October, 1898. 144 p. 23 cm. Brown cloth.

This bitter story is the title piece of a volume of tales and essays that appeared in 1900. It is a study in misanthropy in which Mark Twain carries an almost comic narrative on to a tragic conclusion. Leading citizens of "honest & upright" Hadleyburg claim ownership, on the strength of secret letters that have come to each of them, of a sack, supposed to contain money, that has been left with a bank cashier by a stranger—the corrupter. In the concluding paragraphs the greed of the citizens and the hypocrisy of this American town are laid bare in the sanctity of their church. "The Man that Corrupted Hadleyburg" is one of the strongest sermons against self-righteousness ever preached, and many critics consider it to be Mark Twain's finest short story. Reproduced here is the first page of the manuscript, which was acquired by Pierpont Morgan in 1912, and the final page with the two mottoes and the author's instructions to the printer regarding them.

The Man that Corrupted Hadleyburg.

I.

~~It was fifty years ago~~ It was ~~twenty-three eight or ten~~ many years ago. Hadleyburg was the most honest & upright town in all the region round about. It had kept that reputation unsmirched during three generations, & was prouder of ~~its good name~~ than of any other of its possessions. It was so proud of it, ~~that~~ & so anxious to insure its perpetuation, that it began to teach the principles of honest dealing to its babies in the cradle, & made the like teachings the staple of their ~~education~~ culture thenceforward through all the years devoted to their education. Also, throughout the formative years temptations were kept out of the way of the young people, so that their honesty could have every chance [to harden and solidify, and become a part of their very bone....]

By an act of the legislature—upon prayer & petition—Hadleyburg was allowed to change its name to (never mind what—I will not give it away), & leave one word out of the motto that graced the town's official seal. ~~Un Before Before the removal of that word the motto had read thus: Lead us not into Temptation.~~

It is an ~~once~~ honest town ~~again~~ once more, & the man will have to rise early that catches it napping again. [...]

Mark Twain

Vienna, October, 1898.

109

concentrated it upon Pudd'nhead, and Pudd'nhead's election was a walk-over.

By act of the legislature — upon prayer and petition — Hadleyburg was allowed to change its name to (never mind what — I will not give it away), and leave one word out of the motto that graced the town's official seal.

Before the removal of that word the motto had read thus:

Lead us not into Temptation.

It is an honest town once more, and the man will have to rise early that catches it napping again.

Former motto.   *Revised motto.*

#B.   Mark Twain

Vienna, October, 1898.

The word above the line closing paragraph. SLC

The Man That Corrupted Hadleyburg.

I.

It was many years ago. Hadleyburg was the most honest and upright town in all the region round about. It had kept that reputation unsmirched during three generations, and was prouder of it than of any other of its possessions. It was so proud of it, and so anxious to insure its perpetuation, that it began to teach the principles of honest dealing to its babies in the cradle, and made the like teaching the staple of their culture thenceforward through all the years devoted to their education. Also, throughout the formative years temptations were kept out of the way of the young people, so that their honesty could have every chance

73

BRET HARTE

"Three Partners." Autograph manuscript signed, dated Arford House, Headley, Hants. 19th May. 96. 125 leaves. 22.5 cm. Red morocco.

Short-story writer, poet and novelist (b. Albany, N.Y. 1836; d. London, England 1902). Harte wrote many stories, novels and poems based on his life in California, where he worked for 17 years. Among these are *The Luck of Roaring Camp* (1870), which included the stories "M'liss," "The Outcasts of Poker Flat" and "Tennessee's Pardner"; *Gabriel Conroy* (1876); and two volumes of parodies, *Condensed Novels* (1867 and 1902). He wrote two plays, *Two Men of Sandy Bar* (1876) and *Ah Sin* (1877), the latter in collaboration with Mark Twain.

As a young man, Harte was a printer and journalist in San Francisco, and his first work was published in local periodicals and newspapers. It attracted much attention and in 1871 *The Atlantic Monthly* offered him a handsome contract to write for them; he moved East the same year. But his stories soon became much the same in content and plot and he became involved in financial troubles. In 1878, Harte accepted a consular post in Germany and remained there and in the British Isles for the rest of his life—an early American literary expatriate. The English were more receptive to his work than the Americans had been during his years in the East, and he eventually became a considerable figure in English society. Harte left behind him in the United States hostile critics, debts and his family. The reproduction is of the corrected final page of his long story *Three Partners; or, The Big Strike on Heavy Tree Hill*, which was published in 1897. Harte's early stories of California won him fame and influenced writers on the West who followed him. Over one hundred of his manuscripts are in the Huntington Library; the Morgan Library has ten prose and five poetical manuscripts.

"Well," returned Jack, "when the fight was over and ~~we heard the news that Barker's~~ they brought the news to Barker that his wife and her diamonds were burned up at the Hotel—you remember that they said that Mrs ~~Hon~~ Horncastle had saved his boy?"

"Yes," said Demorest, "but what has that got to do with it?"

"Nothing I reckon," said Jack with a slight shrug of his shoulders—"only Mrs Horncastle was the mother of that boy lying there, whom it seems you and I and Barker have helped to kill." [...]

"But God grant that it be not the same prospect of the ~~next~~ five years to come?" ~~said Barker, as he~~ said Demorest. thought of Mrs Horncastle—a free woman! "~~Amen!~~ ~~said~~ Stacy ~~as he dreamed of a~~ [deletion] ~~future~~ started from

a momentary dream of reconstructed future and power. "Amen" he said ~~"Amen," said Demorest, wondering if he should ever see~~ [deletion] ~~again!~~

~~*The End.*~~

~~*Bret Harte*~~

But ~~thought~~ Barker thought how ~~he had found little Sta. asleep that afternoon~~ that afternoon after his agonizing search for his wife's body—he had found little Sta. ~~asl~~ safe and asleep in Mrs Horncastle's lap and smiled.

The End.

Bret Harte

Arford House, Headley, Hants. 19th May. 96

"Well," returned Jack, "when the fight was over and we heard the news that ——'s wife and her diamonds were burned up at the hotel — you remember that they said that Mr. Horncastle had saved his boy?"

"Yes," said Desmond, "but what has that got to do with it?"

"Nothing I reckon," said Jack with a slight shrug of his shoulders, "only Mrs. Horncastle was the mother of that boy — theirs, when you and I and Barker have helped to kill."

*   *   *   *   *   *   *   *   *   *   *

A few hours later when the three partners of Stacy Tree Field sat by the fire in the deserted cabin on Marshalls claim, they were reminded that it was the same proposal before them that they had five years before, for their destruction old cabin.

"But God grant that it be not the same purpose of the five years to come?" said Desmond.

. . . again.

The End.

Barker changes have . . . that afterwards after his agonizing search for his wife's body — he had found Stacy . . . and asleep in Mrs. Horncastle's lap and smiled.

The End.

Bret Harte

Chipstone, Headley Hants,
19th May. 96

74

BRET HARTE

"Plain Language from Truthful James." Autograph manuscript signed [n.p., n.d.]. 4 p. 20 cm.

Bret Harte's most famous poem, also known as "The Heathen Chinee," was first published in the *Overland Monthly*, San Francisco, for September 1870. It had been written some months before and was used to fill up some empty space that appeared in that issue of the magazine. The comic ballad tells of a euchre game in which Truthful James and his friend Bill Nye try to cheat the Chinese gambler Ah Sin, but are themselves outslickered by the Oriental. It became immediately and instantly popular and was reprinted throughout the United States and abroad; it was issued in book form and set to music, and soon became the best-known verse of the post-Civil War era. Harte was strongly opposed to racial prejudice in any form and, in spite of certain lines in the poem, was disgusted by the harsh treatment of Chinese immigrant workers in California.

This manuscript was written out by Harte, probably during one of his visits to Boston, for the autograph album of Mrs. James T. Fields, wife of one of his publishers. The first and last pages are shown here.

Plain Language from Truthful James

Which I wish to remark— / And my language is plain— / That for ways that are dark / And for tricks that are vain, / The heathen Chinee is peculiar / Which the same I would rise to explain. /

Ah Sin was his name; / And I shall not deny / In regard to the same / What that name might imply, / But his smile it was pensive and child like, / As I frequent remarked to Bill Nye. /

It was August the third; / And quite soft was the skies: / Which it might be inferred / [That Ah Sin was likewise. / ...]

[But the floor it was strewed, / Like the leaves on the strand, / With the cards that Ah Sin had been hiding, /] In the game he did not understand. /

In his sleeves, which were long, / He had twenty four packs— / Which was coming it strong / Yet I state but the facts; / And we found on his nails, which were taper, / What is frequent in tapers—thats wax. /

Which is why I remark / And my language is plain, / That for ways that are dark / And for tricks that are vain, / The heathen Chinee is peculiar— / Which the same I am free to maintain. /

—Bret Harte

75

THOMAS BAILEY ALDRICH

"The Ballad of Babie Bell." Autograph manuscript signed [n.p., n.d.]. 7 leaves. 21 cm. Red morocco.

Poet, essayist, novelist and editor (b. Portsmouth, N.H. 1836; d. Boston, Mass. 1907). Aldrich is best remembered for his semiautobiographical novel *The Story of a Bad Boy* (1870); "Marjorie Daw" (1873), a short story with a surprise ending; and *The Still-water Tragedy* (1880), a mystery novel that introduced a "private eye" (an inept one) several years before the appearance of Sherlock Holmes. He was editor of *The Atlantic Monthly* from 1881 to 1890, a period in which the magazine won praise in London as "the best edited magazine in the English language."

"The Ballad of Babie Bell" was written about 1855 when Aldrich, aged 19, was a clerk in a New York office; it was published in 1859 and has appeared in many anthologies. Reproduced here are the first and last pages of a fair copy of the poem written out in purple ink at a later date. In general, his poems have delicacy, charm and a high degree of craftsmanship.

In 1865, Aldrich moved to Boston, which became his home for the rest of his life. He was then young, handsome, witty, with an attractive wife, and combined these qualities and assets with those of a conservative proper Bostonian. Aldrich traveled widely but was totally unconcerned with social and political developments of his time, except what he considered to be uncontrolled immigration. He maintained high standards of taste and championed purity of style in the English language. There is a special collection of Aldrich materials in Harvard University Library.

The Ballad of Babie Bell.

I.

Have you not heard the poets tell / How came the dainty Babie Bell / Into this world of ours? / The gates of heaven were left ajar: / With folded hands and dreamy eyes, / Wandering out of Paradise, / She saw this planet, like a star, / Hung in the glistening depths of even,— / Its bridges, running to and fro, / O'er which the white-winged Angels go, / Bearing the holy Dead to heaven. / She touched a bridge of flowers,—those feet, / So light they did not bend the bells / [Of the celestial asphodels. / ...]

We parted back her silken hair: / We wove the roses round her brow, / White buds, the summer's drifted snow — / Wrapt her from head to foot in flowers! / And thus went dainty Babie Bell / Out of this world of ours! /

Thomas Bailey Aldrich.

The Ballad of Babie Bell

I.

Have you not heard the poets tell
How came the Saintly Babie Bell
Into this world of ours?

The gates of heaven were left ajar:
With folded hands and dreamy eyes,
Wandering out of Paradise,
She saw this planet, like a star,
Hung in the glittering depth of even,—
Its bridges, running to and fro,
O'er which the white-winged Angels go,
Bearing the holy Dead to heaven.
She touched a bridge of flowers,—those feet,
So light they did not bend the bells

We parted back her silken hair;
We wove the roses round her brow,—
White buds, the summer's drifted snow,—
Wrapt her from head to foot in flowers!
And thus went dainty Babie Bell
Out of this world of ours!

Thomas Bailey Aldrich.

76

WILLIAM DEAN HOWELLS

Autograph letter signed, dated Cambridge, Mass., Dec. 28, 1874,
addressed to Henry Adams. 1 p. 20.5 cm.

Man of letters (b. Martin's Ferry, Ohio 1837; d. New York City 1920). During his long life Howells wrote many volumes of plays, travel books, literary criticism, poetry and autobiography, but he is best remembered for his novels. Among these are *Their Wedding Journey* (1872), *The Lady of the Aroostook* (1879), *The Rise of Silas Lapham* (1885), *A Hazard of New Fortunes* (1890) and *A Traveler from Altruria* (1894). He was associated with both the *Atlantic* and *Harper's Magazine*, and was president of the American Academy of Arts and Letters from 1909 until his death. He had a keen interest in social and economic problems, and served as U.S. consul in Venice during the Civil War.

In this letter Howells tells the eminent historian that he is sending him an article by [Edward Howard] House in printed slips. He also recalls Adams' remarks on a "professed Titian" portrait of a Priuli, and offers the information that both Lorenzo and Girolamo Priuli had been Doges of Venice in "Titian's prime." Adams has annotated the letter in his characteristic hand, sending it to the unidentified doctor who owns the painting. Titian does not appear to have done a portrait of a Priuli and nothing more is known of this picture. Howells autograph materials may be found in many libraries but Harvard University Library has an especially large collection.

---

3 Feb. Dear Doctor The enclosed relates to your Tiziano. Yrs truly Henry Adams

Dec. 28, 1874. My dear Adams: I send the whole of House's article in printed slips, under another cover.

After I had heard your account, the other evening, of the professed Titian, I had the curiosity to look if any Priuli had been Doge in the painter's time. I found two: Lorenzo, 1556–9; Girolamo, 1559–67. These reigns were in Titian's prime. I should like very much to see that picture, some time. Yours very truly W.D. Howells.

EDITORIAL OFFICE OF

THE ATLANTIC MONTHLY.

The Riberside Press,
CAMBRIDGE, MASS.

Dec. 28, 1874.

My dear Adams:

I send you the whole of Stones, article in printed slips, under another cover.

After I had heard your account, the other evening, of the proposed Titian, I had the curiosity to look if any Prinli had been Doge in the painter's time. I found two: Lorenzo, 1556–9; Girolamo, 1559–67. These reigns were in Titian's prime. I should like very much to see that picture, come time.

Yours very truly
W. D. Howells.

Dear Doctor
The enclosed relates to your Tiziano.
Yrs truly
Henry Adams

3 Feb.

I.

77

JOHN BURROUGHS

"Recent Phases of Literary Criticism." Autograph manuscript signed
[n.p., c. 1899]. 62 p. 22.5 cm. Brown morocco.

Naturalist, essayist, poet and critic (b. Delaware Co., near Roxbury, N.Y. 1837; d. on a train crossing Ohio 1921). Burroughs published many books, among which are *Notes on Walt Whitman, as Poet and Person* (1867), written in part by Whitman himself; *Wake-Robin* (1871); *Winter Sunshine* (1875); *Birds and Poets* (1877); *Leaf and Tendril* (1908); and *The Summit of the Years* (1913). His books and lectures, his natural history collections and his capacity for friendship made him a national figure, with a host of friends and admirers, many of whom visited him at his rustic cabin on the Hudson River. His biographer, Clara Barrus, wrote that "during the last four decades of his life, John Burroughs was probably more sought after, had more of a personal following, more contacts with readers, both through correspondence and in person, than any other American author has had, and, probably, more than any other author of modern times."

In his critical writings Burroughs was strongly influenced by the work of Emerson, whom he also met and talked with on several occasions. This essay, of which the final page with signature is illustrated, was sold to the *North American Review* in 1899 for 75 dollars, and was published in book form in *Literary Values* (1902). One reviewer of this book said that Burroughs wrote as engagingly on "mere literature" as on the robin, the squirrel or the honey-bee. Burroughs was employed in Washington, D.C. at the same time as Walt Whitman; they became close friends and had a considerable literary influence on one another. The Morgan Library has the autograph manuscript of the revised edition of his work on the poet, *Whitman, a Study* (1896). Burroughs went to the woods searching for spring flowers instead of attending Lincoln's second inauguration. He wrote, "I thought it more desirable to see Spring inaugurated than President Lincoln, significant and gratifying an event as the latter is." A number of manuscripts and papers by Burroughs were sold at auction after his death; his letters and manuscripts are now owned by many American libraries.

With institutionalism goes the divine right of Kings, the sacredness of priests, the authority of forms & ceremonies, & the slavery of the masses; with individualism goes the divinity of man the sacredness of life, the right of private judgement, the decay of traditions & forms & the birth of the modern spirit. With the former one goes stateliness, impressiveness, distinction; with the latter other vigor, seri-ousness, originality as well as the empty, the moribund, the despotic; with the other goes vigor, seriousness, originality, as well as the loud, the amorphous, the fanatical. If we gain in power & vitality through individualism, we are apt to lose in dignity & proportion & vice versa

John Burroughs

With institutionalism goes the divine right of kings, the sacredness of priests, the authority of forms & ceremonies, & the slavery of the masses; with individualism goes the ~~divinity of man~~ the sacredness of life, the right of private judgement, the decay of traditions & forms & the birth of the modern spirit. With the ~~former~~ one goes stableness, impressiveness, distinction; ~~with the latter the empty, the moribund, the vigor, seriousness, originality~~ as well as ~~jitter~~ despute; with the other goes vigor, seriousness, originality, as well as the loud, the amorphous, the fanatical. If we gain in power & vitality through individualism, we are apt to lose in

78

FRANCIS HOPKINSON SMITH

"Colonel Carter of Cartersville." Autograph manuscript and typescript
signed [n.p., n.d.]. 200 p. 20 cm. Brown morocco.
Autograph letter signed, dated [New York] Jan" 1915, addressed to
J. P. Morgan, about this manuscript. 2 p. 23.5 cm.

Author, engineer and artist (b. Baltimore, Md. 1838; d. New York City 1915). His novels include *Colonel Carter of Cartersville* (1891), *Tom Grogan* (1896), *Caleb West, Master Diver* (1898) and *Kennedy Square* (1911). He wrote and illustrated several books of travel sketches.

Smith came to writing late in life (he was 53 when his first novel appeared) after a highly successful career as a marine engineer; he had built Race Rock lighthouse off New London, Conn. and the foundations for the Statue of Liberty. Work as an engineer left him but little time for his hobby of painting, but his artistic ability and industry eventually gained him membership in the prestigious Tile Club, which included Edwin Austin Abbey, Elihu Vedder and William Merritt Chase. His writings and paintings attracted more and more attention and he devoted much time to these pursuits; his first novel, *Colonel Carter of Cartersville*, was a series of character portraits, often in dialect, of people of the South. The Colonel is an impoverished but not disheartened Virginia gentleman. The tale was so successful that Smith devoted the remainder of his life to literature, drawing upon his experiences as an engineer and his travels as an artist. He presented this manuscript to J. P. Morgan in 1915 after the granting of his request to write his own name on a blank page bound in the Morgan autograph manuscript of Dickens' *A Christmas Carol*, his favorite story. With the manuscript of *Colonel Carter* came the letter to Mr. Morgan, the second page of which is also reproduced here. Comparatively few of Smith's letters and papers appear to have survived and these are distributed among a number of American libraries.

The night after the eventful dinner in Bedford Place, the colonel accompanied by ~~all of~~ his guests ~~except Yancey and the Judge except Yancey and the Judge~~ had alighted at a ~~great country house with~~ dreary ~~southern~~ way station, crawled into a lumbering country stage and with Chad on the box as pilot had stopped before a great house ~~with with which~~ that loomed up in the flare of the lantern with ghostly ~~white patterns~~ trailing vines and tall chimneys outlined against the stars.

Thereupon the entire party went to bed.

[Here is also one of the programs of its dramatic presentation at Palmer's Theatre] in 1894. Nothing for a long time has given me as much pleasure as that this my first book—one which probably is best known—should find a resting place in your beautiful library. With my sincere personal regards, Your friend   F. Hopkinson Smith

Jan" 1915.

79

SIDNEY LANIER

*Autograph letter signed, dated Baltimore, Md., March 22ᵈ 1875,
addressed to James Maurice Thompson. 4 p. 20 cm.*

Poet and musician (b. Macon, Ga. 1842; d. Lynn, N.C. 1881). Author of *Tiger-Lilies* (1867), a novel based on his experiences in the Civil War; *Poems* (1877); *The Science of English Verse* (1880), a study of the relationships between poetry and music; and *The English Novel* (1883). Among his best-known single poems are "The Song of the Chattahoochee," "The Marshes of Glynn" and "A Ballad of Trees and the Master." He played the flute with great skill and was praised by Theodore Thomas and Leopold Damrosch.

This letter, of which the first and last pages are shown, was written to Maurice Thompson, the Indiana author, whose first book, *Hoosier Mosaics*, was to be published later in 1875. In February, Lanier's poem "Corn" had been published in *Lippincott's Magazine*, and it attracted much attention; it was the beginning of his career as a poet. In this letter he refers to an earlier publication as a "boyish squib," and thanks Thompson for his interest in "Corn." Poor health and economic hardships following the Civil War prevented Lanier from devoting much time to poetry, but he is, nevertheless, remembered as a major poet of the American South. A very large collection of Lanier manuscripts and related materials is in the Library of Johns Hopkins University, where he held a lectureship.

---

64 Center St. Baltimore, Md. March 22ᵈ 1875. My dear Sir: Your letter was delayed in reaching me, and I hasten to express the pleasure with which I make your acquaintance.

I fancy it is a somewhat vague association which makes you connect me with Scott's Monthly, and the Rebel poets. I am guiltless of Scott's, except one boyish squib published therein some time after the war. During the war I wrote nothing: being like yourself a boy. [...]

[I send you a copy of the Magazines, and congratulate you with all my] heart thereupon. Pray send me whatever you print, or at least let me know when it appears.

I shall be always glad to hear from you, and am, dear Sir, Very truly yours   Sidney Lanier. / Mʳ James Maurice Thompson

64 China St.
Baltimore, Md.
March 23 - 1875.

80

JOHN FISKE

"The Everlasting Reality of Religion." Autograph manuscript signed
[n.p., n.d.]. 38 p. 26.5 cm. ¾ red morocco.

Philosopher and historian (b. Hartford, Conn. 1842; d. Gloucester, Mass. 1901). Author of *Myths and Myth Makers* (1872), *The Outlines of Cosmic Philosophy* (1874), *The American Revolution* (1891) and *Life Everlasting* (1901). Fiske's most important work was to interpret in the United States the philosophy of evolution. As an historian he concentrated on politics and battles, with little attention to economic and social forces; his works, written with great charm of literary style, were widely read. He was also a popular and dedicated lecturer.

This essay was published as the third and final chapter of Fiske's *Through Nature to God* (1899), a book dedicated "To the beloved and revered memory of my friend Thomas Henry Huxley." Before publication he used the essay as a lecture. Fiske prepared his manuscripts with great care, even to writing out a title page with imprint; he revised carefully and generally found few corrections necessary. The text illustrated here, the first page of the essay, is about Voltaire's château at Ferney and introduces the theism of the great writer. After Fiske's death it was said of him in *The Nation*, "philosophers were inclined to think of him at his best as an historian, and historians to urge that he was primarily a philosopher." Fiske, who weighed over 300 pounds, was also known as the largest author in America. The principal repository of his manuscripts is Harvard University Library; the Morgan Library has seven manuscripts and other autograph material is in Princeton University Library.

~~Nature's Eternal Lesson.~~
~~The Everlasting Reality of Religion.~~
The Everlasting Reality of Religion.

I.

"Deo erexit Voltaire."

The visitor to Geneva, whose studies have made him duly acquainted with the ~~richest~~ most interesting ~~and most potent~~ human personality of all that are associated with that historic city, will ~~surely~~ never leave the place without making a ~~loving~~ pilgrimage to the chateau of Ferney. In that refined and quiet rural homestead things still remain very much as on the day when the aged Voltaire left it for

the last visit to Paris, where his long ~~and noble~~ life was worthily ended amid words and deeds of ~~affectionate and and reverent~~ affectionate homage. One may sit down at the ~~little~~ table where was written the most perfect prose, perhaps, that ever flowed from ~~human~~ pen, and look about the little room with its evidences of plain living and high thinking, until one seems to recall the ~~vanished Master that quaint~~ eccentric figure of the vanished Master, with ~~its~~ his flashes of shrewd wisdom and ~~matchless~~ caustic wit, ~~its boundless intellectual curiosity~~ his insatiable thirst for knowledge, ~~its devotion~~ his consuming hatred of bigotry and oppression, ~~its~~ his merciless contempt for shame, ~~its~~ his boundless enthusiasm [of humanity.]

Nature's Eternal Lesson.

The Everlasting Reality of Religion.

The Everlasting Reality of Religion.

I.

"Deo erexit Voltaire."

The visitor to Geneva, whose studies have made him
duly acquainted with the ~~richest~~ most interesting ~~and most potent~~ human
personality of all that are associated with that historic city,
will ~~surely~~ never leave the place without making a loving
pilgrimage to the chateau of Ferney. In that refined and
quiet rural homestead things still remain very much as on
the day when the aged Voltaire left it for the last visit to
Paris, where his long ~~and noble~~ life was worthily ended
amid words and deeds of ~~affectionate~~ affectionate ~~and~~ homage.
One may sit down at the ~~little~~ table where was written the
most perfect prose, perhaps, that ever flowed from ~~human~~ pen, and
look about the little room with its evidences of plain living and
high thinking, until one seems to recall the ~~vanished Master~~
~~worththat going~~ eccentric ~~figure~~ of the vanished Master, with his caustic
wisdom and ~~matchless~~ ~~his~~ wit, ~~its~~ his insatiable thirst for knowledge, his flashes of shrewd
~~its devotion~~ his consuming hatred of bigotry and oppression,
~~its~~ his merciless contempt for shams, ~~its~~ his boundless enthusiasm

81

AMBROSE BIERCE

Autograph letter signed, dated Berkeley, Calif., 14 August 1893,
addressed to Laurens Maynard. 3 p. 18.5 cm.

Author and journalist (b. Meigs County, Ohio 1842; d. in Mexico 1914?). Among his works are *Cobwebs from an Empty Skull* (1874), short and satirical fables; *Tales of Soldiers and Civilians* (1891), reissued as *In the Midst of Life* (1898); *The Cynic's Word Book* (1906), reissued as *The Devil's Dictionary* (1911).

Little is known of Bierce's childhood beyond the fact that he was the son of a farmer. He enlisted with the 9th Indiana Infantry in the Civil War, and served with distinction. After the war he moved to San Francisco to join a brother, and to begin a career of journalism. His first short story appeared in the *Overland Monthly* in 1871. In 1872, Bierce, newly married, moved to England. Three volumes of sketches and articles were published there under the pseudonym "Dod Grile," and he established his reputation as a biting satirist. Bierce returned to San Francisco in 1876, writing for the *Wasp*, the *Argonaut*, and later for William Randolph Hearst's *Examiner*. His finest stories of the supernatural, classics of their genre, appeared in *Can Such Things Be?* (1893), a volume which is mentioned in the last two pages of a letter to the publisher Laurens Maynard, which are reproduced here. In his last years Bierce visibly tired of life. In 1913 he journeyed into revolutionary Mexico with the prediction that he would not return. His prediction was correct. The chief repository of Bierce manuscripts is the Huntington Library.

[. . .] The other book that you ask about is ~~about~~ *soon to be published by the Cassell Publishing Company New York, under the title of "Can Such Things Be?"*

Other recent books of mine are "Black Beetles in Amber," Western Authors Publishing Company, San Francisco, and "The Monk and the Hangman's Daughter"; F. J. Schulte & Co., Chicago. The latter house is bankrupt, and whether the former is selling any books or not I do not know.

I am very truly yours, Ambrose Bierce.

208 California St., San Francisco.

The other being that I am soon to ——— by the Sunset Publishing Company New York, under the title of "Can Such Things Be?"

Other recent books I name my "Black Beetles in Amber," Western Authors' Pub. Fishing Company, San Francisco, and "The Monk and the Hangman's Daughter"; F. J. Schulte & Co., Chicago. The latter house is bankrupt, and whether the former is still ing any books or not I do not know.

very sincerely yours,
Ambrose Bierce.

82

HENRY JAMES

"The Impressions of a Cousin." Autograph manuscript signed, dated [n.p.] April 3, 1883. 116 p. 25.5 cm. Brown morocco.

Novelist (b. New York City 1843; d. London, England 1916). By any standards, Henry James is one of the great figures in the history of the novel. He published a large number of stories and novels, from *A Passionate Pilgrim* (1875) and *Roderick Hudson* (1876) to *The Ivory Tower* and *The Sense of the Past* (both 1917). Some of his best-known titles are *The American* (1877), *The Europeans* (1879), *Daisy Miller* (1879), *Washington Square* (1881), *The Portrait of a Lady* (1881), *The Bostonians* (1886), *The Aspern Papers* (1888), *What Maisie Knew* (1897), *The Two Magics* (1898, with the famous story, "The Turn of the Screw"), *The Wings of the Dove* (1902), *The Ambassadors* (1903) and *The Golden Bowl* (1904).

James's father, of the same name, was independently wealthy and used his leisure to write on religious and social questions from a Swedenborgian standpoint; the novelist's brother William became a world-famous philosopher and psychologist. Henry James, Sr. gave his children much of their education in Europe and, after 1875, young Henry became a permanent resident abroad. His prolific writings effected a seamless merger between an intricate, highly qualified style and a hypersensitivity to the small nuances manifested by relations between human beings and between cultures. James's many novels form the nucleus of his reputation, but he was equally distinctive as a writer of short stories and as a critic. The year before his death he became a British subject.

"The Impressions of a Cousin" is the story of how a young American woman is cheated of her inheritance by her trustee, whom she loves and refuses to prosecute. James wrote the story within a few months of the death of his father, at a time when complications of inheritance were much on his mind. It was published in two parts in *The Century Magazine* at the end of 1883, and reprinted in book form in 1884, as the first tale in *Tales of Three Cities*. The bulk of James manuscripts and many letters are deposited in Harvard University Library.

The Impressions of a Cousin.

New York, April 3ᵈ 1873. *There are moments when I feel that she has asked too much of me—especially since our arrival in this country. These three months have not done much toward making me happy here. I don't know what the difference is—or rather I do, and I say that only because it's less trouble. It is no trouble, however, to say that I like my native land less; and New York less than Rome; that, after all, is the difference. And then there's nothing to sketch! For ten years I have been sketching, and I really believe I do it very well. But how can I sketch Fifty-third Street? There are times when I even say to myself, How can I live in even endure Fifty-third Street? When I turn into it from the Fifth Avenue the vista seems too hideous—the vulgar, uniform narrow, impersonal houses, with the dry, hard tone of their brown stone, a surface as uninteresting of as that of sand-paper; their steep, stiff stoops, giving you such a climb to the door, their lumpish balustrades, and porticoes, and cornices, turned out by the hundred and adorned with heavy excrescences—such an eruption of ornament and such a poverty of effect. [...]*

The Impressions of a Cousin.

New York, April 3d 1873. There are moments when I feel that she has asked too much of me — especially since our arrival in this country. These three months have not done much toward making me happy here. I don't know what the difference is — or rather I do, and I say that only because it's less trouble. It is no trouble, however, to say that I like New York less than Rome; that, after all, is the difference. And there there's nothing to sketch! For ten years I have been sketching and I really believe I do it very well. But how can I sketch Fifty-Third Street? There are times when I say to myself, How can I today endure Fifty-Third Street? When I turn into it from the Fifth Avenue the vista seems too hideous — the narrow, impersonal houses, with the dry, hard tone of their brown stone, a surface as uninteresting as that of sand-paper; their steep, stiff stoops, giving you such a climb to the door, their lumpish balustrades, porticoes and cornices, turned out by the hundred and adorned with heavy excrescences — such an eruption of ornament and such a poverty of effect. I suppose my impression would seem very pretentious if my body rose to lead this meandering record of personal feeling; and I should be asked why an expensive up-town residence is not as good as a shiny Italian palazzo. My answer of course is that I can sketch the palazzo and I am do nothing with the up-town

83

HENRY JAMES

"Project of Novel by Henry James." Typescript signed, dated [n.p.] September 1ˢᵗ 1900. 90 p. 24.5 cm. Red cloth box.

The first edition of Henry James's novel *The Ambassadors* was published in London on 24 September 1903 and the first American edition followed in November. A serial version was published in *The North American Review* from January to December 1903. The book has a complicated textual and bibliographical history to which this typescript contributes. It is a scenario for *The Ambassadors* with the title in James's hand and is signed and dated by him. Although James is known to have written a scenario for his *Sense of the Past*, this seems to be the only scenario to have survived. This outline, itself of Jamesian proportions, was sent to James B. Pinker, the literary agent, and to publishers, specifically to Harper & Bros. With the scenario in the collection is an opinion from Henry Mills Alden, a veteran Harper's editor, which reads in part, "The tissues of it are too subtly fine for general appreciation. It is subjective, fold within fold of a complex mental web, in which the reader is lost if his much wearied attention falters. . . . I do not advise acceptance." Nevertheless, Harpers did publish the finished novel. James considered *The Ambassadors* to be his best book and used material from this scenario in the final product.

a total of 100,000. But I should very much like my option of stretching to 120,000 if necessary—that is, adding an Eleventh and Twelfth Parts. Each Part I rather definitely see in Two Chapters, and each very full, as it were, and charged—like a rounded medal-lion, in a series of a dozen, hung, with its effect of high relief, on a wall. Such are my general lines. Of course there's a lot to say about the matter that I haven't said—but I have doubtless said a great deal more than it may seem to you at first easy to find your way about in. The way is really, however, very straight. Only the difficulty with one's having made so very full a Statement as the present is that one seems to have gone far toward saying all: which I needn't add that I haven't in the least pretended to do. Reading these pages over, for instance, I find I haven't at all placed in a light what I make of the nature of Strether's feeling—his affian-ced, indebted, and other, consciousness—about Mrs. Newsome. But I need scarcely add, after this, that everything will in fact be in its place and of its kind.

Henry James

September 1st 1900.

Project of Novel by Henry James

It occurs to me that it may conduce to interest to begin with a mention of the comparatively small matter that gave me, in this case, the germ of my subject—as it is very often comparatively small matters that do this; and as, at any rate, the little incident in question formed, for my convenience, my starting-point, on my first sketching the whole idea for myself.

A friend (of perceptions almost as profound as my own!) had spoken to me, then—and really not measuring how much it would strike me or I should see in it—something that had come under his observation a short time before, in Paris. He had found himself, one Sunday afternoon, with various other people, in the charming old garden attached to the house of a friend (also a friend of mine,) in a particularly old-fashioned and pleasantly quiet part of the town; a garden that, with two or three others of the same sort near it, I myself knew, so that I could easily focus the setting. The old houses of the Faubourg St.-Germain close round their gardens and shut them in, so that you don't see them from the street—only overlook them from all sorts of picturesque exorescences in the rear. I had

84

HENRY JAMES

Autograph letter signed, dated [London,] Tuesday, Dec. 18ᵗʰ [1894],
addressed to Dr. William Wilberforce Baldwin. 4 p. 17.5 cm.

Dr. Baldwin was James's Florentine friend and physician. He was a gifted healer and heart specialist who attended a generation of traveling Americans as they passed through Italy, including Mark Twain, William Dean Howells and Edith Wharton, and set up a number of health spas or clinics in various parts of southern Italy. From a record in Dr. Baldwin's casebook, which the physician told him about during a walking trip in Tuscany, James found material for his story "The Pupil," concerning a small boy with a weak heart, who suffered from parental neglect, and of his attachment for his tutor.

This letter to Dr. Baldwin, written shortly after the latter's arrival in England to treat members of the Astor family, is brief, witty and to the point; although it is written in James's large, bold hand, it is not otherwise typical of his usually long and labored epistles. The first and last pages are reproduced.

Tuesday, Dec. 18ᵗʰ   34, De Vere Gardens. W. My dear Baldwin. I both rejoice in you & pity you—the latter for having to race across Alps & Appenines, to say nothing of convulsed channels, to weary your delicate [flesh or to please bloated Billionaires.] . . . [Shant you be here Thursday? To] lunch or dine with me? I hope you are not ½ dead. Damn your influenzas—healer of others. In frantic haste—Yours always—Henry James

34, DE VERE GARDENS. W.

Tuesday, Dec. 185

1891

My dear Balestier.

I too rejoice in your return for

[remainder of letter in largely illegible handwriting]

Yours always

Henry James

85

JULIAN HAWTHORNE

Autograph diary, containing entries from May 1857 to October 1859, written as a boy in England and while on tours of Scotland and Italy. 100 p. 23.5 cm. ¾ brown leather.

Novelist and biographer, son of Nathaniel Hawthorne (b. Boston, Mass. 1846; d. San Francisco, Calif. 1934). Among his novels are *Bressant* (1873), *Garth* (1877), *Archibald Malmaison* (1884) and *A Fool of Nature* (1896). Writings on his family include *Nathaniel Hawthorne and His Wife* (1884) and *Hawthorne and His Circle* (1903), which are perhaps his finest books. Many of his novels sold well but his attitude toward his books was mainly commercial and he had little regard for them as literature. Nevertheless he enjoyed writing more than his chosen profession of engineering.

Julian Hawthorne spent most of his early years in Europe, where he was educated by his father and met many famous writers and artists. Perhaps it was his father's journalizing that led young Hawthorne to keep this diary. In spite of the youth of the writer, it contains much information of value about the Hawthorne family and their friends. The entry shown for August 5, 1859, with portions of the entries for the days before and after, is mainly concerned with his aquarium. He has also learned to swim. The largest collection of the manuscripts and papers of Julian Hawthorne is in the University of California Library, Berkeley.

[I have kept my aquarium in an imense earthen pot full of water, But for some reason or another I have] had to change the water every day. This time I have placed almost all the animals in separate jugs of sea-water, each with a bit of sea-weed.

I have one other grand thing to put down and that is that I have learned to swim, and can now swim quite a distance.

Julian Hawthorne

Friday August 5 1859

This morning when I got up I went down stairs and took my sea-anemonies out of their little aquariums and put them into the large one. One of the sea-anemonies I put into it last night, because its aquarium was not pure. I hope the water in the large pot will remain good for I have put a great deal of seaweed into it and there are sand and

rocks all about. All the sea-anemones are in, and look very well. I found an alive sea-urchin yesterday, but I found a dead one this morning. Its water was not pure, and there were some sea-anemones in with it. The sea weed is covered with oxygen bubbles even when the sun is not shining on them. I have put one soldier-crab in, and he has not done any harm, but has sat quietly under the sea weed all this morning in the same place, or about it. I am not allowed to go out this morning because I have got a cold, but I shall go with papa this afternoon and will write about it tomorrow morning

Saturday Morning August 6 1859

I am now writing of my yesterdays' walk with Papa. We started about half past three, and we walked towards Whitby as far as the [little town of Marsk[e] where there is a road which leads from there to Redcar.]

had to change the water every day. This time I have placed almost all the animals in separate jars of sea-water, each with a bit of sea-weed.

I have one other grand thing to put down and that is that I have learned to swim, and can now swim quite a distance.

Julian Hawthorne

Friday August 5 1859

This Morning when I got up I went down stairs and took my sea-anemonies out of their little aquariums and put them into the large one. One of the sea-anemonies I put into it last night, because its aquarium was not pure. I hope the water in the large pot will remain good for I have put a great deal of seaweed into it and there are sand and rocks all about. All the sea-anemonies are in, and look very well. I found an alive sea-urchin yesterday, but I found a dead one this morning. Its water was not pure, and there were some sea-anemones in with it. The sea weed is covered with oxygen bubbles even when the sun is not shining on them. I have put one soldier-crab in, and he has not done any harm, but has sat quietly under the sea weed all this morning in the same place, or about it. I am not allowed to go out this morning because I have got a cold, but I shall go with papa this afternoon and will write about it to-morrow morning

Saturday Morning August 6 1859

I am now writing of my yesterday's walk with Papa. We started about half past three, and we walked towards Whitby as far as the

86

JOEL CHANDLER HARRIS

Autograph letter signed, dated Atlanta, Ga., 21 June. 1884, addressed to William Carey. 2 p. 23 cm.

Author and journalist (b. near Eatonton, Ga. 1848; d. Atlanta, Ga. 1908). His first book, *Uncle Remus; His Songs and His Sayings* (1881), was the first of ten Uncle Remus books, of which only the later volumes were aimed specifically at children; they attracted many readers in both North and South. Harris also wrote *Mingo, and Other Sketches in Black and White* (1884); *Sister Jane* (1886) and *Gabriel Tolliver* (1902), both novels; and *Free Joe* (1887) and *Tales of the Home Folks in Peace and War* (1898).

Joel Chandler Harris was an illegitimate child, who kept his mother's surname. At the age of 14 he began work as printer's devil for Joseph Addison Turner's weekly newspaper *Countryman*; Turner played the major role in the boy's education as a writer. Harris continued as a journalist throughout his life, including 24 years on the staff of the Atlanta *Constitution*. He wrote many volumes of Georgia sketches and stories but his permanent fame was achieved in the persona of Uncle Remus. All his books gave painstaking attention to the subtleties of middle-Georgia black speech; the question of the stories' sources in black and European folklore is a much more complicated one. Outside his family and a circle of old friends and neighbors, Harris was a shy, retiring man who rarely ventured beyond the borders of his beloved native state. The lighthearted letter from Harris reproduced here is written to William Carey, the waggish Irish wit, who was assistant editor of *The Century*. When he was on the staff of *Scribner's Magazine*, Carey had the editorial inspiration to change the title of Frank Stockton's famous short story from "The King's Arena" to "The Lady or the Tiger?" The letters and manuscripts of Joel Chandler Harris are mainly in the Emory University Library, Atlanta.

From the collection of Mr. C. Waller Barrett at the Alderman Library, University of Virginia, Charlottesville, Virginia.

1884: 21 June. My Dear Mr. Carey: The name of the author of the song—an extract from which you enclose with your letter—will be well known to you when you get to be a little older. It is old Father Time. In other words, it is a song which a hundred generations ~~have~~ (more or less) have had a hand in composing. I have no doubt that parts of it existed in Chaucer's time It belongs to the oral literature of the people a great mass of which is waiting for a sympathetic collector. Your version has been somewhat doctored, The first line should be "Oh," said the chickadee, hopping in the grass." The last line of the woodpecker stanza should be "And ever since then my head's been red." I wrote to Mr. Johnson the other day about a sketch entitled "Free Joe." Curiously enough, I had arranged

to make Free Joe sing a stanza that belongs to your song—"Oh," said the Blackbird to the Crow, / "What makes the white folks shoot us so? / For, you know, since we've been born / It's been our trade to pull up corn." /

The song runs on at great length, describing various episodes, but I can recall no other stanza. I shall hunt it up and send it to you. There is another beginning: The Jaybird died with the whooping-cough / The Killdee died with the colic—/ (Oh, ladies, aint you sorry?) / The pa'tridge had his tail pulled out / And couldn't go to the frolic—/ (Oh, ladies, won't you marry?) / [...]

Faithfully yours   Joel Chandler Harris

The Constitution,
ATLANTA GA
EDITORIAL ROOMS.

1884:
21 June.

My dear Mr Cary:

The name of the author of the song—an extract from which you enclose with your letter—will be well known to you when you get to be a little older. It is old Father Time. Another word, it is very which had a hand in composing. I have no doubt that facts of it existed in Chaucer's time. It belongs to the oral literature of the people—a great mass of which is waiting for a sympathetic collector. You never heard a somewhat dictated. The first line should be

"Oh," said the chickadee, hopping in the grass."

The next line of the woodpecker songs should be

"And you rine than my head's burned."

Just to the follow the other sing about

Which entitled "The Jay": Coming enough, I beg enough to make the jay dig a thing a that which to you ring—

"Oh," said the Blackbird to the Crow,
"What makes the white police doctors is?
For you know, since we've been born
It's been our luck to pull up corn."

The song runs on at great length, describing various episodes, but I can recall no other stanza. I shall tack heart it up and send it to you. Here is another beginning:

The Jaybird died with the whooping cough
The Killdee died with the colic—
(Oh ladies, ain't you sorry!)

The first of his tail pointed out
And couldn't get to the polic—
(Oh ladies, won't you marry?)

Queerly enough, I am continually appealing to find these things in Shakespeare. I will in my end I endeavor all the Shakespearean connotations together and take them in an accurate pin among the people. I wonder people. In one such I could commit them that the ding are the sharpest the very essence of simplicity. But what warrant have you given me to insist my anger I into your minds in this manner? You asked me a plain question, and here I am about to bestow upon me the world. My excuse is that your enclosure has carried me away back to the old days.

Faithfully Yours
Joel Chandler Harris

87

EMMA LAZARUS

"Success." Autograph manuscript of the poem signed [n.p., n.d.].
1 p. 20 cm.

Poet, translator and essayist (b. New York City 1849; d. New York City 1887). She wrote *Poems and Translations* (1867); *Admetus and Other Poems* (1871), written in her teens; *Alide: An Episode of Goethe's Life* (1874); *Songs of a Semite* (1882) and a series of poems "By the Waters of Babylon," published in *The Century Magazine* for March 1887, which showed the influence of Whitman. She also translated the poems and ballads of Heinrich Heine.

Emma Lazarus was a precocious child born to a prosperous Sephardic family. Her early poems were fragile and romantic but in the 1880s, in the wake of Russian pogroms, she took up with vigor the cause of Jewish rights. *Songs of a Semite* contains some of her finest work. She is remembered today for her sonnet "The New Colossus," inscribed on the pedestal of the Statue of Liberty, which includes the lines "Give me your tired, your poor, / Your huddled masses yearning to breathe free." There are few Lazarus manuscripts and letters in public collections but The New York Public Library and Columbia University Library have some.

Success.

Oft have I brooded on defeat and pain, / The pathos of the stupid, stumbling throng. / These I ignore to-day and only long / To pour my soul forth in one trumpet strain, / One clear, grief-shattering triumphant song, / For all the victories of man's high endeavor, / Palm-bearing, laureled deeds that live forever, / The splendor clothing him whose will is strong. / Hast thou beheld the deep, glad eyes of one / Who has persisted and achieved? Rejoice! / On naught diviner shines the all-seeing sun. / Salute him with free heart and choral voice, / Midst flippant, feeble crowds of spectres wan, / The bold, significant, successful man. /

Emma Lazarus.

Success.

Oft have I brooded on defeat and pain,
  The pathos of the stupid, stumbling throng.
  These I ignore to-day and only long
To pour my soul forth in one trumpet strain,
One clear, grief-shattering, triumphant song,
For all the victories of man's high endeavor,
Palm-bearing, laureled deeds that live forever,
The splendor clothing him whose will is strong.
Hast thou beheld the deep, glad eyes of one
  Who has persisted and achieved? Rejoice!
On naught diviner shines the all-seeing sun.
Salute him with free heart and choral voice,
Midst flippant, feeble crowds of spectres wan,
The bold, significant, successful man.

Emma Lazarus.

88

SARAH ORNE JEWETT

"The Failure of David Berry." Autograph manuscript signed [n.p., n.d.].
Pages 1 and 39 (concluding) only. 2 p. 20.5 cm.

Novelist, short-story writer and poet (b. South Berwick, Me. 1849; d. South Berwick, Me. 1909). She is best known for her books on Maine life, especially *Deephaven* (1877), her fictional name for South Berwick, and *The Country of the Pointed Firs* (1896), and by numerous short stories in *Harper's, The Century* and *The Atlantic Monthly*. Although a writer of regional stories, her reputation as a careful, incisive author was by no means confined to the New England area; her work was well received by the Boston literary circle, and she was a recognized author on her trips to Europe with Mrs. James T. Fields, where she became acquainted with Tennyson, James and Du Maurier.

As a child her writing ability was encouraged by her father (a country physician), who instilled in her the beauty of careful observation and assimilation of the natural phenomena of the New England town. Her formal education was limited by her poor health, but her literary education more than made up for it. A paced and meticulous writer, she "nibbled all round her stories like a mouse." Her images of the Maine coastal life are characterized by their preciseness and clarity. "The Failure of David Berry," typical of her style, was first published in *Harper's Magazine* in June 1891; the first and last pages are reproduced here. There are large collections of manuscripts and letters of Sarah Orne Jewett at Colby College Library and Harvard University Library.

The Failure of David Berry.

Mr. David Berry used to keep his shop in a small wooden building in his own yard and worked steadily there a great many years—being employed by a large manufacturing company in Lynn at soling and heeling men's boots. There were just such small shoeshops as his scattered among the villages and along the country roads, most of the farmers knew something of the shoemaking trade, and they and their sons worked in their warm little shops in winter when they had nothing else to do, and so added a good deal of ready money to their narrow incomes. The great Lynn teams, piled high with clean wooden shoe boxes, ~~that~~ came

and went along the high ways at regular times to deliver and collect the work. Many of the women bound shoes and sometimes, in pleasant [. . .]

[. . .] came back, took his jacknife out of his pocket and scratched the verse from the wall. Somehow there was no getting rid of one's thoughts about the old man. He had laughed once and told some body that David Berry could travel all day in a peck measure, but now it seemed as if David Berry marched down upon him from the skies with a great army of those who owed no man anything but love, and had paid their debt.

Sarah O. Jewett

came back, took his jackknife out of his
pocket and scratched the rose from
the wall. Somehow there was no getting
rid of one's thoughts about the old man.
He had laughed over and told some
body that David Berry could trace
all day in a poor measure, but not
it seemed as if David marched down
upon him from the skies with a
great army of those who owed no
man anything but love, and had
paid their debt.

Sarah O. Jewett

The Failure of David Berry

By Sarah Orne Jewett

Mr. David Berry used to keep his shop in
a small wooden building in the village
and worked steadily there a great many
years - being employed by a large manufacturing
company in Lynn at soling and heeling
men's boots. There were just such small
shoe shops as his scattered among the
villages and along the country roads of
most of the farmers knew something
of the shoemaking trade, and they
and their sons worked in their warm
little shops in winter when they had
nothing else to do, and so added a
good deal of ready money to their
narrow incomes. The great Lynn
teams, piled high with shoe boxes,
came and went along the high way
at regular times to deliver and collect
the work. Many of the women
bound shoes and sometimes, in pleasant

89

JAMES WHITCOMB RILEY

"Karl Schronz's Christmas Story. 'Dot Leedle Poy of Mine.'"
Autograph manuscript signed [written in Indianapolis late in 1875].
3 p. 21 cm.

Poet and journalist (b. Greenfield, Ind. 1849; d. Indianapolis, Ind. 1916). Some of his representative books, often a mixture of verse and prose, are *The Old Swimmin'-Hole* (1883), *Afterwhiles* (1887), *Old Fashioned Roses* (1888), *Pipes o' Pan at Zekesbury* (1888), *Rhymes of Childhood* (1890), *Book of Joyous Children* (1902), *The Raggedy Man* (1907) and *When the Frost is on the Punkin* (1911). The "Hoosier Poet" was at his best in dialect verse that was characterized by humor, sincerity and pathos.

Although he had contributed verse to various journals, Riley's career began in 1877 when he joined the staff of the *Indianapolis Journal*, where he remained for 11 years. In later years Riley built up a national reputation as a public reader of his poetry and prose; his appearances were enhanced by his abilities as an actor and humorist and sometimes marred by his intemperance. Many of his poems were written for and about children, with whom he was a great favorite. His dialect poem "Karl Schronz's Christmas Story," the last page of which is reproduced here, was written before Riley began to have trouble with printers unable to read his handwriting and had to develop an engraving-like script. It was first published in *People*, an Indianapolis paper, on January 1, 1876, and was collected in *Green Fields and Running Brooks* (1893). A very large group of Riley's manuscripts and letters is in the Lilly Library, Indiana University.

[. . .] *Unt gotten vorse unt vorser, unt dumble on der bed,— / Unt ven der doctor seen id he kind o' shake his head, / Unt veel his bulse unt visper,—"Der poy is a dyin"* . . . *— / You dink I could believe id?* . . . Dot leedle poy of mine? /

I dold you, friends, dots someding,—der last time dot he speak, / Unt say "Goot bye, Kriss Kringle!"—Ot make me feel so veak / I yoost kneel down unt drimble, unt bursted

oud a cryin'— / "Mine Gott, Mine Gott in Himmel! dot leedle poy of mine!" / [. . .]

Der sun vont shine dot Christmas! Off dot leedle poy had lived— / No deeferin—for Heaven vas his leedle Christmas-giv'd; / Unt der rooster unt der candy, unt me unt my Katrine / Unt der Jay-bird is a vaiting for dot leedle poy of mine. /

J. W. *Riley.*

Vit candies, nuts unt raisins: vnt I buy a leedle drum
Dot I vant to hear 'im rattle ven der Christmas morning come;
Vnt a leedle schmall tin rooster dot would crow so fine
Ven he squeeze 'id in der morning — dot leedle poy of mine.

Vnt vile ve vas a freezin', dot leedle poy vake oud —
I tought he been a dreamin' Kris Kringle vas aboud,
Vnt he say, — "Dots him! I see 'im mit der stars dot make der shine" —
Vnt vent keep on a cryin' — dot leedle poy of mine —

Vnt gotten vorse unt vorser, unt dumble on der bed, —
Vnt ven der doctor seen id he kind o' shake his head,
Vnt veel his pulse unt visper, — "Der poy is a dyin'" —
You dink I could believe id? — Dot leedle poy of mine?

I dold you, friends, dots someding, — der last time dot he speak,
Vnt say "Goot bye, Kriss Kringle!" — Ot make me feel so veak
I yoast kneel down unt drimble, mit bursted and a cryin' —
"Mine Gott. Mine Gott in Himmel! dot leedle poy of mine!"

*   *   *   *   *

Der sun vont shine dot Christmas! Off dot leedle poy had lived —
No deeferin — for Heaven vas his leedle Christmas-giv'd;
Vnt der rooster unt der candy, unt me unt my Katrine
Vnt der jay-bird is a vaiting for dot leedle poy of mine.

J. W. Riley

90

LAFCADIO HEARN

"Notes of a Trip to Izumo." Autograph manuscript signed, dated
[in Japan] Jan. 9ᵗʰ '97. 91 p. 20 cm. Blue cloth case.

Author and journalist (b. Leucadia, Greece, one of the islands in the Ionian group that is also known to Italian and British occupants as Santa Maura, and to modern Greeks as Levkas, 1850; d. Tokyo, Japan 1904). He wrote many books, among which are *Stray Leaves from Strange Literature* (1884); *Some Chinese Ghosts* (1887); *Chita* (1889), the story of the destruction of a Caribbean island by a tidal wave; *Youma* (1890), a novel which describes the devotion of a black girl to the daughter of her deceased mistress: *Two Years in the French West Indies* (1890); *Glimpses of Unfamiliar Japan* (1894); *Japanese Fairy Tales* (1898–1903), a popular favorite; and *A Japanese Miscellany* (1901), the manuscript of which is in the Morgan Library.

Hearn was the son of a Greek mother and an English father, both of whom abandoned him in his early childhood. He was brought up by an aunt in Dublin and sent to Catholic schools in England and France. A school accident blinded him in one eye, and he permanently abused the other with excessive reading; for the rest of his life he was convinced that his appearance was freakish and repulsive. At the age of 19, impoverished, he arrived in America and found a succession of short-lived menial jobs in New York and Cincinnati. Hearn eventually found work on the Cincinnati *Enquirer*, where he revealed great literary talent; his strikingly beautiful prose owes much to the polished style of his favorite French writers, Baudelaire, Flaubert and Gautier. He was dismissed from the *Enquirer* for living with a mulatto woman and migrated to New Orleans, where he did more newspaper work and where his first book, *One of Cleopatra's Nights* (1882), translations from Gautier, was published. For several years he lived in poverty in Martinique. In 1890 Hearn moved to Japan where, despite continuing financial hardships, he enjoyed the first settled life he had ever known; he married a Japanese woman, became a Japanese subject and taught English at the Imperial University. His last books made valuable contributions toward explaining Japanese culture to the West. These travel sketches, of which two pages are reproduced here, were first published in *The Atlantic Monthly* for May 1897. There are large collections of Hearn's letters and manuscripts in the Alderman Library, University of Virginia, Harvard University Library and The New York Public Library.

V.

Hiroshima, Aug. 29ᵗʰ.

. . . At Kabé, while waiting with my Kurumaya to cross the river by the ferry, we were joined by a number of other travellers,—chiefly peasant-women. The ferry-boat was a large solid construction, built to bear loaded wains, and made only a fixed number of trips per hour. Just as we were pushing off, a belated little pilgrim came running, and leaped in lightly,—a boy of perhaps thirteen. [...]

Lafcadio Hearn

Jan. ~~10ᵗʰ~~ 9ᵗʰ '97.

women, satisfied with creative's perpetual poem, and filled with perfect trust in the Buddhist gospel of love! For the New Japan the grave is waiting;— the green capital, so long dreaded, draws to her completion at last. And the question I can not keep asking myself is whether in that respect the New Japan I can be fortunate enough at happier moments to meet with something of the Old.

Lafcadio Hearn

Jan. 1st '97.

V.

— Hiroshima, Aug. 29th.

...at Kobe, while waiting with my Kurumaya to cross the Kunozawa... we were near the ferry, we were joined to a number of other travellers,— chiefly peasant-women. The ferry-boat was a large solid construction, built to bear loaded trains, and made only a number of trips per hour. Just as we were pushing off, a belated little pilgrim came running, and leaped in eighties,— a boy perhaps in eighties... He was all in white from head to foot after the fashion...

EUGENE FIELD

"Casey's Table d'hote." Autograph manuscript signed, dated Dec. 28, 1888. 5 p. 25 cm. Brown morocco.

Poet, humorist and newspaperman (b. St. Louis, Mo. 1850; d. Chicago, Ill. 1895). His books include *The Tribune Primer* (1882), *A Little Book of Western Verse* (1889), *Second Book of Verse* (1892), *The Love Affairs of a Bibliomaniac* (1896) and *Songs and other Verse* (1896). From 1883 until his death Field was on the staff of the Chicago *Morning News* (later *Record*), where he wrote a column, "Sharps and Flats." Much of the material in his columns found its way into his books.

Field spent most of his early years in New England but always considered himself to be a Westerner. He was an incorrigible practical joker and prankster; at other times he was deeply, almost pathetically, sentimental. The father of eight children, he had a great love for the poetry and games of childhood. On his first trip to Europe in 1872 he developed a passion, which remained throughout his life, for collecting rare and beautiful books and prints.

Opposite is a facsimile of the final page of the original draft of one of Field's most popular and nostalgic Western dialect poems. It was first published in *A Little Book of Western Verse*. Field manuscripts and letters are in many libraries, but especially the Alderman Library, University of Virginia, Amherst College Library and the Washington University Library, St. Louis.

And you, ~~Oh long-loved~~ O cherished brothers, ~~that are a~~ sleepin' way out ~~there~~ west / With ~~them~~ Red Hoss mountain ~~standin' guard~~ huggin' you close to its lovin' breast— / Oh, do you dream in your last sleep of how we used to do— / Of how we ~~worked and~~ [deletion] ~~and saved 'nd worked 'nd~~ worked our little claims together, me 'nd you? / Why, when I saw you last, a smile was restin' on your face— / ~~I would to God~~ Like ~~As if~~ you wuz glad to sleep forever in that lon~~ly~~ely place; / And so you wuz, and ~~so~~

I'd be, too, if I ~~wereuz~~ sleepin' so, / But ~~a~~ bein' how a brother's love ~~f'r brother~~ aint for the world to know— / ~~So And when I have~~ Whenever I've this heartache and this chokin' in my throat, / I lay it all to thinkin' of Casey's tabble dote. /

Eugene Field.

Dec. 28, 1888

And you, a cherished brother, sleepin' way out west

With Red Hoss mountain huggin' you close to its lovin' breast —

Oh, do you dream in your last sleep of how we used to do —

Of how we worked our little claims together, me 'nd you?

Why, when I saw you last, a smile was restin' on your face —

Like as if you wuz glad to sleep forever in that lonely place;

And so you wuz, and I'd lay too, if I wuz sleepin' so,

But bein' how a brother's love ain't for the world to know —

So whenever I've this heart ache and this chokin' in my throat,

I lay it all to thinkin' of Casey's tabble dote.

— Eugene Field.

Dec. 28, 1888

92

WILLIAM SYDNEY PORTER
(O. HENRY)

Autograph letter signed with initials, dated Austin, Texas, April 28, 1885, addressed to "Dear Dave." 8 p. 24.5 cm.

Short-story writer, poet and journalist (b. Greensboro, N.C. 1862; d. New York City 1910). Although he published pieces in newspapers and periodicals before the turn of the century, O. Henry did not publish his first book, *Cabbages and Kings*, until 1904. Other books by him include *The Four Million* (1906), *The Trimmed Lamp* (1907), *The Voice of the City* (1908) and *The Gentle Grafter* (1908). He also founded a humorous weekly, *The Rolling Stone* (1894–95).

Though O. Henry is most commonly thought of as a New York writer, he never saw the city until he was almost 40. For 15 years he lived in Texas, working at odd jobs, leading a sociable life and developing a career as a journalist. In 1896 he was accused of embezzlement from a bank where he had worked as teller, and made the mistake of fleeing to Honduras. Returning to Texas to visit his mortally ill wife, he was arrested and sentenced to a five-year prison term, of which he served three years and three months (1899–1901). Following this, Porter moved to New York City, where he began pouring out, in casual profusion, the stories that brought him steadily increasing fame.

This early letter of no pretension, of which the first and last pages are reproduced here, was written to one of Porter's Texas pals. It shows at least a few of the qualities O. Henry invested in his stories—an amiable, humorous turn of mind, a concern with odd human incidents, a taste for slang. His cottage in Austin is now an O. Henry Museum. There are collections of his manuscripts and papers in the University of Texas Library and in Baylor University Library, as well as in several other institutions.

April 28, 1885 Dear Dave, I received your letter in answer to mine, which you never got 'till sometime after you had written.

I snatch a few moments from my arduous labors to reply. The Colorado has been on the biggest boom I have seen since '39. In the pyrotechnical and not strictly grammatical language of the Statesman,— The cruel, devastating flood swept on, a dreadful holocaust of swollen, turbid waters, surging and dashing in mad fury which have never been equalled in human history.

A pitiable sight was seen the morning after the flood. Six hundred men, out of employment were seen standing on the banks of the river, gazing at the rushing [stream, laden with debris of every description. . . .]

Charlie Cook is well, and Jim Glover is as gay and debon-

nair and ne plus ultra as ever.

Shoemaker is taking photographs, now, instead of fifteen cent cigars, and Governor Gibbs is in the city, and Slick Johnson has gotten back from New Orleans, and also Dr. Goodwin, and Tom Smith shot at a burglar, and hit a street lamp and another fellow says he did it himself while full, and John Watts ducked Mose in the bath tub, and Joe has reformed again, and Mrs. Pryors guinea flew through the house, and Jones has got a joke about it, and nobody can see the joke, and Jess Randolph is well, and dude Smith has joined the club and going straight to—well, and Scuddy is an end man, and Lord, what an end man!, and I don't know nothin else to write, and there's no accounting for the decision of a petit jury or Yours truly W.S.P.

OFFICE OF

J. HARRELL, JR.

Successor to M. Brahl.

DEALER IN

CIGARS, TOBACCO & SMOKERS' ARTICLES.

OLD CLOCK BUILDING.

Austin, Texas, April 28 1889

Dear Sam,

I received your letter in answer to mine, which you never got till sometime after you had written, but I await a few moments from my address labors to enjoy the Colorado, has been on the English train I have been since 339.

In the hypochondriacal and not strictly from matured longings of the Philistian. The cruel, devastating flood surges on, a dreadful holocaust of civilian, tinkled valets, religious and dashing in mad fury which have never been questioned in human history.

A pitiable sight was seen the morning after the flood. Six hundred men, out of employment, were seen dashing on the banks of the river, gazing at the troubled...

Charlie Cook is well and his love is as gay and ever as never as ever ne plus ultra.

Sylvester is taking physical exercise now, instead of fifteen cigars a day, and ... Loomis thinks he is in the city, and ...

Dick Johnson has gotten back from New Orleans and also Dr. Goodwin, and Tom Smith shot at a burglar, and hit a civil lamp and another fellow.

Dingo he did it himself while full, and John Nolte ended there is the Even Club, and Joe Hawkeford again, and Miss Payne gives slewanway the band, and Jones has got ... about it, and nobody can see the joke, and Jeff Randolph is well, and Oscar Smith has joined the club and going straight to well, and Scuddy is an old maid, and God, who an old man, and I don't know nothing due to write, and thus in according to the decision of a fool going to Glory fully.

W.P.

93

CLYDE FITCH

"Barbara Freitchie   The Frederick Girl   a comedy in Four Acts by Clyde Fitch." Autograph manuscript signed and inscribed "Virginia Gerson from Clyde Fitch. 1899." 170 p. 21.5 cm. Red cloth.

Playwright (b. Elmira, N.Y. 1865; d. Châlons-sur-Marne, France 1909). Author of over 50 plays, of which the best-known are *Beau Brummell* (1890), written for Richard Mansfield; *Barbara Frietchie* (1899); *Captain Jinks of the Horse Marines* (1901), in which Ethel Barrymore first appeared as a star; *The Truth* (1907); and *The City* (1909).

Barbara Frietchie (Fitch spelt the surname in several different ways) was first produced in New York in 1899 with Julia Marlowe in the title role. She was unlike the lady of fourscore years and ten in Whittier's poem which inspired this drama, and played the role as a youthful heroine. But in the manuscript page reproduced here Stonewall Jackson speaks Whittier's description "yon gray head." Fitch wrote that he "endeavored merely to picture in an imaginary story some of the spirit and atmosphere of a certain period of our history, using the personality of 'Barbara Frietchie' as best lending itself" to his purpose. The manuscript is written in both ink and pencil, often in apparent haste, and has many corrections and additions. Fitch was a friend and neighbor of the Morgan family and in 1922 Virginia Gerson, who designed the costumes for *Barbara Frietchie*, gave this manuscript to J. P. Morgan for his library, so that a play by Fitch might be "in that rare company." Miss Gerson was also an artist, author and Fitch's friend and biographer. Fitch was one of the first American playwrights to publish his plays with some regularity, although a few remain unpublished; *Barbara Frietchie* was published in 1900. The success of the drama evoked a Weber and Fields parody entitled *Barbara Fidgetty*. Amherst College Library has the largest collection of Fitch manuscripts and letters.

Barbara Freitchie   The Frederick Girl   a comedy in Four Acts by Clyde Fitch / Virginia Gerson from Clyde Fitch. 1899. [...]

[Barbara] leans over picks up the flag, & waves it singing "My Country 'tis of Thee!" (in the same key as they are singing Dixie)

STONEWALL JACKSON *Halt! Who touches a hair of that yon [?] gray head, dies like like a dog! March on.*

The soldiers start marching at once, & singing at the same time. The people half of them singing with the soldiers, & half yelling at Barbara; who has continued singing in an exalted frenzy

Barbara Frietchie
The Frederick Girl
a comedy in Four Acts
by
Clyde Fitch

94

FINLEY PETER DUNNE

Autograph letter signed, dated "Chicago Journal" Dec 12 1898,
addressed to [John Kendrick] Bangs. 2 p. 21.5 cm.

Journalist, humorist and political commentator (b. Chicago, Ill. 1867; d. New York City 1936). He is best known for his series of books in which Mr. Dooley, the Irish saloon keeper on Archey Road, of undiminished brogue, criticizes current events, the social scene and political leaders. The first of these was *Mr. Dooley in Peace and in War* (1898) and the last *Mr. Dooley on Making a Will* (1919). His books had a great popular success and his work was admired by such intellectual figures as Henry Adams and Henry James. In one of his articles he wrote, "Pierpont Morgan calls in wan iv his office boys, th' prisidint iv a national bank, an' says he, 'James,' he says, 'take some change out iv th' damper an' r-run out an' buy Europe f'r me,' he says. 'I intind to re-organize it an' put it on a paying basis,' he says."

Dunne was the son of an Irish carpenter and, after graduating from high school, went into newspaper work. He began writing a column quoting the opinions of a fictional Irish saloon keeper, Colonel McNeery, in 1892. The next year McNeery underwent a change of name to Martin Dooley, and over the next years Dunne's mouthpiece, Mr. Dooley, became a national figure—and America's favorite political analyst. John Kendrick Bangs, to whom this letter of Dunne's is written, was editor of the humor departments of *Harper's Magazine* and *Harper's Bazaar*; he published many volumes of humorous pieces, the best-known being *A Houseboat on the Styx*. Not many letters and manuscripts of Dunne appear to have survived and these are distributed in a number of libraries.

From the collection of Mr. C. Waller Barrett at the Alderman Library, University of Virginia, Charlottesville, Virginia.

Dec 12 1898   Dear Mr Bangs: Mr Small sends me your letter & I beg to thank you for your interest in my work. My friends on the newspaper have been zealous in shipping my incog. so you need not hesitate on that account. But I am afraid I can't promise anything for the Drawer at present. Running a newspaper & trying to feed copy to a hungry syndicate leave me very little time for other work & that is taken up with a cloud of letters that would make Rush Ashmore dizzy. As the author of a really popular book you may have some notion of what happens in this respect to the author of even a mildly popular one.

At the same time I appreciate it as a very high honor to be asked to write for the Drawer under your direction & to assure you that if I do anything—of Dooley—outside the stories I have already agreed to write it will be for you. Sincerely   F. P. Dunne

CHICAGO JOURNAL

1878

Dec 12

Dear Mr Banks: Mr Small handed me your letter & I beg to thank you for your interest in my work. My friends on the newspaper have been jealous in slipping my income so you need not hesitate on that account. But I am afraid I can't promise anything for the drama at present. Running a newspaper & trying to feed a hungry syndicate leaves me very little time for other work that is to say with a closed letter that would make Ruth behave the 557, & at the author for Ralf

popular work you may have some notion of what happen in this respect to the author. Given a weekly popular one felt the same time lappreciate it in every high hour to be asked to write for the drama under your direction & assume you that if I do anything of sorts — consider the stories I have already agreed to write it will be for you.

Sincerely,
F. P. Dunne

95

EDWIN ARLINGTON ROBINSON

*Autograph letter signed, dated Cambridge [Mass.] 30 August, 1899,
addressed to James Barstow. 4 p. 17.5 cm.*

Poet (b. Head Tide, Me. 1869; d. New York City 1935). His poetry includes *The Torrent
and the Night Before* (1896); *Children of the Night* (1897), with some poems from his
earlier volume and some of his best such as "Luke Havergal" and "Richard Corey"; *Captain Craig* (1902); *The Man Against the Sky* (1916); *Lancelot* (1920); *Tristram* (1927),
which finally brought Robinson some fame and financial independence; *Cavender's
House* (1929); and *Talifer* (1933). Robinson's early years were a struggle against restlessness, loneliness, and financial insecurity. About 1905, President Theodore Roosevelt
took an interest in his work and secured him a post as an inspector in the New York subway, then in the course of construction.

This letter to his boyhood friend, James Barstow, literary editor of the Kansas City
Star, was written from Cambridge, Mass., where Robinson was employed as a clerk about
six weeks before he left for New York. Robinson had been offered this same post on the
Star but turned it down. Barstow was a great admirer of Robinson's poems and reprinted
six of them in the newspaper. There are important collections of Robinson's manuscripts
and letters in the Colby College Library, Harvard University Library and The New
York Public Library.

---

*1716 Cambridge Street—Cambridge, 30 August, 1899 My
dear James—I have changed my roost as, you will see, or
have seen, and am once more in my old house—where I
lived when a victim of German B and French Ia. Chug
has gone to Camp where I trust he is making himself indispensable and generally agreeable. I am not there this
year, having too much to do and too many things to think
of.—I received a copy of The* Star *containing [one of my
specimens of transcendent poesy....]*

*[Write once in a] while and tell me how your new geographical shirt fits your delicate Eastern torso. You never
say anything about Kansas City except an occasional vague
word on the subject of beer.*

*For me, in my present condition, I find Cambridge an
excellent summer resort. Sincerely yours   E. A. Robinson*

whole and tell me how your new geographical
shirt fits your delicate Eastern torso. You
never say anything about Kansas City except an
occasional vague word on the subject of beer.

Find me, in my present condition, — I find
Cambridge an excellent summer resort —

Sincerely yours
E. Ash Palmer

17/8 Cambridge Street —
Cambridge, 20 August 1895

My dear James —

I have changed my mode
of your while life, a London, and
have now run in my old haunts — where
I lived with a review of German
Bass Punch &c. — Along Las
you to change when I wish —
he is very happily independent
and friendly agreeable. I am not
there this September, but my to visit
to do and to my things to
thunder City. — I remind a
copy of the Stein contain

96

FRANK NORRIS / HAMLIN GARLAND

"Blix." New York, Doubleday & McClure, 1899. Presentation copy with inscription from the author, Frank Norris, to Hamlin Garland, probably written in 1900, and Garland's autograph account of the circumstances of the presentation, written in the same volume.

Norris was a novelist and journalist (b. Chicago, Ill. 1870; d. San Francisco, Calif. 1902). His novels include *Moran of the Lady Letty* (1898), *McTeague* and *Blix* (both 1899), *The Octopus* (1901) and *The Pit* (1903).

Norris studied art in Paris but soon became aware of his commitment to literature, and returned to take courses at the University of California and at Harvard. As a journalist he visited Africa and covered the Santiago campaign for *McClure's Magazine*. On his return from Cuba he finished and published *McTeague*, a realistic romance influenced by Zola which is his strongest work. *Blix* is based on his courtship and his struggle for literary recognition. His most ambitious work (unfinished at his death) was to have been a trilogy on wheat which began with *The Octopus*, a California novel on the growing of wheat, continued with *The Pit*, a Chicago tale of the wheat in commerce, and was to have ended with "The Wolf," about wheat consumed in a famished old-world village. There is no large collection of Norris letters and manuscripts but some are in the Alderman Library, University of Virginia.

Hamlin Garland was a short-story writer and novelist (b. West Salem, Wis. 1860; d. West Salem, Wis. 1940). His books include *Main-Travelled Roads* (1891), *A Member of the Third House* (1892), *Jason Edwards* (1892), *Rose of Dutcher's Coolly* (1895), *The Captain of the Gray-Horse Troop* (1902), *A Son of the Middle Border* (1917) and *A Daughter of the Middle Border* (1921).

Garland's literary position as a chronicler of the Middle Border and a pioneer in realism have earned him a high place among American authors, even though his books have more power than polish. After an unhappy childhood during which his parents wandered through the Midwest, Garland studied and taught oratory in Boston and made the acquaintance of many prominent men of the time. He returned to the West in 1887 and produced books that were a record of a bygone era, had the spark of life and crusaded for social justice. Large numbers of Garland's papers are in the University of Southern California Library.

To Mr. Hamlin Garland. Very Sincerely   Frank Norris

One day as I went into the office of Doubleday Page and Co I saw Frank Norris sitting at a desk bent over some M.S. I knew him but slightly had met him once or twice but I had just read "McTeague" and was powerfully moved by it. This must have been about New Years 1900. As I was about to pass Norris I stopped and shook hands and asked him for an autograph in "Blix." There was only the "Sample Copy" in the house and so he wrenched it from the shelf and put his name in it. This was the beginning of our more intimate acquaintance.

Hamlin Garland

BLIX

To Mr. Hamlin Garland.

Very Sincerely

Frank Norris

One day as I went into the
office of Doubleday Page and Co
I saw Frank Norris selling a
dull book over some MS. I knew
him and slightly knew the
one or two books that had put him
"Me Teague" and was consequently
mystified. He was then his own
about his own 1900. As I was
about to pass him I stopped
and shook hands and asked him
for an autograph in "Blix". This
was only his "sample copy." He
then asked to be introduced from
his shelf and put his name in it.
This was the beginning of our more
intimate acquaintance.

Hamlin Garland

97

STEPHEN CRANE

"The Red Badge of Courage. An Episode of the American Civil War.
By Stephen Crane." Autograph manuscript signed [n.p., c. 1893–94].
176 p., written on paper of various sizes.

Novelist, short-story writer, poet and war correspondent (b. Newark, N.J. 1871; d. Baden-weiler, Germany 1900). His books include *Maggie: A Girl of the Streets* (1893); *The Black Riders* (1895), poems, partly epigrammatic, which had an influence on the early imagist anthologies; *The Red Badge of Courage* (1895); *The Little Regiment* (1896); *The Open Boat* (1898), one of his finest short stories; *Active Service* (1899), a novel of the Greco-Turkish War on which he and Cora Taylor reported for the New York *Journal; War is Kind* (1899), his second volume of poetry; *The Monster* (1899); and *Wounds in the Rain* (1900), memories of the Spanish-American War.

Crane grew up in an atmosphere of Methodism and journalism in both of which his family was active. He rebelled against Methodism but took to writing and to the experience of life with such frenzy that it eventually cost him his health and wasted his undoubted genius. He died in his twenty-ninth year but he left behind him a body of work that assures him a permanent place in American literature. *The Red Badge of Courage* is Crane's greatest work. It first appeared in the Philadelphia *Press* in December 1894, in a shortened and syndicated version that was repeated in many newspapers; the first book and complete edition was published in 1895. The novel is a psychological study of a soldier under stress during a crucial battle of the Civil War and the conversion of his character from cowardice to heroism. The first page of the autograph manuscript is reproduced. Crane letters and manuscripts can be studied in Columbia University Library and the Alderman Library, University of Virginia.

From the collection of Mr. C. Waller Barrett at the Alderman Library, University of Virginia, Charlottesville, Virginia.

The Red Badge of Courage.

An Episode of the American Civil War.

By Stephen Crane.

The cold passed reluctantly from the earth and the retiring fogs revealed an army streched out on the hills, resting. As the landscape changed from brown to green the army awakened and began to tremble with eagerness at the noise of rumors. It cast its eyes upon the roads which were growing from long [deletion] troughs of liquid mud to proper thoroughfares. A river, amber-tinted in the shadow of its banks, purled at the army's feet and at night when the stream had become of a sorrowful blackness one could see, across, the red eye-like gleam of hostile camp-fires set in the low brows of distant hills.

Once, Jim Conklin a certain tall soldier developed virtues and went resolutely to wash a shirt. He came flying back from a brook waving his garment, banner-like. He was swelled with a tale he had heard from a reliable friend who had heard it from a reliable truthful cavalryman who had heard it from his trust-worthy brother, one of the orderlies at division head-quarters. Conklin He adopted the important air of a herald in red and gold.

"We're goin' t' move t'morrah—sure," he said.

The Red Badge of Courage.
An Episode of the American Civil War.
By Stephen Crane.

The cold passed reluctantly from the earth and
the retiring fogs, revealed an army stretched out on the hills,
resting. As the landscape changed from brown to
green the army awakened and began to tremble
with eagerness at the noise of rumors. It cast
its eyes upon the roads which were growing
from long ~~adult~~ troughs of liquid mud to
proper thoroughfares. A river, amber-tinted in
the shadow of its banks, purled at the army's
feet and at night when the stream had become
of a sorrowful blackness one could see across,
the red eye-like gleam of hostile camp-fires
set in the low brows of distant hills.

Once, ~~Jim Conklin~~ a certain soldier developed virtues and
went resolutely to wash a shirt. He came fly-
ing back from a brook waving his garment, banner-like. He was swelled with a tale he had
heard from a reliable friend who had heard it
from a ~~reliable~~ truthful cavalryman who had heard
it from his trust-worthy brother, one of the orderlies
at division head-quarters. ~~He~~ He adopted the important air of a herald in red and gold.

"We're goin' t' move t'morrah—sure," he said

98

PAUL LAURENCE DUNBAR

Autograph letter signed, dated Library of Congress, Washington, D.C. 2/17/98, addressed to Mrs. A. S. Lanahan. 4 p. 23 cm.

Poet (b. Dayton, Ohio 1872; d. Dayton, Ohio 1906). His books of poems include *Lyrics of Lowly Life* (1896), with an introduction by William Dean Howells; *Lyrics of the Hearth-side* (1899); *Lyrics of Love and Laughter* (1903) and *Lyrics of Sunshine and Shadow* (1905). Dunbar was the first black to write in Negro dialect, which had previously been used by a variety of white Southern writers; although he was not from the deep South, he excelled them all in the use of language.

Dunbar was the son of ex-slaves; his father escaped from a plantation in Kentucky, and served in the Civil War with the 55th Massachusetts Infantry. On graduating from high school (where he was the only black student) Dunbar took a job as an elevator operator. He wrote occasional poems for newspapers and, in 1893, printed a book of poems, *Oak and Ivy*, at his own expense. His second book, *Majors and Minors* (1895), was partly paid for by friends. It came to the attention, a year later, of William Dean Howells, who gave it an enthusiastic review in *Harper's Weekly*. This brought Dunbar to national attention and Howells wrote an introduction for his next and best-known book, *Lyrics of Lowly Life*. Dunbar traveled to England on a lecture tour, married and worked for 15 months as an assistant in the Library of Congress, on whose stationery he wrote this letter to a Mrs. Lanahan who had asked for information about the poet. She received in return a fine biographical account, of which pages one and four are reproduced here. Dunbar wrote prolifically, both poetry and some unsuccessful novels, despite progressively worsening health, and died while still a young man. The most important Dunbar collection is in the Ohio Historical Collection.

From the collection of Mr. C. Waller Barrett at the Alderman Library, University of Virginia, Charlottesville, Virginia.

Washington—D.C. 2/17/98 Mrs. A. S. Lanahan, Dear Madam:—Your favor of recent date is at hand. In answer I must say that my life has been so uneventful that there is little in it to interest anyone.

I was born at Dayton, Ohio twenty-five years ago. Attended the common school there and was graduated from the high school. This constituted my "education."

My parents and grand parents had been slaves in Kentucky. My great grand parents on the eastern shore of Maryland.

I began writing early, when about 12, but published nothing until I was fourteen. Then the fever took me, and I wrote ream upon [ream of positive trash when I should have been studying Euclid....]

I continued reading, published Lyrics of Lowly Life, went to England where in spite of the opposition which British sentiment offered to my having a woman-manager, I had a most enjoyable time. There my book was handsomely republished. and there [deletion] in the heart of a typical English home among the hills of Somerset, I finished my novel "The Uncalled" which is to appear in the May Lippincott's. A book of short stories mostly of Kentucky life will also appear in March.

I have tried to be as full as possible without being prolix.

Thanking you for your interest, I am Sincerely Yours Paul Laurence Dunbar.

Washington D.C. 2/7/98

Mrs. A. S. Lanehaus

Dear Madame:—

Your favor of recent date is at hand. In answer I must say that my life has been so uneventful that there is little in it to interest anyone. I was born at Dayton, this twenty-five years ago. My parents were at the common schools and now hardihood firms the light school. This consisted of my parents and of several slaves of Maryland. I began writing early, when about '12, but published nothing until I was fourteen. Then the first poem left me, and I wrote soon after

that his contributin was a copy. I enclosed reading, published Lyric of Lowly Life, sent to England. Other in spite of the offering, which British reviewed offered to buy, should a ... copyright laws. There are not then now the best of a special English home among the titles of Lowrie't, 9 friends. "The macaroni" is my novel. The which is to appear in the ... supplement. A book of that stories recently of Kentucky life will also appear in march. I have tried to be as frank as I could in what relates being highly.

Thanking you for your interest, I am, sincerely yours,

Paul Laurence Dunbar

Complete Checklist

of American Literary Autographs in The Pierpont Morgan Library

In citing authors' names, parentheses are used to supply (1) maiden names of married women, even when these names were an integral part of their normal bylines—*example:* Howe, Julia (Ward); (2) pseudonyms, which are also placed within quotation marks—*example:* Browne, Charles Farrar ("Artemus Ward"); (3) variant forms of names actually used in bylines—*example:* Stockton, Francis (Frank); and (4) original foreign forms of names—*example:* Follen, Charles (Karl). Square brackets are used to enclose names or parts of names not regularly used by the authors in their bylines—*examples:* Alcott, [Amos] Bronson; White, E[lwyn] B[rooks].

The following bibliographical abbreviations are used here and in the main part of the book: Acs (autograph card signed), Ad (autograph document), Ads (autograph document signed), Al (autograph letter), Als (autograph letter signed), An (autograph note), Cs (card signed), Ds (document signed), Ls (letter signed), n.d. (no date), n.p. (no place), p. (page/pages), Tls (typed letter signed), v. (volumes). The numbers in parentheses refer to the total number of items immediately preceding; these numbers are followed by the range of dates of the items.

ABBOTT, JACOB, 1803–1879. "Report on Story Book Engravings," 1 p.; Als (38) 1851–1856 and n.d., including 37 to Harper & Bros.

ADAMS, ABIGAIL (SMITH), 1744–1818. Als (6) 1784–1816.

ADAMS, BROOKS, 1848–1927. Als 28 May 1896 to Worthington C. Ford.

ADAMS, CHARLES FRANCIS, 1835–1915. Als 28 April 1879 to David A. Wells.

ADAMS, HENRY, 1838–1918. Als 24 October 1887 to Paul L. Ford.

ADAMS, JOHN, 1735–1826. Als, Al, Ls, Ds (26) 1767–1822.

ADAMS, JOHN QUINCY, 1767–1848. "A Plague in the Forest. A Fable," 4 p.; verses by Gray and Young, 2 p.; Als, Ls, Ds (25) 1796–1842 including 9 to Lafayette.

ADAMS, SAMUEL, 1722–1803. Als, Ds (11) 1772–1794.

ADAMS, WILLIAM TAYLOR ("OLIVER OPTIC"), 1822–1897. *Richard Humble* (fragment), 1 p.

AGASSIZ, JEAN LOUIS [RODOLPHE], 1807–1873. Als (2) 1849 and n.d. including 1 to H. D. Thoreau.

ALCOTT, [AMOS] BRONSON, 1799–1888. Als (3) 1863–1874.

ALCOTT, LOUISA MAY, 1832–1888. *Jack and Jill* (fragment), 1 p.; "My Kingdom," 2 p.; Als (3) 1862, 1864 and n.d.

ALDEN, HENRY MILLS, 1836–1919. Als, Tls (10) 1873–1906 including 5 to Harper & Bros.

ALDRICH, THOMAS BAILEY, 1836–1907. "Among the Studios," 16 p.; "The Ballad of Babie Bell," 7 p.; "Castles," 3 p. (Fields Album); "Destiny," 1 p.; "Identity," 1 p. (Fields Album); "Kismet," 1 p.; "My Cousin the Colonel" (fragment), 2 p.; "Nourmandee," 13 p.; "The Parcae," 1 p.; "The Song in Wyndham Towers," 1 p.; "With Men like Lowell," 3 p. (Lowell Album); *Wyndham Towers,* 75 p.; Als (3) 1874–1889.

ALGER, HORATIO, 1834–1899. "How Johnny bought a Sewing-Machine," 14 p.; Als 21 November 1879 to Robert Bonner.

ALLEN, ETHAN, 1738–1789. Als 28 December 1778 to Watson & Goodwin.

ALLEN, JAMES LANE, 1849–1925. Autograph appreciation of J. R. Lowell, 2 p. (Lowell Album); Als 25 November 1905 to W. W. Baldwin.

ALLEN, PAUL, 1775–1826. Als (3) 1806–1813 to Henry Wheaton.

ALLIBONE, SAMUEL AUSTIN, 1816–1889. Als (2) 1860, 1871.

ALLSTON, WASHINGTON, 1779–1843. Als (2) 1834, 1841.

AMES, FISHER, 1758–1808. Als (2) 1791, 1792.

ANTIN, MARY, 1881–1949. Als 28 March 1922.

APPLETON, THOMAS GOLD, 1812–1884. Als (2) to William Wetmore Story.

ARTHUR, TIMOTHY SHAY, 1809–1885. Als 13 November 1855.

AUCHINCLOSS, LOUIS STANTON, 1917– . *Richelieu* (autograph manuscript and corrected typescript), 307 p.

AUDEN, W[YSTAN] H[UGH], 1907–1973. Review of Hindemith's *A Composer's World,* 5 p.

AUDUBON, JOHN JAMES, 1785–1851. Als (21) 1828–1846 including 9 to Mr. and Mrs. Benjamin Phillips and 9 to John Adamson (with 16 letters from members of the Audubon family).

AUSTIN, MARY (HUNTER), 1868–1934. Als, Tls (7) 1906–1909 to Harper & Bros.

BALLOU, MATURIN MURRAY, 1820–1895. Als 23 October 1852 to Benjamin Perley Poore.

BANCROFT, AARON, 1755–1839. Als 19 August 1822 to John Pierpont.

BANCROFT, GEORGE, 1800–1891. Als (8) 1823–1862 and n.d.

BANGS, JOHN KENDRICK, 1862–1922. Als (2) 1901.

BARLOW, JOEL, 1754–1812. Als 25 August 1791 to Thomas Jefferson.

BARNUM, PHINEAS TAYLOR, 1810–1891. Als (4) 1858–1875.

BARTRAM, JOHN, 1699–1777. "Life & Character of the Chinese Philosopher Confucius," 4 p.

BEECHER, HENRY WARD, 1813–1887. Als (2) 1884 and n.d.

BELKNAP, JEREMY, 1744–1798. Als 24 July 1788 to Jedidiah Morse.

BELLAMY, EDWARD, 1850–1898. Als 1 June 1884 to his wife.

BENÉT, STEPHEN VINCENT, 1898–1943. Als, Tls (2) 1928 and n.d.

BENJAMIN, PARK, 1809–1864. "To an Old Friend," 3 p.; Als (2) 1854 to Harper & Bros.

BIDDLE, NICHOLAS, 1786–1844. Als (4) 1827–1838.

BIERCE, AMBROSE [GWINNETT], 1842–1914? Als 14 August 1893 to Laurens Maynard.

BIRD, ROBERT MONTGOMERY, 1806–1854. Als (in rhyme) 26 February 1839 to the Wistar Family.

BOK, EDWARD W[ILLIAM], 1863–1930. Als 1912 to Ernest Dressel North.

BOOTH, EDWIN [THOMAS], 1833–1893. Als n.d. to J. E. Millais.

BOTTA, ANNE C[HARLOTTE] (LYNCH), 1815–1891. Als 17 July 1845 to Edgar Allan Poe.

BOUCICAULT, DION L[ARDNER], 1820–1890. Als (3) 1854–1876 to Charles or Mrs. Dickens.

BOWDITCH, NATHANIEL, 1773–1838. Als, Ls (2) 1810, 1837.

BOWDOIN, JAMES, 1726–1790. Als 22 January 1787 to Major General Lincoln.

BOYESEN, HJALMAR HJORTH, 1848–1895. "The Little Chap" (fragment), 1 p.; "To J. R. Lowell," 1 p. (Lowell Album).

BRAINARD, J[OHN] G[ARDINER] C[ALKINS], 1796–1828. "So Science Whispered," 1 p. (Fields Album).

BRIGGS, CHARLES FREDERICK, 1804–1877. Als (2) 1859 and n.d. to Harper & Bros.

BROOKS, CHARLES TIMOTHY, 1813–1883. Als 15 September 1855 to Harper & Bros.

BROOKS, NOAH, 1830–1903. Als 19 April 1883 to Gordon L. Ford.

BROOKS, PHILLIPS, 1835–1893. Als (2) 1884, 1889 to Oliver Wendell Holmes and J. R. Lowell (Lowell Album).

BROUGHAM, JOHN, 1810–1880. Als n.d. to Mr. Jackson.

BROWNE, CHARLES FARRAR ("ARTEMUS WARD"), 1834–1867. Als 11 December 1860.

BROWNE, J[OHN] ROSS, 1821–1875. Als (15) 1852–1869 to Harper & Bros.

BROWNELL, WILLIAM CRARY, 1851–1928. *French Art* (chapter I), 29 p.

BROWNSON, ORESTES AUGUSTUS, 1803–1876. Als (2) 1842 and n.d. including 1 to H. D. Thoreau.

BRYAN, WILLIAM JENNINGS, 1860–1925. Autograph testimonial, 1 p.

BRYANT, WILLIAM CULLEN, 1794–1878. "Death of the Flowers," 2 p., with a note by N. P. Willis; "Iliad Book 8ᵗʰ near the conclusion" (translation), 1 p.; "Innocent Girl and Snow-White Flower," 1 p.; "Oh, God! whose dread and dazzling brow," 1 p.; "Monument Mountain," 4 p.; "Painted Cup," 1 p.; "Robert of Lincoln," 3 p.; "Thanatopsis," 2 p. (Fields Album); "These struggling tides of life," 1 p.; "To a Waterfowl," 2 p.; "When he, who, from the scourge of wrong," 1 p.; *Letters of a Traveller*, Series II, nos. 21–24 (Dec. 1857–July 1858), 31 p.; "Old New York," (intro. to a volume of etchings by Eliza Greatorex), 2 p.; Als (12) 1820–1874.

BUNNER, H[ENRY] C[UYLER], 1855–1896. "To a Hyacinth Plucked for Decoration Day," 1 p.

BURNETT, FRANCES (HODGSON), 1849–1924. "Statue," 1 p.

BURRITT, ELIHU, 1810–1879. Als (4) 1843–1873.

BURROUGHS, JOHN, 1837–1921. "Recent Phases of Literary Criticism," 62 p.; "The Return," 1 p.; *Whitman*, 400 p.; "Waiting," 1 p. (Fields Album).

BURTON, WILLIAM EVANS, 1804–1860. Als (3) 1839–1848.

BUSHNELL, HORACE, 1802–1876. Als 5 September 1851 to John Pierpont.

CABLE, GEORGE WASHINGTON, 1844–1925. Greeting to J. R. Lowell, 1 p. (Lowell Album); Als 4 August 1901 to Small, Maynard & Co.

CALHOUN, JOHN C[ALDWELL], 1782–1850. Als (26) 1816–1846 including 17 to Henry Wheaton.

CAREY, HENRY CHARLES, 1793–1879. Als (3) 1847–1853 and n.d.

CAREY, MATHEW, 1760–1839. Als 24 April 1829 to John Griscom.

CARLETON, WILL[IAM McKENDREE], 1845–1912. "The Funeral" (fragment), 1 p.; Als 4 March 1887 to Harper & Bros.

CARMAN, [WILLIAM] BLISS, 1861–1929. Als (7) 1895–1905 and n.d. to Laurens Maynard.

CARRYL, GUY WETMORE, 1873–1904. Als, Tls, (3) 1899, 1901 to Harper & Bros.

CARY, ALICE, 1820–1871. Als 15 September 1868 to Horace Greeley.

CARY, PHOEBE, 1824–1871. "Whittier," 1 p.; Als (2) 1868 and n.d.

CATHER, WILLA [SIBERT], 1876–1947. Als, Tls, Acs, telegrams (131) 1906–1946 including 75 to Elizabeth Shepley Sergeant, 32 to Mr. or Mrs. George Whicher, 10 to Elizabeth Moorhead Vermorcken, 4 to Laura Coombs Hills and 4 to Edward Wagenknecht.

CAWEIN, MADISON [JULIUS], 1865–1914. "The Vikings," 4 p.; Als 29 November 1914 to Belle da Costa Greene.

CHANNING, WILLIAM ELLERY, 1780–1842. "Discourse on Christianity, a Rational Religion," 106 p.; *Duty of the Free States*, parts I and II, 300 p.; Als (31) 1802–1841 and n.d. including 23 to his relatives.

CHANNING, WILLIAM ELLERY, 1818–1901. "Concord Walks" (pencil drafts), 83 p.; "Morrice Lake," 3 p. (Fields Album); notebook containing transcriptions from journals of Thoreau and Emerson, with poetry and miscellaneous notes, 240 p.; Als, Al (3) 1850 and n.d.

CHANNING, WILLIAM HENRY, 1810–1884. Als 7 August 1869 to Horace Greeley.

CHASE, MARY ELLEN, 1887–1973. Als 1 March 1948 to Elizabeth M. Dodd.

CHILD, LYDIA MARIA (FRANCIS), 1802–1880. Als (5)

1842–1844 including 4 to John Pierpont.

CLAPP, HENRY, 1814–1875. Als 27 April 1846 to John Pierpont.

CLARK, LEWIS GAYLORD, 1808–1873. Als (11) 1855–1856 to Harper & Bros.

CLARKE, JAMES FREEMAN, 1810–1888. Als, Acs (2) 1846, 1866.

CLAY, CASSIUS MARCELLUS, 1810–1903. Als (2) 1846, 1884.

CLEMENS, SAMUEL LANGHORNE ("MARK TWAIN"), 1835–1910. "Autobiography" (written in 1872 or 1873 for Charles Dudley Warner), 11 p.; "The Back Number: a monthly magazine" (prospectus for a magazine), 5 p.; *A Double-barrelled Detective Story*, 154 p.; *Life on the Mississippi*, 3 v.; *The Man that Corrupted Hadleyburg*, 144 p.; *Pudd'nhead Wilson*, 2 v.; Als, telegram (14) 1892–1909 including 7 to W. W. Baldwin.

COBBETT, WILLIAM, 1763–1835. As (6) 1792–1832.

COFFIN, CHARLES CARLETON, 1823–1896. "Abraham Lincoln's Early Years" (fragment), 1 p.; Als 26 June 1892 to Harper & Bros.

COLDEN, CADWALLADER, 1688–1776. Ds, 1724.

CONE, HELEN GRAY, 1859–1934. "The Gifts of the Oak," 2 p. (Lowell Album).

CONWAY, MONCURE DANIEL, 1832–1907. Als (7) 1858–1907 including 6 to William A. Knight.

COOKE, JOHN ESTEN, 1830–1886. Als (6) 1855–1857, including 5 to Harper & Bros.

COOKE, ROSE (TERRY), 1827–1892. Als 20 April 1872 to Mr. Ward.

COOLIDGE, SUSAN: *see* Woolsey, Sarah Chauncey.

COOPER, JAMES FENIMORE, 1789–1851. *The Deerslayer*, 261 p.; *Satanstoe*, Chapters I–XV, 120 p.; Als (3) 1836–1844.

COOPER, SUSAN FENIMORE, 1813–1894. Als 3 April 1884.

COXE, ARTHUR CLEVELAND, 1818–1896. "Sonnet to John Jay," 1 p.; (Fields Album); Als 8 April 1863 to A. James Faust.

CRANE, STEPHEN, 1871–1900. Als n.d.

CRAWFORD, FRANCIS MARION, 1854–1909. "The Little City of Hope," 68 p.; Als, Tls (3) 1889–1893.

CROCKETT, DAVID (DAVY), 1786–1836. Als 28 November 1833 to Lewis Cass.

CUMMINGS, E[DWARD] E[STLIN], 1894–1962. "the dangerous thing is" (draft with other phrases and notes), 1 p.; album of 46 drawings; Tls, Cs (27) 1940–1963 including 26 to Mrs. Henry T. Curtiss.

CURTIS, GEORGE TICKNOR, 1812–1894. Als (21) 1854–1892 including 17 to Harper & Bros.

CURTIS, GEORGE WILLIAM, 1824–1892. "Family Portraits," 24 p.; "Fashion," 26 p.; "From the Summer Diary of Minerva Tattle," 45 p. (*The Potiphar Papers*, chapter 4); "Introductory," 7 p.; "Music," 13 p.; "Music," 11 p.; "Newport in Winter," 36 p.; Notes on the Egyptian Museum of Doctor Henry Abbott, 4 p.; "An Observation," 4 p.; "Our new Livery, & other things," 44 p. (*The Potiphar Papers*, chapter 2); "A Spring Song," 1 p.; "A Swiss Journal: The Town of Basle," 11 p.; Als (5) 1856–1873.

CUSTIS, GEORGE WASHINGTON PARKE, 1781–1857. Als 22 January 1810 to Col. E. Deneale.

DALY, AUGUSTIN, 1838–1899. Als 11 December 1882 to Mr. Bouton.

DANA, RICHARD HENRY, 1787–1879. "Song—I Saw Her Once," 1 p. (Fields Album); "Sonnet—To a Garden-Flower," 1 p. (Fields Album); "To Mr. and Mrs. Fields," 2 p. (Fields Album); Als (6) 1851–1879 and n.d. including 4 to members of the Wheaton family.

DANA, RICHARD HENRY, 1815–1882. Als (3) 1848–1865.

D'ARUSMONT, FRANCES (WRIGHT), 1795–1852. Als 11 October 1835.

DAVIDSON, LUCRETIA MARIA, 1808–1825. "No! for soft pity," 1 p. (Fields Album).

DAVIDSON, MARGARET MILLER, 1823–1838. "Oh, many an hour," 1 p. (Fields Album).

DAVIS, REBECCA (HARDING), 1831–1910. Als (2) 1878 to Harper & Bros.

DAVIS, RICHARD HARDING, 1864–1916. "Foreword," 5 p.; Als (2) 1892 to Harper & Bros.

DAWES, RUFUS, 1803–1859. Als 25 June 1858.

DE FOREST, JOHN WILLIAM, 1826–1906. Als 19 August 1890 to E. F. Strickland.

DELAND, MARGARET[TA WADE (CAMPBELL)], 1857–1945. Als n.d.

DICKINSON, EMILY [ELIZABETH], 1830–1886. "Distance ——is not the realm of fox," 1 p.; "The sun kept stooping—stooping—low," 1 p.; "Two—were immortal—twice," 1 p.; Als (2) c. 1873, c. 1883.

DICKINSON, JOHN, 1732–1808. Als, An, Ds (9) 1766–1803.

DODGE, MARY [ELIZABETH] (MAPES), 1831–1905. Appreciation of J. R. Lowell, 1 p. (Lowell Album); *Hans Brinker* (fragment), 1 p.; unidentified fragment, 1 p.

DONNELLY, IGNATIUS, 1831–1901. Als (2) 1864, 1865.

DORR, JULIA C[AROLINE] (R[IPLEY]), 1825–1913. Als 2 August 1896 to C. E. Hurd.

DOUGLASS, FREDERICK, 1817–1895. Als (5) 1869–1885 and n.d.

DRAKE, JOSEPH RODMAN, 1795–1820. "To fortune," 1 p. (Fields Album).

DRAPER, JOHN WILLIAM, 1811–1882. Als 15 August 1855 to Harper & Bros.

DREISER, THEODORE, 1871–1945. Als, Tls (8) 1921–1945 including 7 to Margaret Carson.

DUGANNE, AUGUSTINE JOSEPH HICKEY, 1823–1884. Als 29 May 1855 to George Palmer Putnam.

DUNNE, FINLEY PETER, 1867–1936. Als, Tls (2) 1893, 1900.

DU PONCEAU, PETER STEPHEN (PIERRE ETIENNE), 1760–1844. Als (10) 1816–1833 including 7 to Henry Wheaton.

DUPUY, ELIZA ANN, 1814–1881. Als 10 September 1855 to Harper & Bros.

DUYCKINCK, EVERT AUGUSTUS, 1816–1878. Als (3) 1851–1857 including 2 to Harper & Bros.

DWIGHT, THEODORE, 1764–1846. Als (3) 1807 and n.d.

DWIGHT, TIMOTHY, 1752–1817. Als 6 May 1784 to Noah Webster.

DWIGHT, TIMOTHY, 1828–1916. Als (3) 1887.

EBERHART, RICHARD, 1904– . "Baudelaire," 1 p.

EDWARDS, JONATHAN, 1703–1758. Als 6 August 1753 to Joseph Bellamy.

EGGLESTON, EDWARD, 1837–1902. Appreciation of J. R. Lowell, 1 p. (Lowell Album).

ELIOT, JOHN, 1604–1690. Ds (2) 1624, 1655.

ELIOT, T[HOMAS] S[TEARNS], 1888–1965. "Defense of the Islands," 1 p.; Als, Tls (22) 1928–1948, including 21 to E. McKnight Kauffer.

ELLET, ELIZABETH FRIES (LUMMIS), 1818–1877. Als (3) n.d.

ELLIS, EDWARD SYLVESTER, 1840–1916. Tls 23 February

1899 to Helen F. Levy.

EMERSON, RALPH WALDO, 1803–1882. "Behavior" (from *Conduct of Life*), 119 p.; "Considerations by the way" (from *Conduct of Life*), 141 p.; "Eloquence," 122 p.; "Progress of Culture," 10 p.; "Remarks at Kansas Relief Meeting," 39 p.; transcripts of speeches delivered, poems read, etc. at John Brown Memorial Meetings at Salem and Concord, 1859–1860, copies in the hands of Thoreau, Emerson, F. B. Sanborn, and others, 125 p.; "Days," 1 p. (Fields Album); "Ever the poet from the land," 1 p.; "Hymn sung at the completion of the Concord Monument," 1 p.; "The Titmouse," 6 p.; "Unbar the door since thou the opener art" (from the *Rubáiyát*), 2 p.; copy of the first portion of Chaucer's "The Doctor's Tale," 1 p.; Als (19) 1838–1876 and n.d. including 6 to or about H. D. Thoreau.

ENGLISH, THOMAS DUNN, 1819–1902. "The Beggar's World," 4 p.; "Ben Bolt," "Hurrah for You, Old Glory" and "Ruins," together 10 p.

EVERETT, ALEXANDER HILL, 1790–1847. Als (3) 1831–1841.

EVERETT, EDWARD, 1794–1865. Als (56) 1821–1862, including 30 to Henry Wheaton.

FAY, THEODORE SEDGWICK, 1807–1898. Als (21) 1832–1852 including 18 to Henry Wheaton or his wife.

FESSENDEN, THOMAS GREEN, 1771–1837. Als 4 November 1810 to Parker Cleveland.

FIELD, EUGENE, 1850–1895. "Casey's Table d'hote," 5 p.; "The Christmas Stocking," 1 p.; "Doctors," 7 p.; "Modjesky as Cameel," 10 p.; "When I was broke in London in the fall of '89," 4 p.

FIELDS, ANNIE (ADAMS), 1834–1915. Als, Acs, telegram (11) 1892–1908 including 7 to Harper & Bros. and 4 to W. W. Baldwin; album of autograph letters and poems by English and American authors collected by Mrs. Fields (see listings under individual authors).

FIELDS, JAMES T[HOMAS], 1817–1881. "Stanzas" (fragment), 1 p.; Als (6) 1855–1878 including 3 to Harper & Bros.

FISKE, JOHN, 1842–1901. *Destiny of Man Viewed in the Light of his Origin*, 63 p.; *Discovery and Spanish Conquest of America*, 3 v.; *Idea of God*, 80 p.; *Life Everlasting*, 32 p.; *Through Nature to God* ("Mystery of Evil," 35 p.; "Cosmic Roots of Love," 37 p.; "The Everlasting Reality of Religion," 38 p.); Als (2) 1878, 1889.

FITCH, [WILLIAM] CLYDE, 1865–1909. *Barbara Freitchie*, 170 p.

FLINT, TIMOTHY, 1780–1840. Als 20 February 1836 to John Pierpont.

FOLLEN, CHARLES (KARL) [THEODORE CHRISTIAN], 1796–1840. Als (2) 1834, 1839 to John Pierpont.

FORCE, PETER, 1790–1868. Als 25 August 1835 to James Greenleaf.

FORESTER, FRANK: *see* Herbert, Henry William.

FRANKLIN, BENJAMIN, 1706–1790. Notes for his autobiography, 4 p.; minutes of a meeting of the Library Company (fragment), 1 p.; "The Ugly and Handsome Leg," 3 p.; Als (40) 1746–1787, including 15 to William Strahan (with 10 letters from his son William to the same), 11 to Peter Collison and 1 to M. Le Veillard (with 16 letters from William Temple Franklin and 2 from Benjamin Franklin Bache, all addressed to the same).

FREEMAN, DOUGLAS SOUTHALL, 1886–1953. *Lee's Lieutenants* (fragment of chapter 42), 10 p.

FREEMAN, MARY E[LEANOR] (WILKINS), 1852–1930. "A Humble Romance" (fragment), 1 p.; Als, Tls, Acs (13) 1893–1928 including 12 to Harper & Bros.

FRÉMONT, JESSIE (BENTON), 1824–1902. Als (4) 1878 to Harper & Bros.

FRÉMONT, JOHN CHARLES, 1813–1890. Als (8) 1850–1899 and n.d.

FRENCH, ALICE ("OCTAVE THANET"), 1850–1934. Als 30 November 1901 to Small, Maynard & Co.

FROST, ROBERT (LEE), 1874–1963. "To E. T.," 1 p.

FROTHINGHAM, OCTAVIUS BROOKS, 1822–1895. Als 8 August 1883 to J. R. Lowell.

FULLER, [SARAH] MARGARET, MARCHESA OSSOLI, 1810–1850. Als (3) 1850 and n.d. including 1 to H. D. Thoreau.

FURNESS, HORACE HOWARD, 1833–1912. Appreciation of J. R. Lowell, 2 p. (Lowell Album); Als (2) 1889, 1896.

GALLAGHER, WILLIAM DAVIS, 1808–1894. Als 28 July 1840 to Lewis J. Cist.

GALLOWAY, JOSEPH, 1731–1803. Ds 24 July 1774.

GARLAND, HAMLIN, 1860–1940. Als (24) 1897–1910 and n.d.

GARRISON, WILLIAM LLOYD, 1805–1879. "The Free Mind," 1 p.; another copy, 1 p. (Fields Album); Als (3) 1844–1873.

GAYARRÉ, CHARLES ETIENNE ARTHUR, 1805–1895. Als 12 June 1860 to Franklin Bacheller.

GEORGE, HENRY, 1839–1897. Als (2) 1880, 1884 to David A. Wells.

GERSTÄCKER, FRIEDRICH WILHELM CHRISTIAN, 1816–1872. Als 13 March 1855 to Harper & Bros.

GILDER, RICHARD WATSON, 1844–1909. "On seeing the MS of Keats' 'Endymion,'" 1 p.; Appreciation of J. R. Lowell, 1 p. (Lowell Album); Als (3) 1889–1907.

GILLETTE, WILLIAM [HOOKER], 1853–1937. Als, Acs, Tls (16) 1889–1928 including 5 to Harper & Bros.

GILMAN, DANIEL COIT, 1831–1908. Als 20 December 1871 to W. Reich.

GODKIN, EDWIN LAWRENCE, 1831–1902. Als n.d.

GODWIN, PARKE, 1816–1904. Als (6) 1851–1876 including 2 to Harper & Bros.

GOODRICH, SAMUEL GRISWOLD ("PETER PARLEY"), 1793–1860. Als (9) 1847–1854 including 8 to Harper & Bros.

GOULD, HANNAH FLAGG, 1789–1865. "The Dying Revolutionary Soldier," 3 p. (Fields Album).

GREELEY, HORACE, 1811–1872. "The Crystal Palace and its lessons," 9 p.; "Edward Everett," 6 p.; "Recollections of a Busy Life—No. XXXIII. Europe—The World's Exposition," 7 p.; Als, Ads (21) 1848–1872 including 4 to H. D. Thoreau and 1 casting an electoral ballot for Lincoln.

GREENE, GEORGE WASHINGTON, 1811–1883. Als 25 October 1847 to Henry Wheaton.

GREY, ZANE, 1875–1939. "The Rube," 36 p.; Als 14 December [c. 1930] to Harper & Bros.

GRISWOLD, RUFUS WILMOT, 1815–1857. Als (3) 1841–1848.

HALE, EDWARD EVERETT, 1822–1909. Appreciation of J. R. Lowell, 3 p. (Lowell Album); "Of the Chief:—and To Him," 2 p. (O. W. Holmes tribute); "The Old South Meeting House" (fragment), 2 p.; "Ten times one is ten," 1 p.; Als (4) 1872–1902 and n.d.

HALE, SARAH JOSEPHA (BUELL), 1788–1879. Als, Ls (37) 1837–1878 including 33 to Harper & Bros.

HALLECK, FITZ-GREENE, 1790–1867. "Marco Bozzaris," 6 p. (Fields Album); "Twilight," 1 p.; Als (5) 1836–1866.

HALPINE, CHARLES GRAHAM, 1829–1868. Als (4) 1852–

1868 and n.d.

HAMILTON, ALEXANDER, 1757–1804. Als, Ads (9) 1781–1794.

HARBEN, WILL[IAM] N[ATHANIEL], 1858–1919. Als, Tls (4) 1903–1910 to Harper & Bros.

HARLAND, MARION: see Terhune, Mary Virginia (Hawes).

HARPER, FLETCHER, 1806–1877. Ds 1836.

HARPER, JAMES, 1795–1869. Als (2) 1852, 1853.

HARPER, JOSEPH HENRY, 1850–1938. Als 3 April 1900 to G. H. Putnam.

HARRIS, JOEL CHANDLER, 1848–1908. Tls 6 July 1901 to Mr. Stedman.

HARTE, [FRANCIS] BRET[T], 1836–1902. "Boom of the Calaveras Clarion," 14 p.; "Chatelaine of Burnt Ridge," 32 p.; "How Santa Claus came to Simpson's Bar," 44 p.; "Postmistress of Laurel Run," 23 p.; "A Sappho of Green Springs," 60 p.; "A Secret of Telegraph Hill," 39 p.; "Their Uncle from California," 32 p.; "Three Partners," 125 leaves; "Treasure of the Redwoods," 15 p.; review of A. F. Evans' Our Sister Republic, a Gala Trip through Tropical Mexico, 25 p.; "Fate," 1 p.; "A Greyport Legend (1797)," 3 p.; "Legend of Glen Head," 3 p.; "Plain Language from Truthful James (The Heathen Chinee)," 4 p. (Fields Album); tribute to O. W. Holmes, 1 p. (Holmes Album); Als (4) 1879–1884.

HAWTHORNE, JULIAN, 1846–1934. "Garth: a Novel" (fragment of Ch. XXI: Fermentation), 1 p.; diary of 1857–1859, 100 p.; notebook containing materials relating to his father including 14 p. of "Grimshawe Fragments," extracts of letters and 19 p. of "Nathaniel Hawthorne Described by his Son"; notebook containing printed and autograph materials concerning Julian's works including 22 p. of "Perdita" and "Memorandum of letters," 1892, together 170 p.; notes on the MS of Septimius Felton, 1 p.; Als, Tls, Ls (3) 1871–1895.

HAWTHORNE, NATHANIEL, 1804–1864. "The Ancestral Footsteps," 88 p.; The Blithedale Romance, 206 p.; "Civic Banquets," 38 p.; Dr. Grimshawe's Secret (early draft in the hand of his wife), 20 p. with 2 fragments of the final manuscript, 125 p.; Dolliver Romance, chapters II–III, 25 p. with fragment, 2 p.; "Feathertop," 20 p.; Ghost of Dr. Harris, 13 p.; review of Orville Dewey's The Old World and the New, 5 p.; title page and contents to The Scarlet Letter, 2 p.; Septimius Felton (fragments), 20 p. with draft, 57 p., and complete manuscript, 92 p.; Tanglewood Tales for Girls and Boys, 146 p.; "There was an old boy," 1 p.; miscellaneous notes, 6 p.; diary with entries for 1856, 60 p.; journal kept jointly with his wife, 2 v.; notebooks: American, 1835–1853, 4 v.; English, 1853–1858, 7 v., French and Italian, 1858–1862, 5 v.; Als (21) 1819–1862 including 6 to his mother, sisters or wife and 2 to Thoreau (with 16 letters from his wife including 1 to Thoreau and 13 to their daughter Una).

HAY, JOHN [MILTON], 1838–1905. Als (2) 1898, 1905.

HAYNE, PAUL HAMILTON, 1830–1886. Als 24 January 1878 to Harper & Bros.

HEARN, [PATRICIO] LAFCADIO [TESSIMA CARLOS], 1850–1904. "About Faces in Japanese Art," 68 p.; "At Hakata," 31 p.; A Japanese Miscellany, 2 v.; "The New Civilization," 82 p.; "Notes from a travelling-Diary," 76 p.; "Notes of a trip to Izumo," 91 p.; "The Story of Mimo-nashi-Hoïchi," 47 p.; Als (19) 1890–1900 including 4 to Harper & Bros.

HEDGE, FREDERIC [HENRY], 1805–1890. Als (2) 1851 to John Pierpont.

HELPER, HINTON ROWAN, 1829–1909. Als 10 March 1871 to Gen. Carlos Butterfield.

HENRY, O.: see Porter, William Sydney.

HERBERT, HENRY WILLIAM ("FRANK FORESTER"), 1807–1858. Als (2) 1845.

HERNDON, WILLIAM HENRY, 1818–1891. Als 15 December 1869 to Charles H. Hart.

HIGGINSON, THOMAS WENTWORTH, 1823–1911. "Women and Men. Women & Men in Conference" (fragment), 2 p.; Als (5) 1878–1892 including 2 to Harper & Bros.

HILDRETH, RICHARD, 1807–1865. Als (4) 1851–1855 to Harper & Bros.

HOLLAND, JOSIAH GILBERT, 1819–1881. Als (16) 1859–1871.

HOLMES, OLIVER WENDELL, 1809–1894. The Autocrat of the Breakfast-Table, parts IV–XII, 306 p.; "Letter from a Man to a Woman," 3 p.; "Medicine in Boston," 39 p.; tribute to J. R. Lowell, 4 p.; biographical sketch of John L. Motley, 10 p.; speech at the memorial meeting for Bayard Taylor, 2 p.; corrected proofs of an autobiographical sketch, 2 p.; "Avis," 3 p.; "Come to me," 1 p.; "Farewell to Agassiz," 4 p.; "A few can touch the magic string," 1 p.; "In memory of Fitz-Greene Halleck," 2 p.; "Last Leaf," 3 p.; "Lexington," 3 p.; "Lord of the Universe," 1 p.; "My Aviary," 1 p.; 'Old Ironsides," 1 p.; "The Old Man Dreams," 3 p.; "On Lending a Punch-Bowl," 3 p.; "Song of '29," 4 p.; "Sun and Shadow," 1 p.; "Through my North Window," 1 p.; "Toast to Wilkie Collins," 1 p.; "The voice of God is calling," 1 p.; "The Voiceless," 1 p.; lines written for the Brooklyn and Long Island Fair, 1 p.; Als (28) 1856–1893; "Tributes to Oliver Wendell Holmes on his 75th Birthday, forming the Holmes number of The Critic," 1884 (original manuscripts from the contributors).

HOPKINSON, FRANCIS, 1737–1791. Als, Ads (3) 1778–1786.

HOSACK, DAVID, 1769–1835. Als (5) 1824–1830 and n.d. including 3 to William Vaughan.

HOVEY, RICHARD, 1864–1900. "Hanover Winter-Song," 1 p.; autograph notes, 4 p.; Als 22 September 1898.

HOWE, JULIA (WARD), 1819–1910. "Army Hymn [Battle Hymn of the Republic]," 2 p. (Fields Album); Als (3) 1872–1901.

HOWE, SAMUEL GRIDLEY, 1801–1876. Als (4) 1847–1871 including 2 to Horace Mann.

HOWELLS, WILLIAM DEAN, 1837–1920. "A Letter of Introduction. Farce" (fragment), 2 p.; "My Times and Places. An Autobiography," 5 p.; Als (12) 1873–1920 including 4 to Harper & Bros. and 3 to W. W. Baldwin.

HUTTON, LAURENCE, 1843–1904. "Shakespeare's Comedies by E. A. Abbey" (review; fragment), 1 p.; Als (10) 1890–1892 to Harper & Bros.

INGERSOLL, CHARLES JARED, 1782–1862. Als (5) 1816–1844 including 2 to Henry Wheaton.

INGERSOLL, ROBERT G[REEN], 1833–1899. Als 15 October 1877 to Charles Stowe.

INGRAHAM, JOSEPH HOLT, 1809–1860. Als (7) 1857–1858 to Harper & Bros.

IRVING, WASHINGTON, 1783–1859. A Conquest of Granada, 2 v.; Life of George Washington (fragments from v. IV–V), c. 100 p.; last will and testament (copy), 2 p.; Als (13) 1817–1856 and n.d.

IRVING, WILLIAM, 1766–1821. Als (3) 1814 to Henry Wheaton.

JACKSON, HELEN [MARIA (FISKE)] HUNT, 1830–1885. Als 2 April 1884 to Mrs. Quinton.

JAMES, HENRY, 1811–1882. Als (3) 1843 and n.d. including 1 to H. D. Thoreau.

JAMES, HENRY, 1843–1916. The Ambassadors (typewritten

outline), 90 p.; "The Impressions of a Cousin," 116 p.; Als, Ads, Acs, telegrams (78) 1887–1905 and n.d. including 73 to Mr. or Mrs. W. W. Baldwin.

JAMES, WILLIAM, 1842–1910. Als (3) 1903, 1908 and n.d.

JARVES, JAMES JACKSON, 1818–1888. Als (18) 1853–1855 to Harper & Bros.

JEFFERSON, JOSEPH, 1829–1905. Als (4) 1880–1903.

JEFFERSON, THOMAS, 1743–1826. Als, Ls, Ds (50) 1781–1824.

JEWETT, SARAH ORNE, 1849–1909. "The Failure of David Berry" (fragment), 2 p.; Als (10) 1891–1895 and n.d. including 5 to L. Dresel and 3 to W. W. Baldwin.

JOHNSON, OLIVER, 1809–1889. Als 3 August 1882.

JOHNSON, ROBERT UNDERWOOD, 1853–1937. "The Cost," 2 p.; "Rheims," 3 p.; Als, Tls (6) 1892–1923 including 5 to W. W. Baldwin.

JOHNSON, RICHARD MALCOLM, 1822–1898. "Mrs. Gibble Colt's Ducks" (fragment), 1 p.

KEDNEY, JOHN STEINFORT, 1819–1911. Als 16 February 1895 to J. Pierpont Morgan.

KEESE, JOHN, 1805–1856. Als 29 April 1846 to John Pierpont.

KENNEDY, JOHN FITZGERALD, 1917–1963. Tls 1 October 1962 to the Trustees of The Pierpont Morgan Library.

KENNEDY, JOHN PENDLETON, 1795–1870. *Horse-Shoe Robinson* (fragment), 2 p.; Als (3) 1841, 1864 and n.d.

KEY, FRANCIS SCOTT, 1779–1843. Als 3 May 1813 to Henry Thompson.

LA FARGE, JOHN, 1835–1910. Als (2) n.d.

LANIER, SIDNEY, 1842–1881. Als 22 March 1875 to James Maurice Thompson.

LANMAN, CHARLES, 1819–1895. Als (3) 1841–1847.

LARCOM, LUCY, 1824–1893. "By and by," 1 p.; "His song," 2 p. (Lowell Album); Als (3) 1872 and n.d.

LATHROP, GEORGE PARSONS, 1851–1898. "Sunshine of thine eyes," 1 p.

LAZARUS, EMMA, 1849–1887. "Success," 1 p.

LE GALLIENNE, RICHARD, 1866–1947. "Orestes—Act 2," 6 p.; "Three monthly poets," 19 p.; Als (4) 1895–1921.

LEGARÉ, HUGH SWINTON, 1797–1843. Als (12) 1831–1838 and 3 copies of letters to Henry Wheaton.

LEGARÉ, JAMES MATHEWES, 1823–1859. Als (2) 1853–1854 to Harper & Bros.

LELAND, CHARLES GODFREY, 1824–1903. Als, Acs (7) 1889–1898 to W. W. Baldwin.

LESLIE, ELIZA, 1787–1858. Als (2) 1846 to Bayard Taylor.

LESTER, CHARLES EDWARDS, 1815–1890. Als 30 October 1845 to Mr. Gilman.

LEWIS, SINCLAIR, 1885–1951. Tls 8 January 1935 to Prof. E. S. Oliver.

LINCOLN, ABRAHAM, 1809–1865. "The Bear Hunt," 4 p.; notes for political speeches, 3 p.; Als, Ls (12) 1851–1865, Ads, Ad, Ds (20) 1839–1865.

LINDSAY, [NICHOLAS] VACHEL, 1879–1931. "The Trial of the Dead Cleopatra in her Beautiful and Wonderful Tomb" (corrected typescript), 26 p.; Tls 16 February 1925 to John Drinkwater.

LINTON, WILLIAM JAMES, 1812–1897. Als (2) 1846, 1881.

LODGE, HENRY CABOT, 1850–1924. Als (3) 1879, 1905 including 2 to W. W. Baldwin.

LOGAN, JAMES, 1674–1751. Ads, Ds (2) 1703, 1731.

LONGFELLOW, HENRY WADSWORTH, 1807–1882. "Ah, nowhere is the rose so red," 1 p.; "The Arrow and the Song," 1 p.; "The Children's Hour," 4 p.; "The Day is Done," 1 p.; "Ex-

celsior," 4 p. (Fields Album); "Friends, my soul with joy remembers," 1 p.; "Giotto's Tower," 1 p.; "In the Church at Tarrytown," 2 p.; "The Poet and his Songs," 3 p.; "Prometheus and Epimetheus," 10 p.; "Psalms of Life, stanza 7," 1 p.; "Song," 1 p.; translation of Dante's *Inferno* (fragment), Canto III, 1 p.; facetious market quotations, 12 p.; notes for introduction, 1 p.; Als, Ads (80) 1827–1882 including 35 to Helen M. Bean.

LONGFELLOW, SAMUEL, 1819–1892. Als (2) 1857, 1858 to John Pierpont.

LOWELL, AMY, 1874–1925. Tls (9) 1922–1925 to Belle da Costa Greene.

LOWELL, JAMES RUSSELL, 1819–1891. *A Year's Life* (72 poems), 91 p.; "Dirge," 7 p.; "Hakon's Lay," 2 p.; "Maiden, when such a soul as thine," 1 p.; "To Keats," 1 p.; "The Trustee's Lament," 1 p.; "The Washers of the Shroud," 6 p. (Fields Album); "From the French of Voltaire, to Made. de Châtelet," 2 p.; "Notes," 2 p.; "Books and Libraries" (notes for an address), 2 p.; Als, Al (55) 1852–1886 including 22 to William A. Knight and 8 to William Wetmore Story; "Lowell's Birthday Book—Tributes to J. R. Lowell on his 70th Birthday" (manuscripts from the contributors to the Lowell number of *The Critic*, Feb.–March 1889), 75 p.

MABIE, HAMILTON WRIGHT, 1845–1916. Als, Tls (8) 1900–1912 to Harper & Bros.

McCARTHY, MARY, 1912– . Description of pictures by Fantin-Latour, 5 p.; Als 1945 to E. Jay Rousuck.

McCLURG, ALEXANDER CALDWELL, 1832–1901. Als 2 May 1885 to Harper & Bros.

MACKENZIE, ROBERT SHELTON, 1809–1880. Als 1 October 1836 to William D. Gallagher.

MACLEISH, ARCHIBALD, 1892– . "The Young Dead Soldiers," 1 p.

MADISON, JAMES, 1751–1836. Als, Al, Ls, Ds (32) 1782–1836.

MANN, HORACE, 1796–1859. Als (3) 1853–1855.

MARKHAM, EDWIN, 1852–1940. Tls 4 October 1899 to Herbert Small.

MARVEL, IK: *see* Mitchell, Donald Grant.

MASTERS, EDGAR LEE, 1869–1950. "Anne Rutledge," 1 p.

MATHER, COTTON, 1663–1728. "And Godly in this present world" (sermon), 7 p.; record of three marriages, 1 p.; Als (2) 1712, 1717.

MATHER, INCREASE, 1639–1723. Als 10 January 1710/11 to Sir William Ashurst.

MATHER, SAMUEL, 1706–1785. "Sermon on I Peter II.9," 17 p.

MATHEWS, CORNELIUS, 1817–1889. Als (12) 1841–1847 including 10 to E. B. Browning.

MATTHEWS, [JAMES] BRANDER, 1852–1929. Als 31 December 1891 to Harper & Bros.

MELVILLE, HERMAN, 1819–1891. Als (8) 1849–1854 to Harper & Bros. including 1 written by Alan Melville.

MENCKEN, H[ENRY] L[OUIS], 1880–1956. Tls (3) 1934, 1937 and n.d. including 2 to Prof E. S. Oliver.

MILLER, CINCINNATUS HINER ("JOAQUIN MILLER"), 1839?–1913. Signature to his poem "Dakota," 1 p.

MILLET, FRANCIS DAVIS, 1846–1912. Als (4) 1890–1891 to Harper & Bros.

MITCHELL, DONALD GRANT ("IK MARVEL"), 1822–1908. Tribute to J. R. Lowell, 1 p. (Lowell Album); Als (2) 1869 to Horace Greeley.

MITCHELL, S[ILAS] WEIR, 1829–1914. Als, Al, Tls, An (11) 1897–1905 and n.d. including 8 to W. W. Baldwin.

MOORE, MARIANNE [CRAIG], 1887–1972. Als, Tls, Acs (66) 1949–1962 including 15 on the naming of the Edsel, 19 to David Pleydell-Bouverie, 16 to Mrs. Eugène Reynal, 8 to David Wallace and 4 to E. McKnight Kauffer.

MORRIS, GEORGE POPE, 1802–1864. Als (6) 1854–1859 to Harper & Bros.

MORSE, SAMUEL FINLEY BREESE, 1791–1872. "Description of the original telegraph," 3 p.; Als (4) 1843–1847.

MOTLEY, JOHN LOTHROP, 1814–1877. Als (6) 1856–1869 and n.d.

MOULTON, ELLEN LOUISE (CHANDLER), 1835–1908. "Beauty for Ashes," 2 p.; "The Traveller by Unaccustomed Ways," 1 p.; Als n.d. to Mr. Ford.

MOWATT, ANNA CORA: see Ritchie, Anna Cora (Ogden) Mowatt.

MUIR, JOHN, 1838–1914. Als 9 February 1880.

MUNROE, KIRK, 1850–1930. "A Mud-bespattered Arrival from California" (fragment of chapter III), 2 p.

NASH, OGDEN, 1902–1971. "The Voluble Wheel Chair (for Eugène)," 2 p.

NEAL, JOHN, 1793–1876. Als (c. 225) 1817–1860 to John Pierpont.

NORDHOFF, CHARLES, 1830–1901. Als (7) 1863–1866 to Harper & Bros.

NORTON, ANDREWS, 1786–1853. Als (6) 1821–1847 including 4 to Henry Wheaton.

NORTON, CHARLES ELIOT, 1827–1908. Als (8) 1848–1904.

O'BRIEN, FITZ-JAMES, 1828–1862. Als (2) 1854, 1858 to Harper & Bros.

OPTIC, OLIVER: see Adams, William Taylor.

OSGOOD, FRANCES SARGENT (LOCKE), 1811–1850. "Women's Trust, a Dramatic Sketch" (in the hand of E. A. Poe), 2 p.

OSSOLI, [SARAH] MARGARET (FULLER), MARCHESA: see Fuller, [Sarah] Margaret, Marchesa Ossoli.

OTIS, JAMES, 1725–1783. Als 21 October 1766 to Oliver DeLancey.

OWEN, ROBERT DALE, 1801–1877. Als (2) 1860, 1868 to Horace Greeley.

PAGE, THOMAS NELSON, 1853–1922. "All the Geog'aphy a Nigger wants to know" (fragment), 2 p.; appreciation of J. R. Lowell, 2 p. (Lowell Album); Als (2) 1892, 1894.

PAINE, ALBERT BIGELOW, 1861–1937. Als, Tls (3) 1908–1911 to Harper & Bros.

PAINE, ROBERT TREAT, 1773–1811. Als, Ds (3) 1780–1792.

PAINE, THOMAS, 1737–1809. "On the Descent of England," 2 p.; Als (2) 1789, 1792.

PALFREY, JOHN GORHAM, 1796–1881. Als (3) 1849 and n.d.

PARKER, THEODORE, 1810–1860. Als (6) 1845–1852 and n.d. including 5 to John Pierpont.

PARKMAN, FRANCIS, 1823–1893. "The Arcadian Tragedy" (fragment), 2 p.; Appreciation of J. R. Lowell, 1 p. (Lowell Album).

PARLEY, PETER: see Goodrich, Samuel Griswold.

PARSONS, THOMAS WILLIAM, 1819–1892. "Dirge for those who fell in battle," 1 p. (Fields Album).

PARTON, JAMES, 1822–1891. Als (5) 1858–1868 including 2 to Harper & Bros.

PAULDING, JAMES KIRKE, 1778–1860. Als (2) 1836, 1838.

PAYNE, JOHN HOWARD, 1791–1852. "Sweet Home," 1 p. (Fields Album); Als (2) 1838 and n.d. with autograph copies of letters between Payne and Douglas Kinnaird, 35 p.

PEABODY, ANDREW PRESTON, 1811–1893. Als 15 July 1858.

PEABODY, ELIZABETH PALMER, 1804–1894. Als n.d. to Mrs. Adams.

PEABODY, JOSEPHINE PRESTON, 1874–1922. "Foreboding," "Song," "Song of a rose," 2 p.; "From other days," 1 p.; Als (16) 1890–1900 to Laurens Maynard.

PENFIELD, EDWARD, 1866–1925. Als, telegrams (3) 1891 to Harper & Bros.

PENN, WILLIAM, 1644–1718. Last will and testament, Ads, Ds, Als (7) 1665–1703.

PENNELL, ELIZABETH (ROBINS), 1855–1936. Acs 21 June 1926 to Mrs. T. J. Cobden-Sanderson.

PENNELL, JOSEPH, 1857–1926. Als 5 April 1922 to Mr. Haddon.

PERCIVAL, JAMES GATES, 1795–1856. "Poems," 1 p. (Fields Album); Als (3) 1834–1841.

PETERS, HUGH, 1598–1660. Ds c. 1651.

PHILLIPS, WENDELL, 1811–1884. Als (3) 1854 and n.d.

PIATT, JOHN JAMES, 1835–1917. Als (2) 1869, 1874.

PIERPONT, JOHN, 1785–1866. "Dr. Follen," 1 p.; "E Pluribus Unum," 2 p.; "Exile at Rest," 2 p.; "He is Not There," 4 p.; "Hymn" ["Let the loud trumpet speak"], 2 p.; "Hymn, for 17 Sept. 1830" ["Break forth in song"], 3 p.; "Hymn for the Dedication of a Church" ["O Holy Spirit, who alone"], 2 p.; 'Hymn for Independence, 1850," 2 p.; "Let There Be Light" (autograph?), 13 p.; lines beginning "I suppose, reader, that you understand," 1 p.; lines beginning "On Heaven's sweet light," 1 p.; lines beginning "One mouth and one back," 1 p.; lines beginning "To God, the gracious giver," 4 p.; "One hundred times hath this celestial sphere" (poem delivered at Litchfield Centennial Celebration, 14 Aug. 1851), 30 p.; "Our Country's Call," 3 p.; "Passing Away" (pencil draft and fair copy), 3 p., 4 p.; "They cannot Take Care of Themselves" (2 copies), 1 p., 1 p.; "This fratricidal war" (2 copies), 1 p., 1 p.; "To Mr. A. Morton" ["Morton, I am much beholden"], 4 p.; letters (115) 1810–1866 including 55, 1815–1862, to John Neal. In addition, the Library has 16 boxes of manuscripts, letters and printed materials by or relating to John Pierpont. These contain family correspondence, letters written to Pierpont, about 900 autograph sermons and records of where they were preached, poetical manuscripts (published and unpublished), early Baltimore business papers, law notes, lectures, correspondence relating to his readers and other books, diaries, engagement books, financial records, papers relating to the Hollis Street controversy, notes and letters on the antislavery movement, temperance, phrenology, spiritualism and inventions, photographs, and his last will and testament.

PIKE, ALBERT, 1809–1891. Als 15 August 1877 to Dr. Gunton.

PILLSBURY, PARKER, 1809–1898. Als n.d.

POE, EDGAR ALLAN, 1809–1849. "Annabel Lee," 2 p.; "The Bells," 8 p.; "Dreams," 3 p.; "Hans Phaall," 20 p.; "The Lake," 2 p.; The Literati (notes and drafts entitled "The Living Writers of America"), 8 p.; "Politian," 20 p.; "The Raven" (alterations to stanzas 10 and 11 in Als to J. A. Shea), 1 p.; "System of Doctor Tarr and Professor Fether," 64 p.; "A Tale of the Ragged Mountains" (written on strips, rolled); "Tamerlane," 10 p.; "Ulalume—A Ballad," 5 p.; Als (10) 1841–1849 and n.d.; see also Osgood, Frances Sargent (Locke).

POOL, MARIA LOUISE, 1841–1898. "A Dorset Dunbar" (fragment), 1 p.

PORTER, WILLIAM SYDNEY ("O. HENRY"), 1862–1910. Als 28 April 1885.

POTTER, PAUL MEREDITH, 1853–1921. Als 14 September

1895 to Luther Munday.

POUND, EZRA [LOOMIS], 1885–1973. "Canzone: Of Angels," 2 p.; Tls (2) 1930, 1936.

PRENTICE, GEORGE DENNISON, 1802–1870. Als 31 October 1855 to Harper & Bros.

PRESCOTT, WILLIAM HICKLING, 1796–1859. *History of the Reign of Ferdinand and Isabella* (carbon notes, incomplete), 150 p.; Als (2) 1842, 1846.

PRESTON, MARGARET (JUNKIN), 1820–1897. "The Cathedral," 1 p. (Lowell Album).

PRIESTLEY, JOSEPH, 1733–1804. Als (2), 1774, 1802.

PUTNAM, GEORGE HAVEN, 1844–1930. Tls 22 September 1892 to Harper & Bros.

PYLE, HOWARD, 1853–1911. Als, Tls, etc. (67) 1890–1905 to Harper & Bros.

RANDALL, JAMES RYDER, 1839–1908. "Maryland, my Maryland," 1 p.

RAYMOND, HENRY JARVIS, 1820–1869. Als (6) 1847–1864 and n.d. including 3 to Harper & Bros.

READ, THOMAS BUCHANAN, 1822–1872. "Drifting," 1 p.; "Lines to be kind," 1 p.; "Sheridan's Ride," 4 p. (all in Fields Album).

REDPATH, JAMES, 1833–1891. Als 6 October 1871 to Henry C. Bowen.

REID, WHITELAW, 1837–1912. Als, Tls, Ls (3) 1871–1896.

RICE, ELMER L., 1892–1967. Als 23 January 1957 to The Pierpont Morgan Library.

RILEY, JAMES WHITCOMB, 1849–1916. Poems and articles addressed to Charles H. Phillips, editor of the Kokomo *Tribune:* "Ballad of Smiles and Tears," 1 p.; "Fall Harvest," 1 p.; "Genoine Artickle," 1 p.; "Karl Schronz's Christmas Story. 'Dot Leedle Poy of Mine,'" 3 p.; "Luther Benson," 2 p.; "Marthy Ellen," 3 p.; "Romancin," 3 p., with corrected proof; "This Man Jones," 3 p.; "Tom Johnson's Quit," 4 p.; "When I was a lad," 2 p.; "Bully Boy in Blue," 11 p.; "Dreams," 7 p. with 1 p. corrected proof; "Irrepressible Man at Bay," 10 p.; "Man Who Talks in Initials," 3 p.; "A Solemn Protest" (in the form of a letter to the editor), 12 p.; "Use and Abuse of the Poetic Theme," 7 p.; Als (7) 1879 to Charles H. Phillips.

RIPLEY, GEORGE, 1802–1880. Als (4) 1835–1875.

RITCHIE, ANNA CORA (OGDEN) MOWATT, 1819–1870. Als n.d. to Mrs. Morse.

ROBINSON, EDWIN ARLINGTON, 1869–1935. Als 30 August 1899 to James Barstow.

ROE, E[DWARD] P[AYSON], 1838–1888. "Nature's Serial Story" (fragment), 1 p.; Als 28 December 1887 to H. C. Bowen.

ROOSEVELT, FRANKLIN DELANO, 1882–1945. Tls (2) 1933, 1941 to J. P. Morgan.

ROOSEVELT, THEODORE, 1858–1919. *Autobiography,* 2 v.; "Who should go West?" (fragment), 2 p.; Als, Ls, Acs, Ds (9) 1885–1918.

RUSH, BENJAMIN, 1745–1813. "Account of a Journey to Paris," 32 p.; Als (5) 1781–1812.

SALTUS, EDGAR [EVERTSON], 1855–1921. Als n.d. to Mitchell Kennerley.

SANBORN, FRANKLIN BENJAMIN, 1831–1917. Speeches delivered at John Brown Relief and Memorial Meetings at Salem and Concord, Mass. 1859–1860, in the autographs of Sanborn, R. W. Emerson, H. D. Thoreau, et al., 1 v.; journal, 1854–1855, with records of conversations with Alcott, Emerson, Longfellow and Thoreau, 96 p.

SANTAYANA, GEORGE, 1863–1952. "Sonnet II," 1 p.; Als 3 November 1924 to Pierre la Rose.

SARGENT, EPES, 1813–1880. Als (10) 1850–1878 including 6 to Harper & Bros.

SARTAIN, JOHN, 1808–1897. Als (2) 1848, 1896.

SAXE, JOHN G[ODFREY], 1816–1887. Als (5) 1861–1872.

SCHOOLCRAFT, HENRY ROWE, 1793–1864. Als, Ds (3) 1831–1854.

SCHURZ, CARL, 1829–1906. "Manifest Destiny" (fragment), 2 p.; Als, Acs (81) 1864–1897 including 78 to Harper & Bros.

SCOLLARD, CLINTON, 1860–1932. "To J.R.L.," 1 p. (Lowell Album).

SCOTT, EVELYN [DUNN], 1893–   . Tls 13 February 1935 to Mr. Ballou.

SEDGWICK, CATHARINE MARIA, 1789–1867. Als (11) 1829–1858 including 8 to Harper & Bros.

SEDGWICK, THEODORE, 1746–1813. Als 28 October 1792 to Peter van Schaack.

SEDGWICK, THEODORE, 1811–1859. Als, Ls (9) 1845–1858 including 8 to Harper & Bros.

SEEGER, ALAN, 1888–1916. "Mak Toob," 2 p.; Als n.d. to William Archer.

SEITZ, DON CARLOS, 1862–1935. "The Conquerors," 1 p.

SEWARD, WILLIAM HENRY, 1801–1872. Als, Ls (10) 1839–1867 and n.d.

SHAW, IRWIN, 1913–   . *The Young Lions* (corrected typescript), 7 v.

SHILLABER, BENJAMIN PENHALLOW, 1814–1890. "To J. T. Fields," 3 p. (Fields Album); Als (2) 1870 and n.d.

SIGOURNEY, L[YDIA] H[OWARD (HUNTLEY)], 1791–1865. "The Fiery Deluge Drowns our Wealth," 1 p.; Als (8) 1824–1862.

SIMMS, WILLIAM GILMORE, 1806–1870. Als (4) 1854–1856 and n.d.

SMITH, F[RANCIS] HOPKINSON, 1838–1915. *Colonel Carter of Cartersville* (autograph manuscript and corrected typescript), 200 p.; Als, Tls (14) 1891–1915 including 12 to Harper & Bros.

SMITH, GERRIT, 1797–1874. Als (4) 1842–1870.

SMITH, SAMUEL FRANCIS, 1808–1895. "America," 1 p.; another copy, 2 p. (Fields Album).

SPARKS, JARED, 1789–1866. Als, Al (14) 1820–1855 including 3 to Henry Wheaton.

SPOFFORD, HARRIET ELIZABETH (PRESCOTT), 1835–1921. "Evanescent," 1 p.; "High Days and Holidays," 1 p.; "My Ship at Sea," 2 p. (Fields Album); Als (3) 1868–1881.

SPRAGUE, CHARLES, 1791–1875. "The Winged Worshippers," 2 p. (Fields Album); Als 19 January 1828 to John Pierpont.

SPRAGUE, WILLIAM BUELL, 1795–1876. Als (3) 1830–1852.

STEDMAN, EDMUND CLARENCE, 1833–1908. "From the Doorstep," 1 p.; Als, Tls, Ls (6) 1881–1906 and n.d. including 1 to J. R. Lowell (Lowell Album).

STEIN, GERTRUDE, 1874–1946. Als (2) 1929 and n.d. to Henry-Russell Hitchcock.

STEINBECK, JOHN [ERNST], 1902–1968. "Address before the Swedish Academy on Receiving the Nobel Prize for Literature" (various drafts); *America and Americans,* 129 p.; "Letters to Alicia" (first and second series); *The Short Reign of Pippin IV* (autograph and corrected typescript), 290 p.; *Travels with Charley* (with corrected typescript), 269 p.; *The Winter of Our Discontent* (with corrected typescript), 461 p.; Als, Acs (9) 1937–1966 including 4 to Claire Luce, with typescripts of *Of Mice and Men,* and other materials relating to it.

STEPHENS, ALEXANDER HAMILTON, 1812–1883. Als, Ds (6) 1844–1879.

STEPHENS, ANN S[OPHIA (WINTERBOTHAM)], 1813–1886. Als (6) 1868–1878 to Harper & Bros.

STOCKTON, FRANCIS (FRANK) [RICHARD], 1834–1902. Als, Tls (4) 1884–1894 including 1 to J. R. Lowell (Lowell Album).

STODDARD, RICHARD HENRY, 1825–1903. "Wishing and Having," 2 p.; Als (6) 1858–1906.

STORY, WILLIAM WETMORE, 1819–1895. History of Houdon's life mask of Washington, 2 p.; "The Spanish Armada," 2 p.; Als (9) 1856–1894 including 3 to Harper & Bros. and 1 to J. R. Lowell (Lowell Album) (with 32 letters to Story).

STOWE, HARRIET [ELIZABETH] (BEECHER), 1811–1896. Als (3) 1872–1889 including 1 to J. R. Lowell (Lowell Album).

STREET, ALFRED BILLINGS, 1811–1881. Als 9 May 1851 to John Pierpont.

SUMNER, CHARLES, 1811–1874. Als (9) 1847–1869.

TABB, JOHN BANISTER, 1845–1909. Doggerel verses, 3 p.; Als, Acs (20) 1899–1906 including 14 to Harper & Bros.

TARKINGTON, [NEWTON] BOOTH, 1869–1946. Als (4) 1905–1906.

TAYLOR, BAYARD, 1825–1878. Translation of *Faust*, part II (lacking Act III), 250 p.; "Harpocrates," 4 p.; "Oh deep, exulting freedom," 1 p.; "Haunted Shanty" (from *At Home and Abroad*), 21 p.; Als (6) 1859–1878, including 3 to Horace Greeley. Original pencil sketches (50) and MS materials from his European trip (1844–1846) inserted as extra-illustration to a copy of his *Views A-Foot*; included are letters from Taylor (20) to friends, letters (20) to Taylor, his passport, and MSS of the following poems: "An Autumn Thought," 2 p.; "Dear Mary, all I wish is won!," 1 p.; "The Dearest Image" (2 versions), 2 p., 2 p.; "Homeward Bound," 3 p.; "In Italy," 2 p.; "Oh! Gloomy o'er the welkin's arch," 1 p.; "Poet's Ambition," 1 p.; "Powers' Eve," 2 p.; "Rhine Song," 2 p.; "Rome," 2 p.; "Shadows of Twilight," 1 p.; "Single Sonnet," 1 p.; "Song: The Clouds O'er my Pathway," 1 p.; "Song of the Alp," 3 p.; "Storm is Abroad," 1 p.; "Thoughts Among the Highlands," 2 p.; "To My Mother—From Italy," 2 p.; "To the Ship Victoria," 2 p.; "Tomb of Charlemagne," 2 p.; "Upon the Mountain's Rugged Crest," 1 p.; "We meet, the sons of pilgrim-shires," 1 p.

TERHUNE, MARY VIRGINIA (HAWES) ("MARION HARLAND"), 1830–1922. Als, Tls (2) 1900, 1910 to Harper & Bros.

THANET, OCTAVE: *see* French, Alice.

THAXTER, CELIA (LAIGHTON), 1835–1894. "Tempest," 2 p.; Als 9 November 1872 to W. H. Ward.

THOMAS, EDITH M[ATILDA], 1854–1925. "Doom," 1 p.; "Frailty's Shield," 1 p.; "Name of Lowell" (Lowell Album), 1 p.; Als (5) 1909–1911 to Harper & Bros.

THOMAS, ISAIAH, 1749–1831. Als, Ds (2), 1804, 1820.

THOMPSON, JOHN R[EUBEN], 1823–1873. Als 9 November 1849 to E. H. N. Patterson.

THOREAU, HENRY DAVID, 1817–1862. "Farewell," 2 p.; another version, 1 p.; "Greece," 1 p.; "Guido's Aurora," 1 p.; "I'm Not Alone," 1 p.; "Inspiration," 3 p. (Fields Album); "Music," 2 p.; "My life's a stately warrior horse," 1 p.; "Nature," 2 p.; "The Peal of the Bells," 1 p.; "Pray, to what earth does this sweet cold belong," 2 p.; "Poverty," 2 p.; "Speech of a Saxon Ealderman," 2 p.; "To a Stray Fowl," 1 p.; "Travelling," 1 p.; "Upon the Bank at Early Morn," 1 p.; "What sought they thus afar," 1 p.; "Love of Stories, Real or Fabulous," 4 p.; "Musings," 3 p.; "The Service, Qualities of the Recruit," 23 p. (with letter from Margaret Fuller refusing it for the *Dial*); "Ways in which a man's style can be said to offend," 3 p.; list of authors and titles, 4 p.; speeches delivered at John Brown Relief and Memorial Meetings at Salem and Concord, 1859–1860; "Advantages and Disadvantages of Foreign influence on American Literature," 4 p.; "Autumnal Tints" (fragment), 2 p.; "Life without Principle" (fragment), 2 p.; notes concerning efforts to reconstruct the shipwreck on Fire Island, 1 p.; *Walden* (fragment), 2 p.; autograph survey (plan of John Thoreau's house), 3 p.; "Miscellaneous extracts" (largely on English poetry), 190 p.; "Paragraphs etc., mostly original" (largely on the contrasts of the East and West), 50 p.; "Extracts relative to Canada," 100 p.; "Extracts relative to the Indians," 11 v.; nature notes (observations in prose and in tabular form on phenomena of nature), 110 p.; journal, 1839–1846 (including notes for *A Week on the Concord and Merrimack Rivers*), 140 p.; journals, 1837–1861, 39 v.; Als (10) 1840–1860 (with 16 letters to Thoreau); receipt, 1851.

TICKNOR, GEORGE, 1791–1871. Als (6) 1828–1867 and n.d.

TICKNOR, WILLIAM DAVIS, 1810–1864. Als 4 September 1859 to J. J. Clark.

TILTON, THEODORE, 1835–1907. Als (3) 1870 and n.d.

TORRENCE, [FREDERIC] RIDGELY, 1875–1950. "Three O'Clock (Morning)," 1 p.; Als 11 March 1899 to Laurens Maynard.

TOWNE, CHARLES HANSON, 1877–1949. "Manhattan," 37 p.; "The Quiet Singer (Ave! Francis Thompson)," 4 p.; Als 16 May 1928 to Belle da Costa Greene.

TOWNSEND, GEORGE ALFRED, 1841–1914. Als (2) n.d.

TROWBRIDGE, JOHN TOWNSEND, 1827–1916. "The Vagabond," 6 p. (Fields Album); Als (2) 1866, 1898.

TRUMBULL, JAMES HAMMOND, 1821–1897. Als 13 February 1850 to Thomas W. Williams.

TRUMBULL, JOHN, 1750–1831. Als 23 January 1830 to Noah Webster.

TRUMBULL, JOHN, 1756–1843. "The Second of a series of paintings representing important events of the Revolution," 4 p.; Als, Ds (6) 1788–1831.

TUCKER, ST. GEORGE, 1752–1827. Als (2) 1812, 1820.

TUCKERMAN, HENRY THEODORE, 1813–1871. "Palmer's Statue of the White Captive," 1 p.; Als (11) 1841–1864.

TWAIN, MARK: *see* Clemens, Samuel Langhorne.

UPSON, ARTHUR [WHEELOCK], 1877–1908. "Afloat in Finistère," 1 p.; "The Mystery of Beauty," 2 p.; "The Rezzonico Palace," 1 p.; "Up the Minnesota," 2 p.; Als 26 July 1907 to Laurens Maynard.

VAN DINE, S. S.: *see* Wright, Willard Huntington.

VERPLANCK, GULIAN CROMMELIN, 1786–1870. Als (2) 1820 and n.d.

VERY, JONES, 1813–1880. "Nature," 1 p. (Fields Album).

WALLACE, LEW[IS], 1827–1905. Als (6) 1864–1898 including 3 to Harper & Bros.

WALLACK, JOHN JOHNSTONE (LESTER), 1820–1888. Als (2) 1878, 1885.

WALSH, ROBERT, 1784–1859. Als (3) 1817–1835 including 3 to Henry Wheaton.

WARD, ARTEMUS: *see* Browne, Charles Farrar.

WARNER, CHARLES DUDLEY, 1829–1900. "The Drawer" (fragment), 2 p.; "The Study," 38 p.; Als, Tls (6) 1887–1891 and n.d. including 3 to W. W. Baldwin.

WASHINGTON, GEORGE, 1732–1799. Notes on agriculture, 2 p.; first draft of his inaugural address (fragment), 2 p.; plan of a line of march and order of battle during the Ohio Expedition, 3 p.; Als (50) 1755–1798; Ls (57) 1776–1783 including 35 to George and James Clinton; Ds (6) 1768–1790.

WATTERSON, HENRY, 1840–1921. Als 31 October 1887 to D. A. Wells.

WEBSTER, DANIEL, 1782–1852. Als, Ls (14) 1808–1852 and n.d.

WEBSTER, NOAH, 1758–1843. *Dictionary of the English Language* (incomplete), 450 p. with corrected proofsheets AC–AG; miscellaneous notes and brief essays *on education:* "Remarks on Teaching in Schools," 2 p.; "To the Visitor of the Public Schools in Hartford," 2 p.; "Hurry, Hurry, Hurry," 3 p.; "To the Young of Both Sexes," 4 p.; *on religion:* resolution on proper observance of Sunday, 2 p.; "Errors in the present Version of the Scriptures," 2 p. with other remarks on the same subject, 3 p.; *on politics:* appeal for a law on the registry of voters, 1 p.; *on language, pronunciation and spelling:* notes on his elementary books and dictionaries, including notices of errors to be corrected in future editions, 45 p.; Als (59) 1786–1843 including 18 to his son, William, 3 to his wife and 7 to Hudson and Goodwin (with 25 letters 1784–1829 to Webster).

WENDELL, BARRETT, 1855–1921. Als (3) 1901–1903 including 2 to W. W. Baldwin.

WESCOTT, GLENWAY, 1901– . Als, Tls (2) 1944 to E. McKnight Kauffer.

WETMORE, PROSPER MONTGOMERY, 1798–1876. Als 19 January 1849 to C. W. Lawrence.

WHARTON, EDITH [NEWBOLD (JONES)], 1862–1937. Als (5) 1901–1936.

WHIPPLE, EDWIN PERCY, 1819–1886. Als (6) 1844–1878 including 4 to Harper & Bros.

WHISTLER, JAMES A[BBOTT] McNEILL, 1834–1903. Als (9) 1894 and n.d.

WHITE, ANDREW D[ICKSON], 1832–1918. Als (4) 1882–1894 including 3 to W. W. Baldwin.

WHITE, E[LWYN] B[ROOKS], 1899– . *The Trumpet of the Swan,* with preliminary drafts, sketches, drawings, etc.

WHITE, RICHARD GRANT, 1821–1885. Als (7) 1863–1867 including 4 to Harper & Bros.

WHITEFIELD, GEORGE, 1714–1770. "General account of the first part of my life," 1 v.; Als 12 February 1767 to General Scot.

WHITMAN, WALT, 1819–1892. "American Poets," 3 p.; "Answer me, year of repulses," 1 p.; "Death of Longfellow," 5 p.; "Diary of the War: hospital memoranda (fragment), 23 p.; "Ethiopia saluting the colors," 2 p.; "In General Civilization," 1 p.; introduction for the London edition of *Leaves of Grass,* 14 p.; "O Captain! my Captain!," 1 p.; "Starry Union," 1 p.; "Washington's Monument," 1 p.; another version, 1 p.; Als, Acs (52) 1860–1890 including 7 to his mother, 16 to Mrs. Alexander Gilchrist and 23 to Abby H. Price.

WHITTIER, JOHN GREENLEAF, 1807–1892 "Amy Wentworth," 4 p.; "Anniversary Poem," 1 p.; "As on a wave-washed sand," 1 p.; "Barbara Frietchie," 3 p.; "Bartholdi Statue," 1 p.; "Bolivar," 1 p.; "Burial of Barber," 3 p.; "Burning of Drift-Wood" (corrected proofs, 2 sets, and covering letter); "Call of the Christian," 3 p.; "Captain's Well" (corrected proof); "Crisis," 3 p.; "Easter Lillies," 1 p.; "For M.E.S.," 1 p.; "For the Unveiling of the Statue of Gov. Bartlett" (with corrected proof), 2 p.; "Freedom in Brazil," 2 p.; "Garrison of Cape

Ann," 5 p.; another version entitled "The Spectres of Cape Ann," 3 p.; "General Howard at Atlanta," 3 p.; "Giant's Grave," 4 p.; "Given and Taken," 2 p.; "Great Worship," 2 p.; "Hive at Gettysburg," 2 p.; "Isabella of Austria," 7 p.; "June on the Merrimac," 2 p.; "Legend of the Lake," 6 p.; letters in verse to Lucy Larcom 1866–1870 and n.d.; "Lines on leaving Appledore," 1 p.; "Mabel Martin" (2 versions), 10 p.; "Martha Mason" (corrected proof), 2 p.; "My Birthday," 3 p. (Fields Album); "New England," 3 p.; "On Receiving a Lady's Glove," 1 p.; "Our Master," 6 p.; "Outdoor Reception" (corrected proof); "The Question," 6 p.; "Slaves of Martinique," 3 p.; "Song of Slaves in the Desert," 2 p.; "Spiritual Manifestation," 8 p.; "Sumner," 8 p.; another version, 9 p.; drafts for "Sumner," 22 p.; "Thou art going hence," 1 p.; "To Ann Rebecca," 1 p.; "To Lydia M. Child," 3 p.; "To Mary," 1 p.; "To My Old Schoolmaster," 3 p.; "To Oliver Wendell Holmes," 3 p.; "Trust," 2 p.; "Valuation," 1 p.; "Vathek," 3 p.; "Voices," 5 p.; "Wife of Manoah to her Husband," 3 p.; "Wilson," 2 p.; "Wind of March" (corrected proof and additions); "Within," 1 p.; "You ask a merrier strain," 1 p.; "Interviewers," 3 p.; "Nancy Martin," 2 p.; "Quakerism Defined," 5 p.; biographical sketch of Henry Wilson, 7 p.; reviews of *The Patience of Hope* by Dora Greenwell, 3 p.; review of *Up and Down the Merrimac* by P. S. Boyd, 4 p.; Als (15) 1840–1892, the majority forwarding poems to editors.

WILLARD, FRANCES [ELIZABETH CAROLINE], 1839–1898. Als 12 August 1872 to H. Ward.

WILLIS, NATHANIEL PARKER, 1806–1867. "The Belfry Pigeon," 2 p. (Fields Album); Introduction to *Views A-Foot* by Bayard Taylor, 2 p.; On William Cullen Bryant, 1 p.; "To my aged father," 2 p.; Als (7) 1827–1861 and n.d.

WILSON, EDMUND, 1895–1972. Tls (2) 1971 to Brendan Gill.

WILSON, JAMES GRANT, 1832–1914. Als (2) 1885, 1893.

WILSON, [THOMAS] WOODROW, 1856–1924. Als, Tls (7) 1882–1914 including 4 to Harper & Bros.

WINSOR, JUSTIN, 1831–1897. Als 26 November 1887 to Paul L. Ford.

WINTER, WILLIAM, 1836–1917. Als (4) 1781–1877 and n.d.

WINTHROP, ROBERT CHARLES, 1809–1894. Als (5) 1852–1887.

WINTHROP, THEODORE, 1828–1861. "Northern Lights," 2 p. (Fields Album).

WIRT, WILLIAM, 1772–1834. Als (8) 1810–1831.

WISTAR, CASPAR, 1761–1818. Als 28 May 1816 to Thomas Jefferson.

WITHERSPOON, JOHN, 1723–1794. Als (4) 1773–1791.

WOODWORTH, SAMUEL, 1784–1842. "The Bucket," 1 p.; Als 15 May 1837 to Lewis J. Cist.

WOOLSEY, SARAH CHAUNCEY ("SUSAN COOLIDGE"), 1835–1905. Als 18 July 1872 to Dr. Ward.

WOOLSON, CONSTANCE FENIMORE, 1840–1894. Als (40) 1886–1891 and n.d. to W. W. Baldwin.

WRIGHT, FRANCES (FANNY): see D'Arusmont, Frances (Wright).

WRIGHT, WILLARD HUNTINGTON ("S. S. VAN DINE"), 1888–1939. "What of the Night," 3 p.

YOUNG, STARK, 1881–1963. Als 25 June 1944 to Belle da Costa Greene.

Alphabetical List of Authors

The numbers are those of the 98 specimens reproduced.

American Literary Autographs

FROM WASHINGTON IRVING
TO HENRY JAMES

Herbert Cahoon, Thomas V. Lange, Charles Ryskamp

Noah Webster	James Russell Lowell	Henry James
Charles Brockden Brown	Julia Ward Howe	Joel Chandler Harris
Washington Irving	Walt Whitman	Emma Lazarus
James Fenimore Cooper	Herman Melville	Sarah Orne Jewett
William Cullen Bryant	Edward Everett Hale	James Whitcomb Riley
William H. Prescott	Francis Parkman	Lafcadio Hearn
Ralph Waldo Emerson	Emily Dickinson	O. Henry
Nathaniel Hawthorne	Louisa May Alcott	Clyde Fitch
Henry Wadsworth Longfellow	Horatio Alger	Finley Peter Dunne
John Greenleaf Whittier	Mark Twain	Edward Arlington Robinson
Edgar Allan Poe	Bret Harte	Frank Norris
Oliver Wendell Holmes	William Dean Howells	Hamlin Garland
Harriet Beecher Stowe	Sidney Lanier	Stephen Crane
Henry David Thoreau	Ambrose Bierce	Paul Laurence Dunbar
	plus 30 other authors!	

This book contains excellent reproductions of autographs, letters, poems and signed and unsigned manuscripts of 72 prominent American authors. The earliest example is a letter by Charles Brockden Brown (1808), the latest, a letter by Francis Hopkinson Smith to J. P. Morgan (1915). Focusing, however, on the mid-nineteenth century, this volume illustrates the rise and flourishing of American literature and is a popular guide to literary autographs of this great period. Almost all of the illustrations are chosen from manuscripts in the vast collection of The Pierpont Morgan Library, New York City.

Included are pages from novels, selections from a scenario of *The Ambassadors* by Henry James, an excerpt from a play by Clyde Fitch, poems, inscriptions, dedications, tributes, entries from journals, notebooks and diaries. There are passages from such famous works as Cooper's *Deerslayer,* Hawthorne's *Scarlet Letter* and *Blithedale Romance,* Thoreau's *Walden,* Alcott's *Jack and Jill,* Twain's *Life on the Mississippi* and *Pudd'nhead Wilson,* Crane's *Red Badge of Courage;* poems like Bryant's "Thanatopsis," Emerson's "Concord Hymn," Longfellow's "The Children's Hour" and "Excelsior," Poe's "Ulalume," Holmes's "Old Ironsides," Howe's "Battle Hymn of the Republic," Whitman's "O Captain! my Captain!," Dickinson's "The sun kept stooping," and many more.

The full and informative comments on each entry describe the manuscript and its importance, the life and work of the author, and list the major manuscript collections for him. Transcriptions of the autographs allow you to read them without difficulty. At the end is a checklist of *all* the American literary manuscript holdings from the 17th century to the present in The Pierpont Morgan Library. Charles Ryskamp, Director of the Morgan Library, has written an introduction.

Original Dover (1977) publication in association with The Pierpont Morgan Library. Introduction by Charles Ryskamp. Commentary by Herbert Cahoon, Curator of Autograph Manuscripts. Complete checklist of American literary autographs in the Morgan Library by Thomas V. Lange. 98 plates. 136 illustrations. xii + 212pp. 9⅛ x 12¼.   23548-3 Paperbound